Principles of Macroeconomics

Principles of Macroeconomics

Peter Lewis

STATES
ACADEMIC PRESS
www.statesacademicpress.com

Principles of Macroeconomics
Peter Lewis
ISBN: 978-1-63989-438-3 (Hardback)

STATES
ACADEMIC PRESS

Published by States Academic Press,
109 South 5th Street,
Brooklyn, NY 11249, USA

Cataloging-in-Publication Data

Principles of macroeconomics / Peter Lewis.
p. cm.
Includes bibliographical references and index.
ISBN 978-1-63989-438-3
1. Macroeconomics. 2. Economics. I. Lewis, Peter.
HB172.5 .P75 2022
339--dc23

For more information regarding States Academic Press and its products, please visit the publisher's website www.statesacademicpress.com

Table of Contents

Preface VII

Chapter 1 **Macroeconomics: An Introduction** **1**
a. Circular Flow of Income and Expenditure 7
b. Classical Theory 21
c. Concepts of National Income 38
d. Measurement of National Income 44

Chapter 2 **Aggregate Demand and Supply** **50**
a. Aggregate Demand Curve 50
b. Aggregate Supply Curve 60
c. Phillips Curve 65
d. Deriving AD-AS Curves 76
e. Money Market Equilibrium 83

Chapter 3 **Keynesian Economics: An Integrated Study** **93**
a. Keynes's General Theory of Employment, Interest and Money 100
b. Liquidity Preference 113
c. Marginal Efficiency of Capital 116
d. Keynesian Cross Diagram 119
e. Liquidity Trap 122
f. Neo-Keynesian Economics 123
g. New Keynesian Economics 127
h. Post-Keynesian Economics 140
i. Keynes's Theory of Wages and Prices 145

Chapter 4 **Types of Market Structure** **152**
a. Market Structure 152
b. Monopoly 153
c. Oligopoly 173
d. Duopoly 183

Chapter 5 **Global Financial Scenario** **186**
a. Balance of Payments 186
b. Global Financial Markets 194
c. Foreign Exchange Rate 204
d. Real vs. Nominal Exchange Rate 209

Chapter 6 **Money Supply and Monetary Policy** **214**
a. Fiscal Policy 214

b. Money Creation 216
c. Money Supply 223
d. Determinants of Money Supply 231

Permissions

Index

Preface

The branch of economics which studies the economy of a nation or a region as a whole is called macroeconomics. It deals with the large scale repercussions of micro decisions in terms of gross domestic product (GDP), consumer price index (CPI), unemployment rates and international trade. GDP can be defined as the sum of total money spent by all the citizens of a country in a given year. CPI measures the average change in prices over time that consumers pay for a basket of goods and services otherwise known as inflation. Economic models such as the aggregate-demand aggregate supply, IS-LM model and growth models are studied under it. The key areas of research under this subject are consequences of short-run fluctuations in national income and determinants of long-run economic growth. Over the last few decades, different schools of thought such as Keynesianism, monetarism and Austrian have put forward different views on macroeconomics. A combination of these is used to create the monetary and fiscal policy of any modern nation. This book is a valuable compilation of topics, ranging from the basic to the most complex theories and principles in the field of macroeconomics. It explores all the important aspects of macroeconomics in the present day scenario. Coherent flow of topics, student-friendly language and extensive use of examples make this book an invaluable source of knowledge.

A detailed account of the significant topics covered in this book is provided below:

Chapter 1- The branch of economics which deals with the study of the behavior and performance of the whole economy is called macroeconomics. Its focus is on the aggregate changes in the economy. The topics elaborated in this chapter will help in gaining a brief introduction to the varied facets of macroeconomics as well as its meaning and scope.

Chapter 2- The total amount of goods and services which a company desires to sell at a specified price within a particular economy is known as the aggregate supply. The aggregate demand refers to the total amounts of goods and services that will be purchased at all the price levels possible. This chapter discusses in detail the different aspects of aggregate demand and supply such as aggregate demand curve and aggregate supply curve.

Chapter 3- The different theories and models within macroeconomics which show the ways in which aggregate demand has a significant effect on the economic output and inflation fall under Keynesian economics. The diverse theories and concepts which are studied under Keynesian economics such as Keynes's general theory of employment, interest and money, and Keynesian cross diagram have been thoroughly discussed in this chapter.

Chapter 4- There are different types of markets which are studied within the discipline of macroeconomics. A few of them are monopoly, oligopoly, duopoly, monopsony and natural monopoly. The topics elaborated in this chapter will help in gaining a better perspective about these types of markets as well as information asymmetry and income distribution.

Chapter 5- The global financial scenario encompasses the legal agreements, institutions, and other formal and informal economic factors which enable the international flows of financial capital. This chapter has been carefully written to provide an easy understanding of the varied facets of global financial scenario such as global financial markets and trade linkages between countries.

Chapter 6- The total amount of money which is in circulation, including coins, cash and bank balance, is called money supply. The different decisions which are taken by the central bank of a country for the purpose of controlling money supply and achieving economic growth in a sustainable manner are known as monetary policy. This chapter discusses in detail the different aspects of money supply and monetary policy such as the determinants of money supply and fiscal policy.

I would like to make a special mention of my publisher who considered me worthy of this opportunity and also supported me throughout the process. I would also like to thank the editing team at the back-end who extended their help whenever required.

Peter Lewis

1

Macroeconomics: An Introduction

The branch of economics which deals with the study of the behavior and performance of the whole economy is called macroeconomics. Its focus is on the aggregate changes in the economy. The topics elaborated in this chapter will help in gaining a brief introduction to the varied facets of macroeconomics as well as its meaning and scope.

Macroeconomics concerns with the study of aggregate behavior in an economy, and is policy-oriented part of economics. macroeconomics is concerned with "the behavior of the economy as a whole – with booms and recessions, the economy's total output of goods and services and the growth of output, the rates of inflation and unemployment, the balance of payments, and the exchange rates. Macroeconomics deals with long-run economic growth and with the short-run fluctuations that constitute the business cycle."

Thus, the key concepts that are discussed under macroeconomics are: aggregate price level, total output in the economy, employment and unemployment levels, levels of interest rates, wage rates, and exchange rates, growth rate of output, inflation rates, recessions and booms, trade balance, fiscal and monetary policies, and national debt. Thus, macroeconomics includes "those essentials [that] lie in the interactions among the goods, labour, and assets markets of the economy, and [that] lie in the interactions among national economies whose residents trade with each other."

Importance of Macroeconomics

Macroeconomics is a branch of economics that carries significant value to any entity that is involved in trade and commerce. Macroeconomics principles allow researchers and other experts to predict a number of things related to economic markets and monetary policies. Thus, macroeconomics is necessary to understand the behavior of the entire economy, as a whole. It is necessary to understand the mechanisms which determine the price level and output in the entire economy, the employment and unemployment rates, the trade balance and foreign exchange reserves.

Moreover, it is also necessary to have a special branch of macroeconomics, other than microeconomics because what holds for an individual unit may not hold for the aggregate. For example, there is an increased demand for a good, and an individual firm producing that good decides to produce more. This firm can produce more in the shortrun. However, if all the firms in an industry try to do so, it is not possible, at least not in the short-run because of limited availability of resources, like labour, capital, land, and others. As a result, increased demand for the good will raise the price, without increasing its output. Thus, what is true for an individual firm may not be true for an entire economy. Hence, there is a need to study macroeconomics, as a separate branch of economics.

How to Explain and Solve the Problem of High and Persistent Unemployment in the Economy?

The unemployment rate is the number of jobless individuals who are actively looking for work (or are on temporary layoff), divided by the total of those employed and unemployed. Unemployment becomes a problem for an economy when it is high and persistent. There are evidences of high and chronic unemployment in many countries of the world. For example, during 1930s, unemployment rates were more than 20 percent for several years in US. United Kingdom and France suffered double-digit unemployment rates during 1980s, and in 1992-93 Economists say that According to, each one-point increase in the unemployment rate in an economy is associated with: "920 more suicides, 650 more homicides, 4000 more people admitted to state mental institutions, 3300 more people sent to state prisons, 37,000 more deaths, and increases in domestic violence and homelessness."

Thus, research on macroeconomics focuses on finding solutions for high and persistent unemployment. What are the theories behind unemployment, what are the factors that lead to high and chronic unemploymeRs.nt, how to tackle the problem of chronic unemployment, what should government do as part of their fiscal policy to solve the problem of unemployment, is there any role for central bank to play to curb the problem of unemployment. These are the various questions pertaining to unemployment that are answered in macroeconomics.

How to Explain the Problem of Inflation?

The inflation rate is the percentage rate of increase in the economy's average level of prices. There are evidences in United States when average price level rise by more than 10 percent in 1979 and 1980. In Russia, prices rise by more than 20 percent, and sometimes even 30 percent in a month during 1992. In some Latin American countries, prices rise by more than 1000 percent per year in 1980s, leading to hyperinflations. Rising prices become even more severe problem for an economy when it is coupled with high unemployment rates. During the period of 1970-1984, US economy has undergone a situation of high inflation and unemployment rates.

Thus, macroeconomics studies the reasons why an economy faces period of high inflation rates, and even hyperinflation, what are the ways to keep inflation rates low, without leading to a recession, what are policy changes that are necessary to keep inflation at low levels, coupled with low unemployment rates.

How to Explain an Economic Slowdown in an Economy?

In United States, growth rates in output decline to 2.8 percent during the period of 1970- 1984, when there was a steady growth in output at 3.6 percent during the period of 1953- 1969. Moreover, Japanese economy, on an average grows at a higher rate than the US economy when income per person for Japan reaches US levels only recently. So, questions that arise are, why some economies grew at a higher rate than others, what are the factors that lead to higher growth in some economies, while lower growth in others, is it because of government investment in infrastructure and technology that provides a boost to economic growth or is it something else.

The study of macroeconomics provides answers to these questions. It helps to understand the functioning of a complicated modern economic system. How the aggregate output, price level and unemployment are related in an economy. It analyses the forces which determine economic growth of a country and explains how to reach the highest state of economic growth and sustain it. It helps to bring stability in price level and analyses fluctuations in business activities. It explains the factors that determine international trade, balance of payment crises, fluctuations in exchange rates, and business cycles. It provides policy solutions, both fiscal and monetary policy solutions to control Inflation and deflation, problem of unemployment, business cycles, and low economic growth.

Thus, macroeconomics helps us in understanding the above three questions and their answers, both theoretically as well as empirically. Unfortunately, there is no single answer to these questions. Different economists have their own viewpoints, on the answers to these questions. As a result, macroeconomics has been divided into different schools of thought, starting from classical school of economics, to new Keynesian and new growth theories.

Schools of Thought in Macroeconomics

Among economists there is no agreement on how adjustments to equilibrium levels of output, prices and employment will take place. There are also differences on the views on the sources of economic fluctuations from the equilibrium. Basically, there are two important schools of thought in macroeconomics, and other schools of thought came up from the synthesis of these two schools. These two schools are: classical and Keynesian. Later on, the debate on government intervention and role of central bank gain importance, which give rise to monetarist school of thought. New synthesis came up, leading to two new schools: the new classical school, and the new Keynesians.

Classical Approach

The term "Classical Approach" was coined by John Maynard Keynes to refer to the ideas presented by the economists prior to him, mainly by Adam Smith, David Ricardo, Thomas Malthus, and John Stuart Mill. These economists believed that market, and hence the economy operates on the notion of "supply creates its own demand", the famous Say's Law, named after the economists JB Say. Classical economists view that prices, wages and interest rates are flexible such that market always clear. There will be no excess demand or supply. There will be no unemployment, and the growth will depend on the supply side factors. Classical economists believed in the dichotomy between the real and the monetary sectors of the economy, i.e., due to wage-price flexibility, there is no role of money in the determination of output or income in the economy. Full-employment will always exist without inflation. The mechanism behind the working of the economy towards full-employment was "an invisible hand". Any deviations from the full-employment level of output will be corrected within the economy. There is minimum intervention by the government in maintaining fullemployment level. Government's role is limited only to the maintenance of law and order and defence. They suggested that if there is "Laissez Faire" system of trade, i.e., there is free trade among countries, and hence market forces will determine the output and income in the economy. Hence, the major view of the classical economists is a vertical aggregate supply curve, where due to wage-price flexibility; there is no change in the equilibrium level of income and output. If there is any change in the demand, wages and prices will adjust such that full-employment level of output will be maintained. For instance, in figure, aggregate demand decreases from AD_0 to AD_1, creating excess supply at prevailing price level of P_0. Due to wage-price flexibility, wages will fall in the labour market, and prices will fall in the goods market, bringing the output back to its full-employment level of Y_0. Prices will fall to new lower level of P_1.

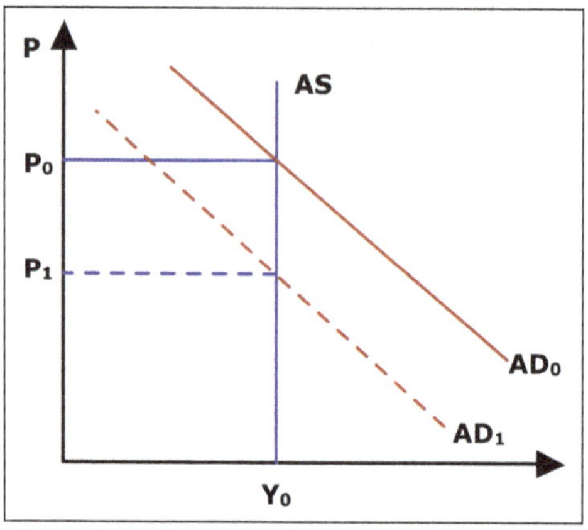

Vertical Aggregate Supply curve by classical economists. Any change in aggregate demand changes the price level, without changing the output and income in the economy.

Keynesian School of Thought

Keynesian school of thought was evolved by John Maynard Keynes in the year 1936 with his book "The General Theory of Employment, Interest, and Money", which revolutionized the macroeconomics. It was after the Great Depression, which continued over a period of 1929 to 1933, that classical economists failed to explain the reason behind the high and persistent unemployment rates, and declining output and income.

It was at that time when Keynes proposed that the reason behind the Great Depression is the low aggregate demand in the economy, which created low levels of income and high levels of unemployment. The concept of Keynesian economics was completely opposite to classical economists. He came up with the notion of "Demand creates its own Supply". Keynes argued that in the short-run, wages and prices are rigid and do not adjust to fluctuations in aggregate demand. Wages are rigid due to various labour market contracts and legislations. Thus, in figure, when aggregate demand falls, wages do not fall immediately, and they are maintained at higher levels only. Consequently, output declines, and there is a recession. In the Keynesian economics, aggregate supply curve is assumed to be horizontal in the short-run, and vertical in the long-run. Thus, Keynes believed that these kinds of business cycles can be managed by active government intervention through fiscal policy (spending more in recessions to stimulate demand) and monetary policy (stimulating demand with lower rates).

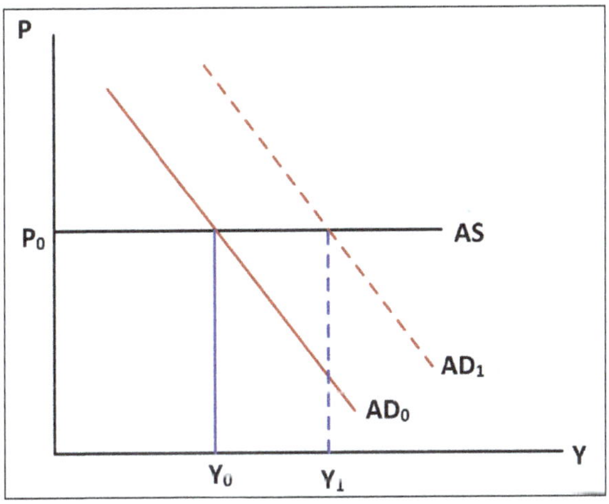

Aggregate supply curve in Keynesian economics in the short-run. An increase in demand increases output, without any change in the price level, due to wage-price rigidity.

Monetaris

Monetarist school of thought evolved after the Nobel Prize winner, Milton Friedman, who argued that in the Keynesian model there is no role of money. He emphasized the role of money supply and the monetary policy in the determination of output and income in the economy. The basis of monetarists was the Keynesian school of thought, and it paved the way of New Classical School of Thought.

Neo-Classical School of Thought

In response to Keynesian economists and monetarists, the neo-classical economists, like John Hicks, Paul Samuelson, and Robert Solow, synthesize the work of Keynesian and classical economists. The revolutionary work was done by Sir John Hicks who came up with the IS-LM Model which integrated the classical and Keynesian ideas on real and nominal macroeconomic variables. The neoclassical growth model by Robert

Solow, known as Solow Model helped in studying the long run growth trajectory of an economy and the attainment of steady state level of growth.

New Classical School of Thought

The New Classical school of thought is built largely on the Neo-classical school. The New Classical School emphasizes the importance of microeconomics and models based on that behavior. Economists like Robert Lucas, Thomas Sargent, Robert Barro, Edward Prescott, and Neil Wallace characterize this school of thought. They believed with the notion of "Rational Expectations", i.e., economic agents act rationally in their own selfinterest to maximize their welfare or profits. They endorsed the wage-price flexibility assumption, and hence believed that market will always clear. The two main issues that are usually discussed in new classical school are rational expectations and real business cycles.

Rational expectation hypothesis, given by Robert Lucas, modeled agents as rational and forward looking. Any policy change will be ineffective, i.e. economic agents would anticipate inflation and adjust to higher price levels before the start of the monetary expansion, that could boost employment and output. Only unanticipated monetary policy could increase employment, and no central bank could systematically use monetary policy for expansion without economic agents catching on and anticipating price changes before they could have a simulative impact.

Real business cycle theory (RBC theory) assumes that business cycle fluctuations can be accounted for by real shocks, rather than nominal shocks. RBC theory sees business cycle fluctuations as an efficient tool in response to the exogenous changes in the real economic variables. They do not represent a failure to market clearance, but the best solution to the structure of the economy. They reject the Keynesian views of government intervention to smoothen out economic short-term fluctuations, and argued that government should concentrate on long-run structural policy changes.`

New Keynesian School of Thought

The New Keynesian School attempts to add microeconomic foundations to traditional Keynesian economic theories. This school of thought includes economists like George Akerlof, David Romer, Olivier Blanchard, and Greg Mankiw. They do not believe that markets clear, but explain why the market fail to clear. They argue that wages and prices are neither rigid nor flexible. They adjust slowly to the shocks. Due to "menu costs", "aggregate demand externalities", and "coordination failure", wages and prices adjust slowly, and even sometimes sticky. Menu costs are the cost to the firm for changing prices and wages. If it is costly for the firm to change the prices they charge and the wages they pay, both wages and price will adjust slowly. Hence, economy wide wage level and price level will not be flexible to adjust to the period of shocks. Aggregate demand externalities include the impact of one firm's price change on the demand for all other firm's product. When one firm lowers the price it charges, it lowers the economy wide average price level, raising the real money balances, and hence the demand for other firms rises. Thus, it is a positive externality to other firms, and hence they are reluctant to reduce their prices, making prices and wages sticky. The problem of coordination failure arises because the leaders, who set the prices, are unable to anticipate the actions of other firms. Similarly, labour unions, which set wages, are unable to see the benefits to other labour unions. As a result, leaders fail to come to an inferior outcome over a preferred outcome, making economy wide average price level and wages are sticky.

New Growth Theories

Beginning in the mid-1980s, many macroeconomists started thinking about long-run "new growth" theories. They were concerned about why sub-Saharan Africa failed to catch up in terms of growth, and why the East Asian Tigers emerge as the booming countries in the word in terms of high growth rates. Thus, they came up with endogenous growth models, which includes technological progress and knowledge spillovers, role of innovation (and protection of this innovation through patents), and therole of human capital formation in growth process. This theory emphasize that an economy can experience high growth rate with the development or imports of technology and innovative ideas for growth. History of a nation does not matter in the growth process. The simplest of these models is the AK model of endogenous growth.

New Synthesis

"New Synthesis" or "New Neoclassical Synthesis" emerges in the 1990s. It is a combination of both new Keynesian and new classical schools. It adapts Real Business Cycle Theories and rational expectation hypothesis from the new classical school, while it adapts nominal rigidities, price stickiness, and market imperfections from the new Keynesian school. Thus, New Synthesis Theory develops Dynamic Stochastic General Equilibrium (DSGE) models. DSGE models formulate hypotheses about the behaviors and preferences of firms and households. These models also include a "stochastic" element created by shocks to the economy.

Circular Flow of Income and Expenditure

In January 2009 the government reported that U.S. real GDP fell at a 3.8 percent annual rate in the fourth quarter of 2008, the sharpest drop since 1982. News reports said nothing about growth of population, capital, or total factor productivity. Instead, they focused on the behavior of individual components of GDP.

Consumption expenditures especially for durable goods like cars, led the decline in total GDP. Exports, also, decreased as U.S. trading partners also slipped into recession. Federal government purchases rose moderately, counter to the trend of other GDP components, but the rise was partially offset by weakness of spending by state and local governments.

The data on investment received special attention. Overall, investment was down; but one category, increases in inventory, was up. While inventory investment helped moderate the total drop in GDP for the fourth quarter, it was taken as a bad sign for the future. At this point in the business cycle, the increase in business inventories did not reflect an optimistic stocking up by businesses to meet growing consumer demand. Instead, it was an unplanned buildup resulting from disappointing sales. Business firms were expected to cut back their orders for goods in the new year until the unwanted inventory buildup was worked off.

The Circular Flow

Figure divides the economy into five main sectors: firms, households, government, financial markets, and the rest of the world. Arrows indicate flows of payments among the sectors. We can begin with the largest and most important set of flows, those representing the incomes that households receive from business firms and the expenditures they make in purchasing goods and services from those same firms.

Gross Domestic Product, Domestic Income and Consumption

At the top of figure we encounter gross domestic product (GDP), a measure of a country's total output of goods and services. The production of goods and services by business firms generates income for the country's households. The bulk of this income consists of wages and salaries. Some is also paid out in interest, rents, and royalties on capital and natural resources owned by households and loaned or sold to firms. Whatever firms have left over, after they have paid all wages and other costs of production, is profit. Profit is earned by the firm's owners, who are a subset of households.

The sum of income received in the form of wages, rents, interest, and profit by all households is known as gross domestic income, or for short, simply domestic income. From the way the circular flow is drawn, it is clear that domestic income and domestic product must be equal, since payments equal to the value of what is produced and sold are paid out to households—either as elements of costs (wages, interest, rents) or as profit (what is left over when cost is subtracted from the value of output).

In figure, which shows the simplest imaginable economy, households immediately spend all the income they receive to purchase goods and services from the firms that pay them their incomes. The corresponding arrow is labeled consumption, which includes all purchases of goods and services for immediate use.

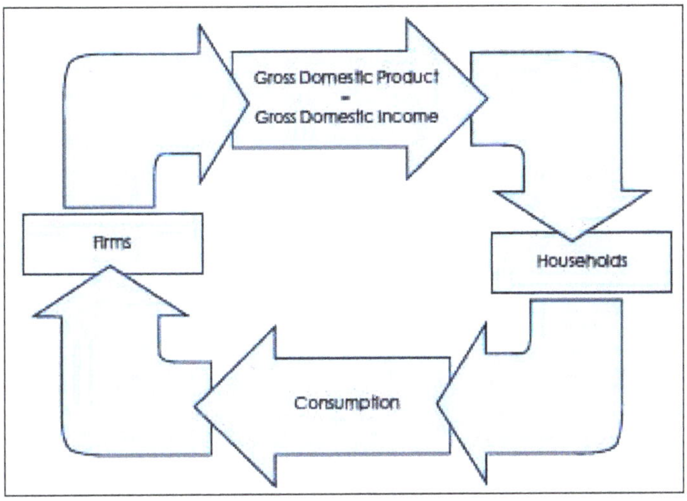

This figure shows flows of income and expenditure for the simplest possible economy. Production, carried out by firms, generates incomes for households in the form of wages, interest, rents, and profits. Households, in turn, immediately spend all of their income on consumption.

Leakages and Injections in a Closed Economy

The economy shown in figure is called a closed economy because it has no connection with the rest of the world. Even in a closed economy, however, the circular flow is not really so watertight as shown in that diagram. Instead of spending all of their income immediately on consumption, part of household income "leaks out" of the basic circular flow as shown in figure. Two types of leakages are shown there.

The first leakage is labeled net taxes. These consist of tax revenues paid by households to government minus transfer payments received by households. Transfer payments mean government payments like pensions, retirement benefits, disability payments, temporary aid to needy families, and so on. In everyday life, we tend to think of retirement benefits or disability payments as another form of income, so we might expect to see them added to the domestic income component of the circular flow. however, economists prefer to think of them more as a sort of "tax rebate" that partially offsets the revenue received by government from households in the form of income taxes, sales taxes, property taxes, and so on.

The second leakage shown in figure is saving. Saving is the part of domestic income that is not used by households to purchase consumer goods or pay taxes. This economic definition of saving differs a little from the everyday idea of saving as money placed in a bank account or mutual fund. Saving, in the economic sense, also includes repayment of debt and spending that builds equity in a home. Also, corporations sometimes retain part of their profit for reinvestment in their operations. Looked at from the point of view of the circular flow, we can consider the retained earnings to be first "earned" by the households who own the firm and then "saved" by those households in the sense that they, as shareholders, approve the idea of using the retained profits for reinvestment.

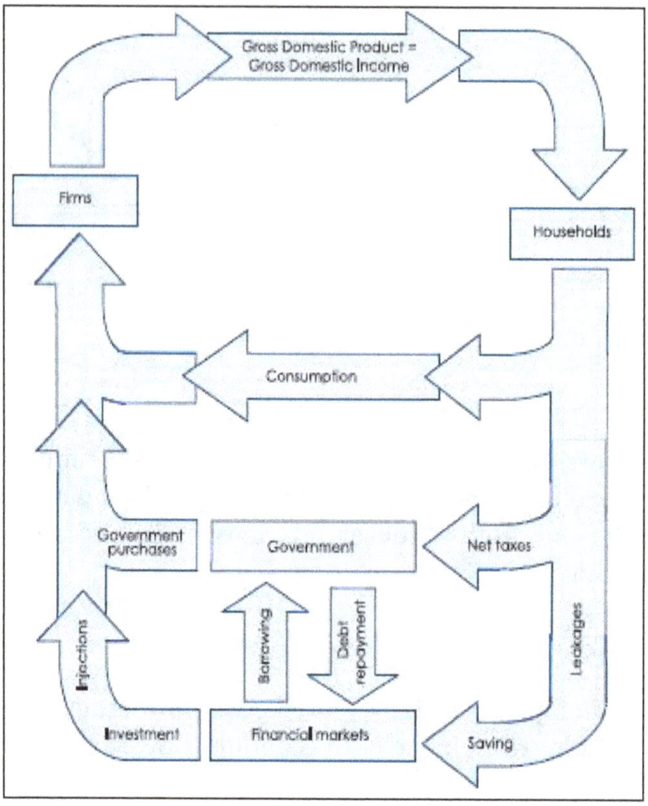

Households do not spend all of their income on consumption. Part of it "leaks out" of the basic circular flow of income and consumption through payments of taxes and through saving. These two leakages are balanced by "injections" of expenditure into the basic circular flow in the form of government purchases and investment. Total leakages (S + T) must equal total injections (I + G) for this simple closed economy.

To match the leakages, figure also shows two injections. Injections are types of expenditure on goods and services that have any origin other than the household consumption that was shown as part of the basic circular flow in figure.

The first injection is government purchases of goods and services or, more simply, government purchases. These include all purchases of goods made by all levels of government (national, regional and local) plus services purchased from contractors and the wages paid to all government employees. Government purchases do not include transfer payments like social security, disability payments, or unemployment compensation. Those items, which are not payments for currently performed services, are subtracted from tax revenue to get the leakage "net taxes." The sum of government purchases of goods and services plus transfer payments is called government expenditures or, sometimes, government outlays.

The second injection is investment. Investment, as the term is understood in macroeconomics, is made up of two components. The first, fixed investment, means purchases of newly produced capital goods—machinery, office equipment, software, farm equipment, construction of buildings used for business purposes, including construction of rental housing, and so on. The second component, inventory investment, means changes in stocks of finished goods ready for sale, stocks of raw materials, and stocks of partially completed goods in process of production. Inventory investment has a negative value if stocks of goods decrease in a given period.

The term investment as used in macroeconomic models is sometimes called economic investment to emphasize that it means expenditures on real productive assets and inventories. Economic investment should not be confused with financial investment, which means purchases of corporate stocks, bonds, and other securities. The latter are not included in GDP because they do not represent new production, but rather are changes in ownership of assets that already exist. When the term investment is used without modifier, it is usually clear from context whether economic or financial investment is meant.

The Role of the Financial Sector

In addition to the leakages and injections figure includes an important box that represents the economy's financial sector. This sector includes banks, mutual funds, insurance companies, and a host of other financial institutions, As an element of the circular flow, the financial sector performs two functions.

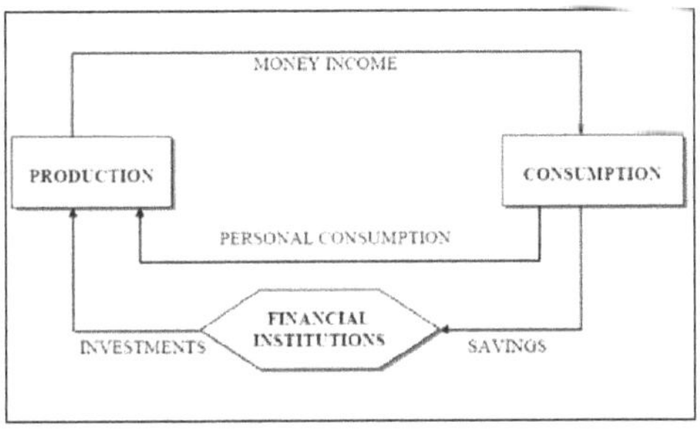

First, it acts as an intermediary in transmitting flows of funds from savers to investors. In most cases, savers do not directly purchase productive assets like machine tools or office buildings. Instead, they make bank deposits, which are used by banks to make loans, buy securities like stocks and bonds, or in other ways indirectly finance the expenditures on capital goods that make up the "investment" arrow in the circular flow diagram.

Second, the financial sector plays a key role in redirecting flows of funds between the private and government sectors of the economy. Without the financial sector, the government would always have to balance its budget, exactly, every year. In terms of the diagram, the amount of funds flowing through the "net taxes" arrow would have to be exactly equal to the flow through the "government purchases" arrow. With the help of the financial sector, the government budget does not have to be balanced.

If government purchases exceed net taxes, the government has a budget deficit. To cover the deficit, the government must then borrow from the private financial sector. In most cases, it does this by selling bonds to private investors through the financial markets. The resulting flow of government borrowing is shown as an arrow running from the financial sector to the government.

On the other hand, the government sometimes collects more in net taxes than it spends on purchases of goods and services. In that case, the budget is in surplus. The surplus funds are used to repay past debt. The result is an arrow from the government sector to the private financial sector. In practice, since there are many units of government—federal, state, and local—at any given time some of them may have budget deficits and others budget surpluses; thus, funds are usually flowing in both ways at once between the financial and government sectors.

In a closed economy like that of figure, which has no links to the rest of the world, the sum of saving plus net taxes must equal the sum of investment plus government purchases, even though the individual leakage and injection items do not have to balance. This fact has important implications for economic policy. If the government runs too large a deficit, borrowing too much from financial markets, not enough saving may be left over to meet the country's investment needs. That can result in a condition of high interest rates and slow growth for the economy as a whole. On the other hand, if the government has a budget surplus, additional funds flow into financial markets that can help keep interest rates low and stimulate private investment. This link between the government budget and private investment does not mean that it is always a mistake for the government to run a deficit. However, we can see even from the simple circular flow that the way the government's budget is managed has important implications for the health of the economy as a whole.

The Open Economy

We do not live in a closed economy. Our economy has many links, both real and financial, with the rest of the world. By adding these links, figure represents the circular flow model for an open economy. The first link that is added to the circular flow for an open economy is another leakage, imports. In everyday life, we are used to thinking of imports as goods flowing into the economy, so it might seem surprising to see imports represented as a leakage, not an injection. However, there is a simple explanation. Remember, the circular low represents flows of money, not flows of physical objects. The leakage represented by the "imports" arrow could perhaps more accurately be labeled "payments for imports of goods and services." Then it would be more clearly seen as what it is: The part of household income that is devoted to purchase of goods and services produced in the rest of the world, rather than in the domestic economy.

Figure also adds a new injection, exports, to match the import leakage. Again, we could more fully describe this item as "payments from the rest of the world for goods and services exported from the domestic economy." It would then be apparent why an arrow representing an injection of funds into the domestic economy represents "exports".

The final detail added to figure is a pair of arrows linking the rest of the world to domestic financial markets. Just as government purchases do not always exactly equal net taxes, resulting in a government surplus or deficit, imports do not always exactly equal imports, resulting in a surplus or deficit of payments with the rest of the world. In the context of the circular flow, we call this external surplus or deficit net exports, which means exports of goods and services minus imports. In everyday discussions, the term net exports is instead called the trade surplus (or the trade deficit if imports exceed exports).

If imports exceed exports, where do domestic purchases get the funds they need to buy all the imports? Only part of the imports can be financed by funds received from exports. The balance must come in the form of financial inflows from the rest of the world, shown in the diagram by an arrow from the rest of the world to domestic financial markets. The most common forms of financial inflows are borrowing from foreign banks or other lenders, and sales of domestic securities like stocks or bonds to foreign investors. Financial inflows are also often called capital inflows. On the other hand, if exports exceed imports, the opposite question arises: How do foreign buyers afford the exports, since only part of them can be paid for by the payments they receive through the "imports" arrow of the circular flow? The answer is that an export surplus must be financed by financial outflows. The most common forms of financial outflows are lending by domestic banks and other financial institutions to foreign borrowers, and purchases of foreign securities like stocks or bonds by domestic investors.

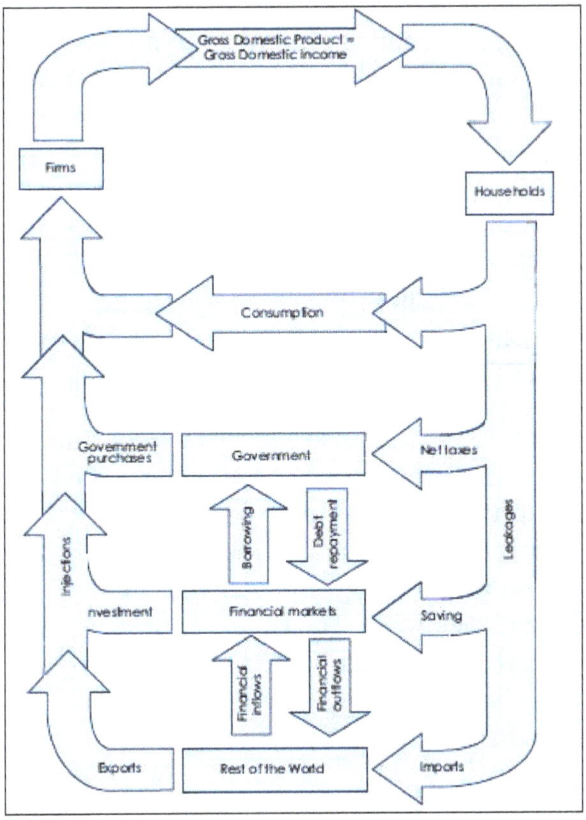

Circular flow in an open economy.

This version of the circular flow represents an open economy that is linked to the rest of the world through imports (a leakage) and exports (an injection). If imports exceed exports, the excess imports must be financed by a financial inflow from the rest of the world. If exports exceed imports, the resulting trade surplus will be balanced by a financial outflow. As was the case in a closed economy, total injections must equal total leakages (S + T + Im = I + G + Ex).

As is the case with government deficits, a country can have financial inflows from some trading partners and financial outflows to others at the same time; thus, both arrows can be in action. From the point of view of the economy as a whole, there will be a net financial inflow whenever net exports are positive and a net financial outflow whenever net exports are negative.

The Balance of Leakages and Injections in an Open Economy

As was the case with a closed economy, individual pairs of leakages and injections do not have to be equal, but total leakages must equal total injections. In equation form,

$$S + T + Im = I + G + Ex$$

It is not possible to explore every possible combination of the way leakages and injections balance, but some important variants are worth mentioning. One possibility is that a country can use a net financial inflow to finance a greater level of domestic investment than would be possible on the basis of domestic saving alone. For example, during much of the nineteenth century, the United States had a persistent trade deficit with Europe and, at the same time, a steady financial inflow that made possible the construction of canals, railroads, and other industrial infrastructure that underpinned the country's rapidly developing economy. More recently, many of the new member states of the European Union are in the same position, with trade deficits and corresponding financial inflows that help finance their economies as they catch up with their wealthier Western European neighbors. In these cases, an external deficit can be a sign of strength, rather than weakness, for an economy.

Another possibility is that a country may use borrowing from abroad not to finance domestic investment but rather to finance a government budget deficit. In terms of the circular flow diagram, such a country would see funds flowing along the arrow from the rest of the world to financial markets, and from there, flowing directly along to the government through sale of government bonds to foreign buyers. A country in this position is said to suffer from the "twin deficit" syndrome. The United States has been in this position, with both government budget deficits and trade deficits, for much of the recent past.

The Determinants of Planned Expenditure

To really understand the economy, we need to be able to explain why GDP or other variables have one value rather than another and why they change over time. In order to do that, we need to look at the choices made by consumers, business managers, and other decision makers.

The Components of GDP

Our starting point is the circular flow of income and product shown in figure. This time our focus is on the total flow of expenditures on goods and services produced by the economy's business firms. These expenditures consist of consumption (by far the largest component) plus purchases of goods and services by government, purchases of investment goods, and expenditures on exported goods and services. Together, these equal gross domestic product, which in turn, equals gross domestic income.

In moving from the circular flow diagram to our macroeconomic model, however, we need to be careful about one detail. The consumption arrow in the diagram represents consumption expenditures on domestically produced goods. A separate arrow representing the "imports" leakage shows consumption of imported goods. In practice, government statisticians do not measure consumption in this way. Instead, the number that they give us in the official national income accounts includes consumption of both domestic and imported consumer goods. The same applies to purchases of imported investment goods by business firms and imported goods used by government. Without adjustment, then, the sum of consumption, investment, government purchases, and exports would overstate expenditures on domestically produced goods and services and, hence, would overstate domestic GDP.

The needed adjustment is, fortunately, very simple. To get an accurate measure of GDP, we simply need to subtract total imports from total measured expenditures. That gives us the following key equation from which we begin construction of our model, in which Q stands for the total quantity of output, that is, GDP, and the final component, Ex - IM, represents net exports:

$$Q = C + I + G + (Ex - Im)$$

Planned versus Unplanned Expenditure

Investment could be broken down into fixed investment and inventory investment. Our next step is to divide inventory investment, in turn, into planned and unplanned components. Inventory investment is considered planned if the level of inventories is increased (or reduced) on purpose as part of a firm's business plan. For example, a retail store might increase inventories in response to growth in the number of customers it serves or the number of branch stores it constructs. Inventory investment is considered unplanned if goods accumulate contrary to a firm's business plan. This happens whenever demand is less than expected so that some goods the firm bought or produced with the intention to sell them, in fact, remain unsold. If demand is greater than expected, so that inventories unexpectedly decrease (or increase at a rate less than scheduled in the business plan), there is negative unplanned inventory investment (disinvestment).

All fixed investment is treated as planned. Total planned investment, then, means fixed investment plus planned inventory investment. All other types of expenditure— consumption, government purchases, and net exports—are also considered to be planned. For that reason, we use the term planned expenditure to mean the sum of consumption, government purchases, net exports, and planned investment. That is shown as the following equation form:

$$E_p = C + I_p + G + (Ex - Im)$$

We can explain the level of planned expenditure, as a whole, by looking at the choices that lie behind each of its components.

Consumption Expenditure

Choices made by consumers have a more powerful effect on the economy than those made by any other group. Consumer expenditure accounts for about two-thirds of GDP in the United States. In some other countries it is a little more, in some a little less; but everywhere consumption is the largest single component of expenditure. What determines the amount of consumer spending?

Among the first economists to pose this question was John Maynard Keynes. he put it this way: "The fundamental psychological law, upon which we are entitled to depend with great confidence is that men are disposed, as a rule and on the average, to increase their consumption as their income increases, but not by as much as the increase in their income." He called the amount of additional consumption, resulting from a one-dollar increase in income, the marginal propensity to consume. For example, if your marginal propensity to consume is .75, you will tend to increase your spending by $750 if your income goes up by $1,000.

This "psychological law" regarding consumption needs a few qualifications if it is to be stated exactly. First, in place of "income," we really should say disposable income. That means the amount of income left after taxes. If a person in one state earns $40,000 and pays $5,000 in taxes, while a person in another state earns $50,000 and pays taxes of $15,000, both would have the same disposable income of $35,000. Other things being equal, we would expect them to spend the same amount on consumption. Second, the relationship between consumption and disposable income is properly stated in real terms. If both prices and nominal disposable income rise in exact proportion, there is no change in real income; so we would expect no change in real consumption expenditure, other things being equal.

Third, the marginal propensity to consume is not equal to the average obtained by dividing total consumption by total income. Instead, there is a minimum level of consumption that people would like to maintain even if their income were zero. Keynes called this "autonomous consumption." Intuitively, you can think of the case of a college student who has no income but maintains a minimum level of consumption by borrowing against future income, or an unemployed person who has no income but maintains a minimum level of consumption by drawing on past saving.

Although income is the principal factor that determines consumption spending, there are certain other factors that also can have an effect. Among them are the following:

- Changes in net taxes (either taxes paid or transfer payments received), which act by changing the amount of disposable income associated with a given total income.
- Changes in consumer wealth, that is, the accumulated value of assets a person owns, is considered apart from current income—One very important example concerns the value of housing, since a home is the biggest asset for many households. In a period when housing prices rise more rapidly than income, as happened in the United States in the early 2000s, consumer spending rises more in proportion to income than it otherwise would.
- Interest rates—If interest rates fall, people can borrow more cheaply and may buy more goods and services on credit. Also, the amount they have to pay in interest on credit cards, mortgages, and other debt decreases, leaving more to buy consumer goods.
- Consumer confidence—In periods when consumers feel secure about their jobs and expect their incomes to rise in line with general prosperity, they tend to spend more for any given level of income. In times of pessimism and insecurity, people tend to be cautious and increase their saving as protection against the expected rainy day.

Planned Investment

The second component of planned expenditure is planned investment. It depends on two principal factors.

First, planned investment depends on interest rates (more specifically, on real interest rates, that is, interest rates adjusted for inflation. The relationship between interest rates and investment is easiest to understand in the case of a business that needs to borrow in order to invest. Suppose you run a construction business, and you are thinking about improving the productivity of your workers by buying a new backhoe, which costs $50,000. Your banker is willing to lend you the money, but you will have to pay 6 percent per year interest, equivalent to $250 per month on the loan of $50,000. If the bank charged 12 percent interest, your monthly interest payments would rise to $500; and you would be less likely to buy the new machine. If the interest rate was just 3 percent, monthly interest payments would be only $125; and you would be more likely to make the investment.

Although it is not so obvious, interest rates also play a role in investment decisions for a company that plans to finance investment from its own retained profits. Suppose that as a result of good profits in the previous year, your construction company had put aside $100,000 in cash. You would not then have to borrow from the bank to buy the backhoe. However, using half of your cash reserves to buy the backhoe still has an opportunity cost that depends on interest rates. For example, if the rate of interest on government bonds is 6 percent, your company could earn $250 per month by using $50,000 of your cash reserves to buy bonds instead of buying the backhoe.8 That is an opportunity cost. If the interest rate were 12 percent per year, your monthly income from the bonds would be $500—a greater opportunity cost—and you would be more tempted to buy the bonds instead of the backhoe.

Interest rates influence investment decisions by consumers as well as business. Residential construction accounts for about a third of all private fixed investment in the United States. When mortgage interest rates are low, as they were in the early 2000s, housing construction booms. The importance of interest rates for investment spending is one of the reasons that we will spend several chapters in this book talking about banking, financial markets, and related topics.

Interest rates are not the only factor influencing investment decisions. The psychological factor of business confidence is also important. By this, we mean the whole complex of expectations and hopes on which firms make their plans for the future. If you expect a boom in the housing market in your area, your construction company is more likely than otherwise to buy that backhoe. If you expect doom and gloom ahead, you'll play it safe by buying the government bonds. Keynes referred to business confidence using the colorful term "animal spirits." In doing so, he wanted to emphasize the fact that business confidence can change quickly for reasons that are hard for economists to measure exactly.

On a global scale, the decision of how much to invest in a given country depends on the country's investment climate, as well as interest rates. Among the conditions that make up a country's investment climate are its tax laws, the amount of "red tape" imposed by the country's bureaucracy, the likelihood that profits will be drained away by criminal gangs or corrupt officials, and the stability of macroeconomic conditions. In countries where the investment climate is good, domestic firms are willing to put profits into expansion of their operations, and international firms are willing to bring in new capital and know-how. In countries where the investment climate is bad, domestic firms send their profits abroad for safekeeping rather than investing them at home, and global business stays away.

Government Purchases

Government purchases are considered to be exogenous in most simple macroeconomic models. This means that they are determined by politics or other considerations that lie outside the model rather than by any variables that are included in the model. Transfer payments and tax revenues, on the other hand, are endogenous in that they depend on the level of real GDP, a variable that is included in the model. During the expansion phase of the business cycle, tax revenues rise and transfer payments, especially for unemployment benefits, fall. During a recession, tax collections fall and transfer payments rise.

Net Exports

The variable net exports is endogenous because it also depends on real GDP. As real GDP increases, both consumers and businesses spend some of their increased income on imported goods. For this reason, net exports tend to fall, and a country's trade deficit tends to widen during the expansion phase of the business cycle.

The exchange rate of a country's currency relative to the currencies of its trading partners is another factor that affects net exports. For example, during the early 2000s, the U.S. dollar weakened relative to the euro, the currency used by the country's major European trading partners. As the dollar weakened, it became easier for U.S. firms to sell their exports in Europe; and, at the same time, imports from Europe became more expensive for U.S. buyers. Consequently, net exports to Europe strengthened. Exchange rates, in turn, are influenced by many factors, including changes in real GDP, inflation, and interest rates.

Equilibrium in the Circular Flow

The market for any single good, say chicken, is said to be in equilibrium when the amount buyers plan to purchase equals the amount that producers supply for sale. When the market for chicken is in equilibrium, there will be no tendency for accumulation or decrease of inventories and no immediate pressure for market participants to change their plans.

The idea of equilibrium as a situation in which there is no unplanned change in inventories can be extended to the circular flow of income and expenditure. When total planned expenditures (consumption plus planned investment plus government purchases plus net exports) equal GDP, total planned purchases will equal total production; and there will be no unplanned inventory change for the economy as a whole. As a result, there will be no pressure from unplanned inventory change to cause changes in production plans. If something happens to increase or decrease total planned expenditures, the equilibrium will be disrupted. Let's see how this process works out as the economy expands and contracts over the business cycle.

An Expansion of Planned Expenditure

Suppose that the circular flow is initially in equilibrium with total planned expenditure exactly equal to GDP. Since goods are being produced at just the rate they are being sold, the level of inventories remains constant from one month to the next. Now suppose that something happens to disturb this equilibrium. For example, suppose that development of new energy-efficient technologies causes an upturn in investment as firms replace obsolete, energy-wasting equipment. As equipment makers increase their output of goods to satisfy the increased investment demand, they will take on more workers. The wage component of national income will increase. Profits of equipment makers are also likely to increase, further adding to the expansion of national income.

We know that when incomes rise, households will increase their consumption expenditure. So far there has been no change in the output of consumer goods; so as consumption expenditure begins to increase, the first effect will be an unplanned decrease in inventories. Only then, when makers of consumer goods see inventories falling, will they modify their production plans to meet the new demand. As they do so, they too will need to hire new workers; and incomes will rise further.

In this way, the original economic stimulus, which began in the industrial equipment sector, spreads through the economy. GDP and domestic income continue to rise, but not without limit. According to the principle of the marginal propensity to consume, people spend only a part of any increase in income on consumer goods, and each round of the cycle of more-production-more-income-more-spending is smaller than the previous one. Before long, GDP reaches a new equilibrium where production and planned expenditure balance, and there are no further unplanned changes in inventories.

The whole process began with an assumed increase in planned investment. By the time the new equilibrium is reached, the total change in GDP will be greater than the original increase in planned investment because it will also include production of additional consumer goods. The principle that a given initial change in planned expenditure changes equilibrium GDP by a greater amount is known as the multiplier effect.

Contraction of Planned Expenditure

The same process operates in reverse if equilibrium is disturbed by a decrease in some category of planned expenditure. For example, suppose a crisis in the Mexican economy reduces U.S. exports to that country. The first effect will be that U.S. makers of export goods will find inventories rising because Mexican importers are not buying as much as they had planned before the crisis. To bring inventories in line with reduced sales, U.S. makers of export goods cut their output. Workers are laid off or work shorter hours, and their incomes fall. As a result, they cut back on consumption expenditures, following the principle of the marginal propensity to consume. When this happens, makers of consumer goods also find that their inventories unexpectedly increase. They, too, cut back on output, and incomes of their workers fall.

As this process continues, GDP and domestic income decrease. They do not decrease without limit, however. Before long a new equilibrium is reached. In the new equilibrium, real GDP will have decreased by a greater amount than the original change in exports. This is an example of the multiplier effect operating in reverse.

The Multiplier Effect and the Business Cycle

The multiplier effect was one of the key ideas in Keynes' General Theory. Coming at the height of the Great Depression, the multiplier effect was immediately seized upon as an explanation for the business cycle.

Reduced to its simplest form, the Keynesian explanation of the Great Depression went something like this. During the 1920s, the U.S. economy entered a boom due to the multiplier effect of huge investment expenditures, especially expansion of automobile production and road building. Then, in 1929, came the Black Friday stock market crash. The crash destroyed business confidence, and investment fell. This time the multiplier effect operated in reverse to produce the Great Depression.

At the same time the multiplier effect seemed to give an explanation of the causes of the Great Depression, it also seemed to suggest a cure. What if the government increased its purchases of goods and services by enough to offset the drop in private investment? Wouldn't this send equilibrium GDP back to its original level? This reasoning gave rise to various attempts to spend the country back to prosperity, for example, by hiring thousands of unemployed workers for service in national parks. The nation did not fully recover from the Great Depression until the start of World War II brought on a further surge in government purchases.

Modern macroeconomics makes a place for the multiplier effect and recognizes that there is an element of truth in the simple Keynesian view of the business cycle. However, the simple multiplier theory is seriously incomplete. One shortcoming concerns changes in the price level over the business cycle. When producers respond to an unexpected decrease in inventories, do they increase real output without changing prices, do they raise prices to take advantage of unexpectedly strong demand, or do they do a little of both? Another problem is that the simple multiplier theory does not consider capacity constraints related to labor inputs, capital, and technology. Does real output respond in the same way to a change in planned expenditure when the economy is operating above its natural level of real output as below it? Still another limitation is that the theory pays too little attention to the role of money and the financial sector.

Classical Theory

A key tenet of the classical theory is that both households and businesspersons desire to maximize their total satisfaction. This means that in their everyday roles as workers and consumers, members of each household seek to attain the highest possible overall well-being, or utility. Thus, in the classical system, households are utility maximizers.

Businesses operate to produce the highest net income for the household entrepreneurs who own them. The net income of any business is its profit flow. Consequently, in the classical theory, businesses are profit maximizers.

Absence of Money Illusion

Consider the following example. A college student has a part-time job at a local fast-food establishment. The manager offers to increase her hourly wage rate from $6.00 per hour to $6.60 per hour, or by 10 percent. At the same time, however, prices of the goods and services that the student purchases have also risen by 10 percent, largely because of hefty increases in college tuition and fees. Thus, given the 10 percent rise in her living costs, the student is no better off in real terms than she was before her wage increase. Suppose, though, that the student nevertheless feels so good about the 10 percent increase in her nominal wages that she offers to work more hours. If she does, she is exhibiting money illusion. This is the inclination for a household or business to alter desired trades of goods, services, or factors of production simply because of nominal price changes.

A central hypothesis of classical theory is that people do not experience such money illusion. Instead, when they make decisions about how much to produce, sell, or purchase, they pay attention only to real variables, which have been adjusted for the price level. In the absence of changes in real quantities, individuals and businesses will not change their market transactions.

Pure Competition

Classical economists recognize that monopoly businesses, such as many electric utilities, exist. Nevertheless, they contend that the predominant mode of interaction among business firms in the aggregate economy is pure competition. Under pure competition, there are sufficiently large numbers of buyers and sellers of a typical good, service, or factor of production that no single buyer or seller can affect the market price of the good, service, or factor of production.

As a result, each buyer and seller is a price taker the buyer or seller takes market prices as "given" and incapable of change by means of purchases or sales initiated by the buyer or seller in isolation. Nonetheless, collective— though typically uncoordinated—purchases or sales of a good, service, or factor of production can change market prices. In other words, the forces of demand and supply determine market prices. These prices, in turn, adjust flexibly to variations in demand or supply.

What are the key assumptions of classical macroeconomic theory? The classical macroeconomic model is based on the idea that people pursue their own selfinterest. It also presumes that people do not experience money illusion, meaning that people recognize that they are no better off with higher nominal wages if prices also are higher. The third key assumption of the classical model is that there is pure competition throughout the economy, meaning that there are a large number of buyers and sellers of goods and services who individually cannot influence market prices.

Any macroeconomic theory must provide an explanation of how many goods and services businesses produce and how many units of factors of production, such as labor, they utilize. The classical theory is no exception. Indeed, the classical theory of production and employment is the benchmark, or starting point of comparison, for all other macroeconomic theories. Consequently, understanding this topic is crucial to comprehending the subject as a whole.

The Production Function

The aggregate production function is a relationship between the quantities of factors of production—labor, capital, land, and entrepreneurship— employed by all firms in the economy and the total production of real output by those firms, given the technology currently available.Here we shall focus on the short run, which is a time horizon short enough that firms cannot vary all factors of production.

Short-Run Production

In the short run firms cannot adjust the amounts of capital, land, and entrepreneurship. The only variable factor of production for firms is the quantity of labor that they employ on an hourly and weekly basis, which we denote N.

There are three measures of the amount of labor that firms employ. One measure is simply the number of people employed during a given time interval. An alternative measure is the total time worked by all people employed by firms, which is just the total hours of work by all employees during a period. Finally, we can measure employment via a combination of these first two measures, known as person-hours.

In the short run firms use labor together with their fixed quantities of other productive factors to produce output. Some firms, such as fast-food restaurants, may use very simple production processes. Others, such as microcomputer manufacturers, may assemble components manufactured at remote points around the world. The aggregate production function sums up the result of these processes as the total quantity of real output of goods and services, y, that results from the use of the total quantity of labor, N, by firms:

$$y=F(N).$$

This expression says that the aggregate amount of real output is a function of the amount of labor employed by all firms in the economy.

Panel (a) of figure displays a sample aggregate production function, F(N). Any point along this function tells us how much real output firms can produce for a given quantity of labor employed. For instance, if firms employ an amount of labor equal to N_1, their total output of goods and services, or real GDP, is equal to y_1. If firms employ a larger quantity of labor, N_2, then naturally they are able to produce a larger amount of real output. Real GDP then would be at a higher level, y_2.

The production function in panel (a) of figure is concave, meaning that it is bowed downward. This means that the production function's slope—the change in output resulting from a change in employment, or "rise" divided by "run"—varies along the function. To see this, note that the slope of the function at the employment level N_1 is given by the slope of the line tangent to the function at this point, or $\Delta y_1/\Delta N$, where the symbol Δ denotes a change in a quantity. But at the higher employment level N_2, the same change in employment, ΔN, yields a smaller change in output, Δy_2. This means that the slope of the production function at the employment level N_2, which is equal to $\Delta y_2/N$, must be smaller than the slope of the production function at the employment level N_1.

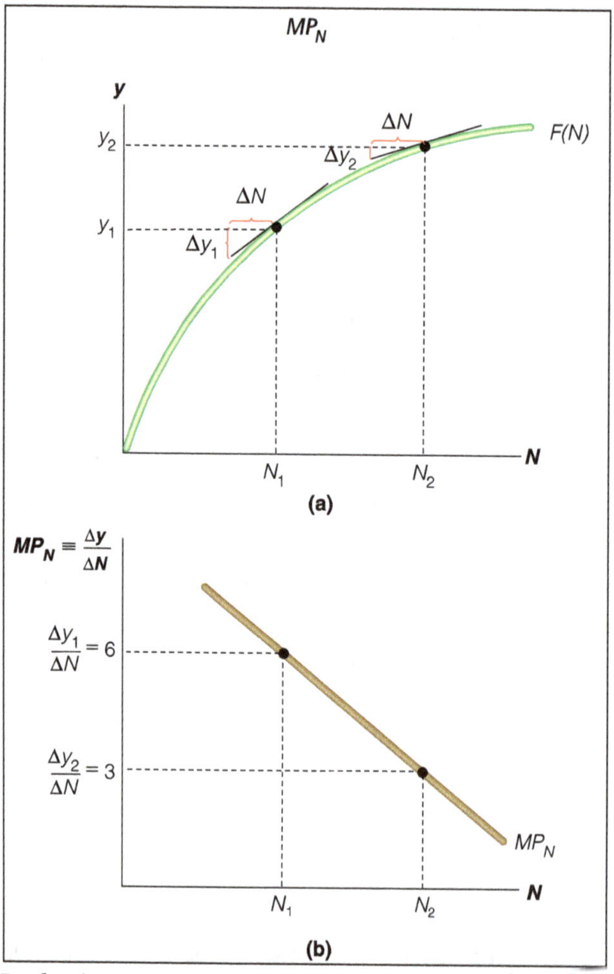

The Aggregate Production Function and the Marginal-Product-of-Labor (MPN) Schedule.

Given a fixed stock of capital and a current state of technology, higher levels of labor employment are necessary to achieve increased production of real output. The bowed, or concave, shape of the production function in panel (a) reflects the law of diminishing marginal returns, which states that total output increases at a decreasing rate for each additional one unit rise in employment of labor. Consequently, as shown in panel (b), the marginal product of labor declines as employment rises.

The Marginal Product of Labor

The decline in the slope of the production function as the amount of labor employed by firms rises is consistent with the law of diminishing marginal returns. This law states that eventually the additional output produced by an additional unit of labor declines as more units of labor are employed by firms. By definition, the slope of the production function, $\Delta y/\Delta N$, is the additional amount of output that firms can produce by employing an additional unit of labor. This is the marginal product of labor, or MP_N. In other words, MP_N $\Delta y/\Delta N$, or the slope of the production function at a given quantity of labor. (The three-barred equals sign ≡ means that a relationship is true by definition; it is an identity.)

Panel (b) of figure graphs the marginal product of labor. At the employment level N_1, the marginal product of labor is equal to $\Delta y1/\Delta N$, or the slope of the production function at this employment level. The value of this slope is assumed to equal 6. If total employment rises to N_2, then the slope of the production function declines to $\Delta y_2/\Delta N$, which is assumed to equal 3; thus, the marginal product of labor is lower at this higher employment level.

The employment levels N_1 and N_2 are just two examples, of course. At employment levels less than N_1, the marginal product of labor would be larger than $\Delta y_1/\Delta N$. At employment levels greater than N_2, the marginal product of labor would be smaller than $\Delta y_2/\Delta N$. At successively greater employment levels between N_1 and N_2, the marginal product of labor would decline. Consequently, there is a downward-sloping set of values for the marginal product of labor that corresponds to the production function shown in panel (a) of figure. This is the marginal-product-of-labor schedule, or MP_N schedule, displayed in panel (b). The MP_N schedule shows the marginal product of labor, or slope of the production function, at any given quantity of labor. Its downward slope reflects the law of diminishing marginal returns.

The Demand for Labor

Because the marginal product of labor measures how much more output an additional unit of labor produces, it is crucial to any firm's decision about how much labor to employ. Another key factor that a firm must consider, of course, is the expense that it must incur by employing a unit of labor. To maximize its profits, a firm must balance the revenue gain from the sale of the additional production generated by another unit of labor against the cost of hiring that labor unit.

Profit Maximization

A profit-maximizing firm produces output to the point at which its marginal revenue (MR), or additional revenue stemming from production and sale of an additional unit of output, equals its marginal cost (MC), or additional production cost that it incurs in this endeavor. If MR exceeds MC at a given level of production, then the firm would earn a positive net profit from the last unit of production. This would encourage the firm to produce more units. If MC exceeds MR, however, then the firm's net profit on the last unit produced would be negative, which would induce the firm to cut back on its production. Consequently, when MR = MC, the firm has produced the output level that ensures positive net profits for every unit of production up to the last unit produced. Thus, the firm has maximized its profit on its total output production.

A central hypothesis of the classical theory is that pure competition prevails, so prices are market determined. Because no single firm can affect the market price, each unit of output that the firm produces by definition yields the same marginal revenue, which is the market price. Therefore, each purely competitive, profit-maximizing firm produces output up to the point at which,

$$MR = P = MC$$

In words, a purely competitive firm produces output to the point at which price equals marginal cost.

In the short run, however, a firm's marginal cost depends on the expense that it incurs by employing its single variable factor of production, labor. The firm's labor expense is the money wage rate (also called the nominal wage rate) that it pays a unit of labor, denoted by W and measured in dollars per labor unit. For instance, suppose that the current market wage rate is W_1 = \$30 per unit of labor. A firm's marginal cost is measured in dollars spent per unit of output produced. Suppose that the marginal product of labor at the firm's current output level is MP_N $\Delta y/\Delta N$ = 3 units of output per unit of labor. Then, to calculate the firm's marginal cost of producing output at the money wage W_1 = \$30 per unit of labor, we divide W_1 by MP_N, which gives MC=(\$30 per unit of labor)/(3 units of output per unit of labor)=\$10 per unit of output. Consequently, marginal cost by definition is equal to W/MP_N.

The Value of the Marginal Product of Labor

This means that we can rewrite a competitive firm's profit-maximizing condition, P MC, as:

$$P = W / MP_N$$

Now, if we multiply both sides of this equation by MP_N, we get,

$$P \times MP_N = (W / MP_N) \times MP_N = W$$

This tells us that another way to express the firm's profit-maximizing condition is:

$$W = P \times MP_N.$$

This is the firm's profit-maximizing rule for employing labor. It says that a purely competitive firm that seeks to maximize its profit should employ labor to the point at which the money wage that the firm pays each unit of labor is equal to the price it receives for each unit of output that labor produces times the marginal product of labor. The price per unit of output times the marginal product of labor is called the value of the marginal product of labor, $VMP_N = P \times MP_N$. For instance, if the market price of a firm's output is \$5 per unit of output and the marginal product of labor is 6 units of output per unit of labor, then the value of labor's marginal product is equal to the product of these two figures, or \$30 pcr unit of labor.

Panel (a) of figure shows how the value of the marginal product of labor typically varies with the amount of labor employed by a firm. We obtain this schedule by multiplying the firm's output price, P, times the MP_N schedule in panel (b) of figure. The result is another downward-sloping schedule, called the value-of-marginal-productof-labor schedule, or VMP_N schedule.

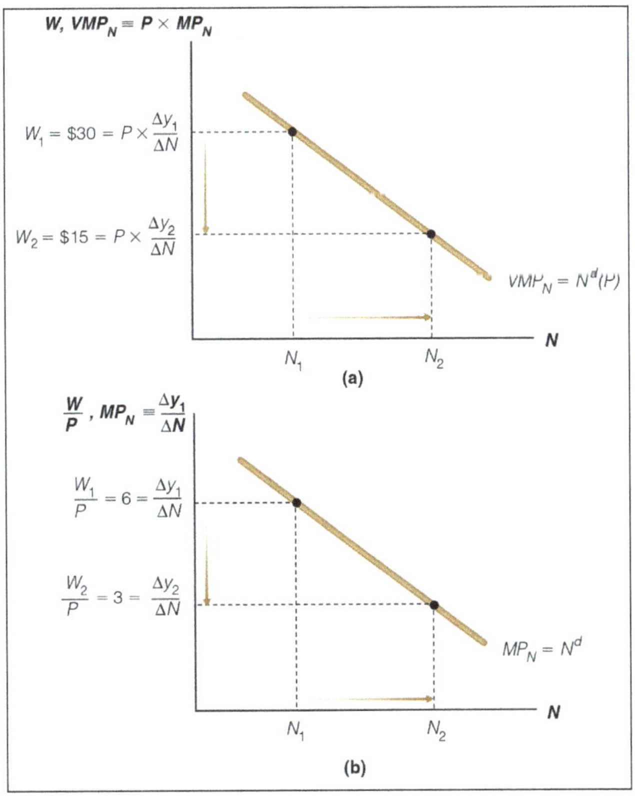

Alternative Labor Demand Schedules for a Purely Competitive Firm.

As panel (a) of figure indicates, if the market wage that the firm must pay each unit of labor it employs is W_1=\$30, then the firm employs labor to the point at which the value of labor's marginal product is equal to $30 per unit of labor, which in the figure implies employment level N_1. At a lower wage rate of W_2 = $15 per unit of labor, however, the firm requires a smaller value of marginal product to maximize its profit, so it increases the amount of labor it employs, to the quantity of labor N_2. A fall in the market wage rate causes the firm to increase the quantity of labor it demands. Hence, the firm decides how many units of labor it desires to employ by moving along its VMP_N schedule. This leads to the following important conclusion.

A profit-maximizing firm employs labor to the point at which the value of labor's marginal product is equal to the money wage. Thus, a fall in the money wage increases the quantity of labor demanded by a firm, as shown in panel (a). Equivalently, the firm hires labor services to the point at which the marginal product of labor is equal to the real wage. Consequently, with an unchanged price level, a fall in the nominal wage induces a decline in the real wage and causes an increase in the quantity of labor demanded by firms, as shown in panel (b).

The VMP_N schedule for a purely competitive firm is that firm's labor demand schedule showing how many units of labor, N, the firm demands at any given money wage, W.

We can rearrange the firm's profit-maximizing condition, $W = P \times MP_N$, by dividing both sides of the condition by P, which yields the expression,

$$W / P = MPN.$$

This expression says that another way of stating the firm's profit-maximizing condition is that the firm should hire labor to the point at which W/P, the real wage that the firm pays, is equal to the marginal product of labor. Panel (b) of figure illustrates this condition for two examples. One example is for the money wage W_1= $30 per unit of labor. Because the price of the firm's output, P, is $5 per unit, the real value of this money wage is $30 per unit of labor divided by $5 per unit of output, or 6 units of output per unit of labor.

In other words, the $30 wage that the firm pays each unit of labor is equivalent to a payment of 6 units of the firm's output. This is the real wage that the firm pays. To maximize its profit, the firm therefore employs labor to the point at which the marginal product of labor is equal to 6 units of output per unit of labor and employs a total of N_1 units of labor. Thus, the firm pays the worker an amount equal to the real value of the labor that the worker provides the firm.

The Firm's Demand for Labor

If the market wage rate were to fall to W_2 = $15 per unit of labor, then the real wage paid by the firm would decline to $15 per unit of labor divided by P = $5 per unit of output, or 3 units of output per unit of labor. Hence, the firm would require the marginal product of the last unit of labor employed to equal 3 units of output, so it would raise its employment of labor to N_2 units. Thus, the firm would demand more units of labor when the real market wage declines. We conclude that the MP_N schedule for a purely competitive firm is that firm's labor demand schedule. This schedule shows how many units of labor, N, the firm wishes to hire at any given real wage, W/P.

In both panels of figure, the same money wage decline, from W_1 = \$30 per unit of labor to W_2 = \$15 per unit of labor, leads to the same increase in desired labor employment by the firm.We may conclude that both schedules depict the same choices by the firm. This makes sense, because in constructing both labor demand schedules, we have worked with the same, single profit-maximizing condition for a purely competitive firm. The only distinction is that the VMP_N schedule in panel (a) is the labor demand schedule if we measure the nominal wage as the factor price of labor, whereas the MP_N schedule in panel (b) is the labor demand schedule if we measure the real wage as the factor price of labor. The labor demand schedule graphed against the money wage, W, in panel (a) depends on the output price P, so we label it $N^d(P)$ to recognize this dependence. The labor demand schedule graphed against the real wage W/P in panel (b) does not depend on the value of P, and so we simply label it N^d.

According to the classical model, what are the determinants of the demand for labor by firms? The demand for labor stems from the marginal product of labor, which is the slope of the aggregate production function. Profit-maximizing competitive firms hire units of labor to the point where price equals marginal cost, which in turn equals the money wage rate divided by the marginal product of labor. Consequently, firms employ labor to the point where the real wage rate equals the marginal product of labor, or at points along the marginal product schedule, which means that the marginal product schedule is the labor demand schedule when the real wage rate is measured along the vertical axis. Alternatively, firms employ labor to the point where the money wage equals the value of the marginal product of labor, meaning that the value-of-marginal-product schedule is the labor demand schedule when the money wage rate is measured along the vertical axis.

The Supply of Labor

All of us strive to find employment in a field in which we can do work that gives us satisfaction. Nevertheless, the time that we devote to work is time that we could otherwise have devoted to leisure activities that we would enjoy. The value we place on leisure time thereby represents an opportunity cost that we incur when we devote our time to work. This is why firms must pay us wages to induce us to devote large chunks of our days to work-related activities.

Measuring Labor Compensation: The Real Wage

Classical theorists focus on the real wage as the relevant measure of the compensation that laborers receive for time that they spend at work. The reason is that the real wage gives the purchasing power of a worker's earnings.

To see why this is true, consider a simple example. During a full year, an individual works 40 hours per week and earns a weekly money wage of $500. Over the course of the year, however, the level of prices of goods and services that the person consumes doubles. By the end of the year, therefore, the $500 weekly wage is worth half as much to the worker as it was at the beginning of the year. Consequently, it is not the money wage alone that matters to a worker. What matters is how many goods and services that money wage can be used to buy. This is why the real wage is the appropriate measure of a worker's compensation for labor time.

The Labor Supply Schedule

Holding all other factors unchanged, the only way that an individual may be induced to give up some leisure time and work more hours is if the real wage increases. Because the real wage is equal to the money wage divided by the price level, W/P, there are two ways that the real wage can rise. One is if the money wage rises relative to the price level; the other is if the price level falls relative to the money wage.

Figure illustrates the effect on an individual's labor supply of a rise in the money wage from an initial value W_1 to a higher value W_2, with the price level unchanged at P_1. As panel (a) shows, this causes the real wage to increase, and the quantity of labor supplied also increases from N_1 to N_2 as workers respond to the higher real wage by giving up leisure time to work. Economists call this the substitution effect stemming from a rise in the real wage, because workers substitute labor for leisure. Note that at sufficiently high real wages, theoretically an income effect could arise: workers' incomes could be high enough that they would prefer to work less so that they could enjoy more leisure time. Most evidence indicates, however, that the substitution effect predominates in the aggregate. Consequently, the labor supply schedule, N^s, typically slopes upward, as in the figure.

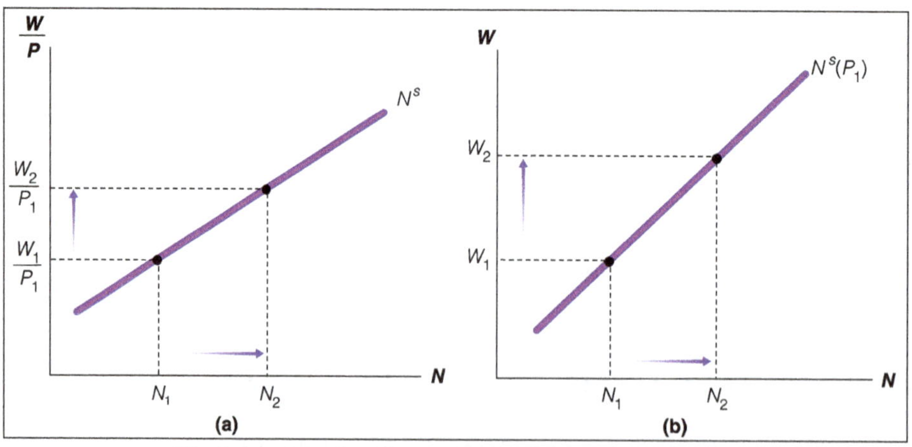

The Labor Supply Effects of a Rise in the Money Wage.

Panel (b) of figure shows another depiction of the labor supply schedule. Here, only the money wage appears on the vertical axis. Again, a rise in the money wage from W_1 to W_2 causes the amount of labor that workers supply to rise from N_1 to N_2. As panel (b) shows, however, this occurs only because the price level has remained unchanged at P_1, so we label this version of labor supply N^s (P_1). In both panels, a rise in the money wage with unchanged prices causes a rightward movement along the labor supply schedule.

An increase in the money wage typically induces a worker to give up leisure time to work. Hence, workers supply more labor as the money wage rises relative to the price level, as shown in panel (a). Therefore the labor supply schedule slopes upward against the real wage. Alternatively, panel.(b) displays this effect of a rise in the money wage for a given price level and indicates that the labor supply schedule also slopes upward if the money wage alone is measured along the vertical axis.

Figure on the following page examines the labor supply effect of a decline in the price level. Panel (a) shows that a fall in the price level, from an initial value P_1 to a lower level P_2, increases the real wage that an individual earns. The effect is the same as if the money wage had risen with prices unchanged: Individuals work more hours, so the quantity of labor supplied increases from N_1 to N_2.

Panel (b) illustrates the effect of a price-level decrease when we measure only the money wage on the vertical axis of a labor supply diagram. Again the money wage remains unchanged. Nevertheless, the fall in the price level causes the real wage to increase, inducing individuals to work more hours and increase the quantity of labor supplied from N_1 to N_2. Consequently, the labor supply schedule in panel (b) shifts to the right as a result of the decline in the price level.

Labor Market Equilibrium and Aggregate Supply

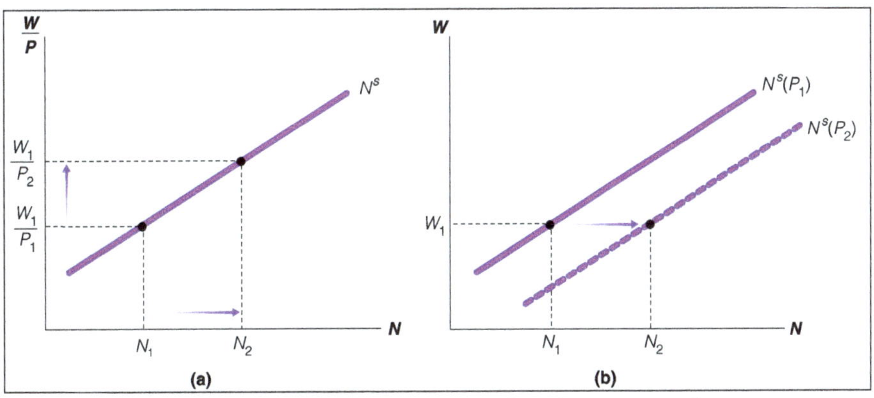

The Labor Supply Effects of a Fall in the Price Level.

The total demand for labor is the sum of the labor demand schedules for all the firms in the economy. Likewise, the total supply of labor is the sum of the labor supply schedules of all people in the economy who participate in the labor force. In the classical system, the interactions among firms and workers through the forces of demand and supply in the labor market determine the equilibrium wage and the equilibrium level of employment.

A reduction in the price level, from P_1 to P_2, with the money wage unchanged, causes the real wage to rise. As a result, workers choose to supply more labor services, as shown in panel (a). Equivalently, panel (b) shows that with the nominal wage unchanged, the fall in the price level induces workers to increase their supply of labor services, so the labor supply schedule graphed against the money wage alone must shift rightward.

Furthermore, the aggregate production function then yields the aggregate level of real output produced in the economy. In addition to providing a theory of the aggregate labor market, the classical labor market theory can help to explain why wages are higher in some industries than in others.

The Price Level, Employment and Real Output

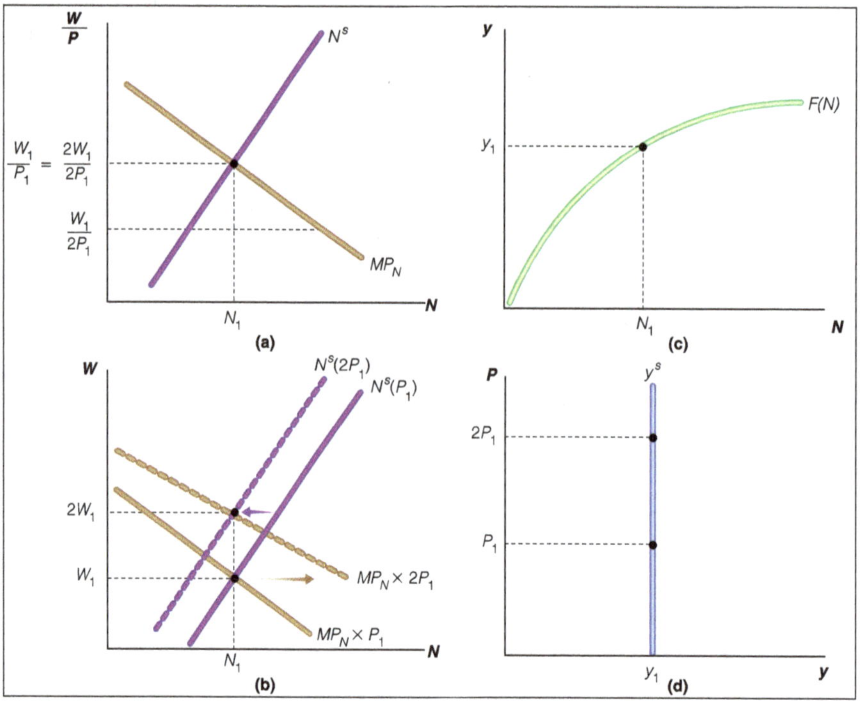

The Effects of a Doubling of the Price Level on the Equilibrium Money Wage, Employment, and Real Output.

Figure depicts the determination of wages, employment, and output in the classical theory. Panels (a) and (b) are alternative illustrations of equilibrium in the labor market. In both panels, an initial equilibrium money wage, W_1, arises at which the quantity of labor demanded by firms is equal to the quantity of labor supplied by workers, given the prevailing price level, P_1. This equilibrium quantity of labor demanded and supplied is the equilibrium employment level, N_1. The aggregate production function in panel (c) then indicates the equilibrium level of real output, y_1, that is produced with this aggregate amount of labor employed. Finally, panel (d) shows that this yields a price level and real output combination of P_1 and y_1.

The price level ultimately is determined in the aggregate market for goods and services. Nonetheless, we can consider the effects of changes in the price level on money wages, employment, and output via a simple, and rather extreme, example in which the price level doubles from P_1 to $2P_1$. In panel (a), this doubling of the price level causes the real wage, which is measured along the vertical axis, to decline by a factor of two, or to half its original value. The result is an excess quantity of labor demanded, because firms would like to hire more workers at the reduced real wage, but individuals are less willing to supply labor to firms. Firms begin to bid up the money wage to induce individuals to supply more labor, and ultimately the real wage returns to its original level. This happens, however, only after the equilibrium money wage has doubled. Consequently, the end result in response to the doubling of the price level is a doubling of the money wage and no change in the equilibrium employment level.

If the price level doubles, then the real wage falls to half its original level in panel (a). At the lower real wage, there is an excess quantity of labor demanded. The money wage is bid upward until labor market equilibrium is reattained. Equivalently, in panel (b) the doubling of the price level doubles the value of the marginal product of labor, and so the demand for labor rises. Workers, however, realize that the real wage has declined and reduce their supply of labor. On net, in both panels (a) and (b), equilibrium employment is unchanged. Thus, equilibrium output also is unchanged, as shown in panel (c). As a result, the increase in the price level has no effect on the production of real output, implying that the aggregate supply schedule in panel (d) is vertical.

Panel (b) of figure provides an alternative illustration of these labor market effects of a doubling of the price level. When the price level doubles, so does the value of marginal product at all firms in the economy. Therefore, labor demand increases, as shown by the rightward shift of the labor demand schedule. At the same time, however, workers perceive that the purchasing power of the money wage is half its previous level, inducing them to reduce their supply of labor. Hence, the labor supply schedule shifts leftward. The result, as in panel (a), is a doubling of the equilibrium money wage. Again, equilibrium employment is unaffected by the rise in the price level. (When all wages adjust flexibly, the classical model indicates that no workers should be involuntarily unemployed; the theory does not rule out unemployment induced by factors that prevent the labor market from reaching equilibrium.

The Classical Aggregate Supply Schedule

Equilibrium employment does not change when the price level doubles, so panel (c) in figure indicates no change in real output. In panel (d), however, there is a new price level–real output combination, $2P_1$ and y_1. This combination, along with the original combination P_1 and y_1, lies along a schedule of price level–real output combinations that is vertical, meaning that any given change in the price level would leave real output unchanged. This vertical schedule is the classical aggregate supply schedule, which is the set of combinations of prices and real output at which the labor market is in equilibrium.

Because the aggregate supply schedule is vertical, we can say that the level of real output is "supply determined." Most economists credit Jean Baptiste Say with first emphasizing this point, which led to the dictum, "Supply creates its own demand." That is, no matter what shape the economy's demand schedule might take, the classical theory of aggregate supply implies that equilibrium real output is determined solely by factors that influence the position of the vertical aggregate supply schedule.

How are the aggregate levels of labor employment and real output of goods and services determined in the classical model? Equilibrium employment occurs at the real wage at which the quantity of labor demanded by firms equals the quantity of labor supplied by households. Equilibrium output then is determined by the aggregate production function. In the classical model, a change in the price level has no effect on equilibrium employment or output, so the classical aggregate supply schedule is vertical.

In the classical system the quantity of real output is determined by the position of the aggregate supply schedule. This feature led to the central classical idea of supply-determined output. Nevertheless, the concept of the aggregate demand for output is crucial to understanding how the price level is determined in the classical theory.

The Demand for Money

The classical economists concluded that the primary factor explaining changes in the price level is variability in the amount of money in circulation, which, in turn, induces variations in aggregate demand. Consequently, a prerequisite to understanding the classical theory of aggregate demand for output is ascertaining how households and businesses decide how much money they desire to hold. Therefore, the classical theory of aggregate demand and price-level determination is developed from a theory of the demand for money.

The Functions of Money

Although we tend to think of money as coins or dollar bills, the classical economists realized that any item that people are willing to accept in exchange for goods and services is money. Modern definitions of money, for instance, include funds that households and businesses hold in accounts in financial institutions such as banks, savings and loan associations, and credit unions.

Money performs four important functions:

- Medium of exchange: The fundamental role of money is as a medium of exchange. When people trade goods and services, they are willing to accept money in exchange. This saves people from having to engage in barter, or the act of exchanging goods and services directly. Barter is a costly process, because it requires locating others willing to exchange items directly. Using money saves on such costs.
- Store of value: A second function of money is as a store of value. An individual can set money aside for later use in purchasing goods, services, or financial assets. While the funds sit idle, they retain value that the individual can draw upon to make the future purchases. For instance, the individual can hold funds in a checking account for several days and then use the funds to buy groceries as needed.
- Unit of account Money's third function is as a unit of account. Households and businesses can value goods and services in terms of money. In addition, people can quote prices of goods and services in money terms. For example, when an individual shops at a U.S. grocery store, the prices of goods are expressed in dollar terms.
- Standard of deferred payment finally, money also serves as a standard of deferred payment. When people reach contractual agreements that require future payments, they specify that the payments will be made with money. Bank loans, for example, specify future dollar repayments.

The Quantity Theory of Money

Although the original classical theorists recognized that money performs these four functions, they viewed money's property as a medium of exchange as the key to explaining why money exists. After all, they reasoned, if money did not function as a medium of exchange, then people could barter goods, services, and financial assets directly. People would not even use money if it did not perform this key function.

For this reason, the classical theory of the demand for money focuses on money's role as a medium of exchange. To understand how much money people desire to hold, the classical economists concentrated on explaining the demand for money for purchases of newly produced goods and services. The transactions-based theory of money demand that they developed is now known as the quantity theory of money. The starting point for the quantity theory of money is the equation of exchange:

$$M \times V = P \times y.$$

In the equation of exchange, M is the nominal quantity of money, or the current-dollar value of currency and checking deposits held by the nonbank public. The term

V represents the income velocity of money, or the average number of times people spend each unit of money on final goods and services per unit of time. Consequently, the left side of the equation of exchange is the value of current-dollar monetary payments for final goods and services. On the right side of the equation, the price level for final goods and services is multiplied by the quantity of output of goods and services. Note, however, that this quantity is also the current-dollar value of monetary payments for final goods and services. Hence, both sides of the equation of exchange must be identical. The equation of exchange is thus an accounting definition, or identity. It states that the product of the nominal quantity of money times the average number of times that people use money to buy goods and services ($M \times V$) must equal the market value of the goods and services that people use the money to purchase ($P \times y$).

An economic identity is a truism. It is not a theory of how people behave. The basis of the quantity theory of money is the Cambridge equation, so named because it was first proposed by Alfred Marshall and other economists at Cambridge University in England. According to the Cambridge equation:

$$M^d \; k \times Y,$$

Where, M^d denotes the total quantity of money all people in the economy wish to hold and k is a fraction ($0 < k < 1$). The Cambridge equation, therefore, says that people desire to hold some fraction of their nominal income as money. the nominal value of real output, $P \times y$, corresponds to the total level of nominal income, Y. This means that the Cambridge equation may also be written as:

$$M^d = k \times P \times y.$$

The idea behind this equation is simple. The fraction k represents the public's desired holdings of nominal money balances relative to total nominal income. For instance, if $k = 0.2$, then people wish to hold 20 percent, or one-fifth, of their nominal income as money. They hold this money in anticipation of exchanges they will make during the coming days and weeks. They allocate the rest of their income to immediate consumption of goods and services. It is for this reason that the theory of money demand is directly related to the classical theory of the aggregate demand for real output.

Aggregate Demand and the Price Level

We now have the essential building blocks that we need to see how aggregate demand and the price level are determined in the classical theory.

The Aggregate Demand Schedule

Suppose that the quantity of nominal money balances supplied through the actions of a central bank is equal to an amount M 1. In equilibrium, all individuals in the economy desire to hold this quantity of money balances, so that:

$$M^d = M_1.$$

The Cambridge equation then indicates that,

$$M_1 = k \times P \times y.$$

If we divide both sides of this equation by k × P, we obtain,

$$M_1 / (k \times P) = y$$

Reversing the two sides of this equation lcaves us with,

$$y^d = M_1 / (k \times P).$$

This is an equation for the economy's aggregate demand schedule. The aggregate demand schedule is all combinations of real output and prices for which households are satisfied holding the available quantity of nominal money balances (M_1 in this example), given their average desired ratio of money holdings, k.

Figure depicts the aggregate demand schedule. As the equation for the aggregate demand schedule indicates, the quantity of real output of goods and services that people wish to purchase declines as the price level rises. This is so because as the price level increases, so do nominal income earnings. According to the Cambridge equation $M^d = k \times Y = k \times P \times y$, individuals will, as a result, desire to hold more money balances, leaving them with less of their income to purchase real goods and services. As a result, the amount of real output demanded falls from y_1 to y_2 when the price level rises from P_1 to P_2. This is a leftward movement along the aggregate demand schedule.

Shifts in the Aggregate Demand Schedule

Two factors can cause the aggregate demand schedule's position to change. One is a change in the quantity of money supplied by the government or by a central bank. As we can see by referring to the equation for the schedule, $y^d\ M_1/(k \times P)$, a rise in the quantity of money to an amount larger than M_1 would increase the right side of the equation. This means that nominal purchasing power available to all individuals in the economy would be higher at any given price level, so people would desire to purchase more real goods and services at any given price level. The aggregate demand schedule would shift to the right, and aggregate demand would rise. In contrast, a decline in the quantity of money would shift the aggregate demand schedule to the left, and aggregate demand would fall.

The other factor that can alter the position of the aggregate demand schedule is a change in k in the Cambridge equation. For example, a technological change might reduce people's desire to demand as much money—for instance, both debit cards and automated teller machines at banks reduce the desire to keep ready cash on hand. In that case, the value of k would decline. People would hold fewer money balances relative to their nominal income, $Y = P \times y$. This would free up income for purchasing goods and services. Referring once more to the equation for the aggregate demand schedule, $y^d M_1 / (k \times P)$, we can see that a decline in k, because it reduces the denominator of the right-hand side of the equation, increases the total purchasing power available to individuals in the economy. Just as an increase in the quantity of money supplied causes a rise, or rightward shift outward, in aggregate demand, so does a decline in the demand for money by individuals. In contrast, a rise in money demand induces a reduction, or leftward shift inward, in aggregate demand.

The graph below shows how real output and the price level are determined in the classical model. What happens if the money stock changes? What occurs if there is a change in technology?

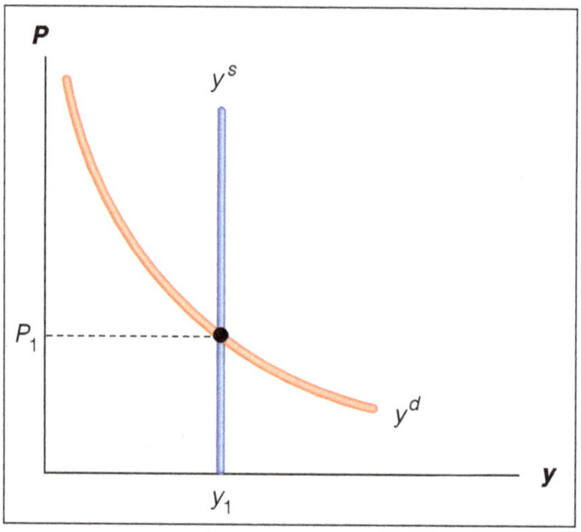

Output-Market Equilibrium in the Classical Model.

The equilibrium price level ensures that the amount of real output that individuals wish to purchase, given the quantity of money and the income velocity of money, is equal to the level of real output produced by firms. This price level corresponds to the point where the aggregate demand schedule crosses the aggregate supply schedule.

Concepts of National Income

Robinson Crusoe Economics

All alone on his tropical island, Crusoe quickly realizes that he doesn't like the way things are developing. His stomach is starting to rumble, his throat is dry and itchy, and he doesn't see any natural shelter from the horrific rainstorms that must occasionally strike the island. Rather than resign himself to his fate, Crusoe decides to take action to alter the unfolding of history, so that events transpire in a manner more to his liking.

Before he can make a sensible decision on how to proceed, Crusoe first needs to see what he has to work with. He climbs to the top of a hill and surveys the island. Crusoe notes that there are plenty of coconut trees, as well as some small streams of running water in the distance. There are several rocks of varying sizes, as well as strong vines. Crusoe's mind begins whirring as he decides what to do first.

At this point we can stop and describe the situation in terms of economic concepts. You probably realized, with Crusoe, why the particular items were relevant to his situation, and would be among the facts that you would consider if you found yourself in Crusoe's place. In economic jargon, Crusoe took an inventory of the goods at his disposal. That is, he appraised himself of the stockpile of physical items available for his use that exhibited scarcity.

After all, Crusoe could have truthfully said, "Hmm, this island is subject to the earth's gravitational pull, meaning I won't drift off into outer space and freeze to death. There is a plentiful supply of oxygen here, meaning I won't suffocate. And the presence of an atmosphere is very good for transmitting sound waves, so that I can hear a storm approaching." These attributes of the island are also extremely useful to Crusoe, and contribute to the achievement of his goals. But Crusoe wouldn't focus on them when formulating his plans, because they aren't scarce. Crusoe doesn't need to economize these general, background conditions the way he needs to exercise stewardship over the coconuts, vines, etc.

The distinctive mark of scarcity is that there are tradeoffs involved. Until he finds another source of food (such as fish after he constructs some tools), Crusoe needs to make sure he doesn't eat his coconuts too quickly. If he decides to use certain rocks in order to make a shelter, Crusoe can't simultaneously use those same rocks when building a fire. And even if the supply of vines is ubiquitous, even so Crusoe must be considerate when cutting them down to make a fishing net, because it takes him time to walk deeper into the jungle and get more vines.

As these examples all demonstrate, Crusoe needs to think through the consequences of his actions whenever his plans involve the rocks, vines, coconuts, and so on. Because these items are scarce, Crusoe might later regret the influence on them, because this will impair his ability to satisfy goals in the future. Items that can help a person achieve his or her goals, and could help the person achieve even more goals if there were more of these items available, are calledgoods. In contrast, background conditions like gravity and oxygen are not (typically) goods in the economic sense, because no action Crusoe takes will render them less useful to the achievement of his goals. Crusoe doesn't need to worry about sprinting too fast and thereby "using up all the oxygen," and he doesn't face any tradeoffs in relying on gravity when knocking down coconuts with a long stick.

Further, there aren't any goals that Crusoe could accomplish, if only he had "more oxygen" or "more gravity." So although oxygen and gravity are necessary for his very life, Crusoe doesn't have to economize on their use, and hence they are not classified as economic goods.

It's important to realize that an object becomes a good when a person incorporates it into his plans. A coconut on the tropical island is not a good because of its physical characteristics per se, but rather because (a) it can serve to alleviate hunger, (b) Crusoe would prefer to not feel hungry, and (c) Crusoe is aware of point (a). If Crusoe were ignorant of the fact that coconuts are edible, then he might not consider them as goods. For a different example, certain plants on the island might have medicinal properties, but if Crusoe doesn't know it, then those plants will not attain the status of economic goods.

Consumer Goods versus Producer Goods

Now that we understand what goods are in general, we can begin to make some distinctions. On the one hand, Crusoe recognizes that there are scarce items that can help him to directly achieve his goals. For example, the running water in the stream can directly quench his thirst, and the coconuts can directly satisfy Crusoe's hunger. Economists call these consumer goods.

On the other hand, there are items that are certainly useful, and which would allow Crusoe to achieve more of his goals if he had more of such items—hence they are goods—but they are not directly useful to him. They are only indirectly useful because they help Crusoe to obtain more consumer goods. For example, a long stick, in and of itself, doesn't do anything for Crusoe, and if it were the only object on the island, Crusoe would not consider it a good at all. But because there are coconuts hanging on trees—some of which are out of Crusoe's reach—suddenly the stick acquires value indirectly. Crusoe now considers the stick to be a good, even though it doesn't directly satisfy hunger, because it indirectly helps him to achieve his goal. Economists call items such as the hypothetical stick producer goods or factors of production or means of production. As with goods in general, the distinction between consumer versus producer goods is in the mind of the acting individual.

Land, Labor and Capital Goods

Even within the class of producer goods, we can make more distinctions. Those producer goods that are the direct gifts of nature are typically called land or natural resources. These include somewhat permanent items such as a flowing stream, or a tree that will yield a flow of coconuts indefinitely; but also included are depletable resources such as a small deposit of tin that Crusoe can use to make cooking pans and fish hooks.

The single most important and versatile producer good is Crusoe's own labor, which is the flow of productive services Crusoe performs with his body. In terms of the logic of economic principles, it would be perfectly sensible to group labor along with other natural resources that provided an indefinite flow of services (with adequate maintenance). However, economists have historically accorded labor special treatment, because labor is the one factor of production that every individual possesses, and also because labor is the one producer good that is required for every production process. When Crusoe devotes his physical efforts toward the indirect satisfaction of goals, he is engaged in labor. On the other hand, if he achieves direct satisfaction of goals through control of his hands, brain, etc., then economists call this leisure. Crusoe will allocate his "body power" among labor and leisure activities, in order to satisfy the goals he considers most important. Historically, economists have referred to the disutility of labor to underscore the fact that individuals directly enjoy leisure, and will only devote some of their scarce time to labor if it allows the achievement (indirectly) of more important ends than the leisure being sacrificed.

Finally, capital goods are those factors of production that were created by people. Every capital good is produced from the combination of (at least one) natural resource and labor. Most capital goods are also produced with the help of (pre-existing) capital goods. For Crusoe on his island, examples of capital goods would be a fishing net that he constructs out of vines and his labor, and a shelter that he creates out of rocks, branches, mud, leaves, and his labor.

Income, Saving and Investment

We now know that Crusoe can separate his world into various types of scarce objects, in the categories of natural resources, labor, capital goods, and consumer goods (which include leisure). Connecting all of these is the flow of time, and Crusoe's understanding of how his actions now can alter his happiness in the future. Specifically, Crusoe can choose to save and invest today, in order to raise his future income.

Income refers to the flow of new consumer goods (and services) that an individual has the potential to acquire during a period of time. Saving occurs when someone consumes less than his income; it is "living below one's means." Investment occurs when ingredients of production are devoted to future income, rather than immediate consumption.

It's easiest to explain with a numerical example. Obviously the following numbers are chosen for simplicity, and serve only to make the scenario concrete enough so that you can really think through the types of tradeoffs Crusoe faces. In that light, suppose that with his bare hands, Crusoe can find an appropriate tree to climb and knock down 1 coconut per hour. If Crusoe devotes 10 hours per day to work, while leaving the rest for leisure (which includes sleep), that means his raw labor can extract 10 coconuts per day from the natural resources available to him on the island. Fortunately, eating 10 coconuts per day provides enough nourishment to maintain Crusoe in decent health. But working 10 hours per day, with no weekend, is hardly an ideal lifestyle. Besides the grueling schedule, Crusoe knows that if he should ever become sick or injured, he could easily die because of the vulnerability of his hand-to-mouth existence.

There is a solution. Crusoe is a disciplined and resourceful man, and realizes that the ability to save and invest can greatly improve his standard of living. Soon after assessing his situation on the island, Crusoe begins saving 20% of his income every day. In other words, Crusoe continues to work 10 hours per day, day in and day out, gathering (earning) 10 coconuts per day. But he only eats (consumes) 8 coconuts each day, and sets aside (saves) 2 coconuts out of each day's income.

After living below his means in this fashion for 25 days, Crusoe has accumulated a stockpile of 50 coconuts. From that point on, he once again resumes eating 10 coconuts per day—he consumes his full paycheck every day, as it were. The main reason Crusoe stopped accumulating additional coconuts is that he discovered their taste begins to suffer five days after being knocked down from the tree. Therefore, Crusoe has settled into a comfortable routine: Every day he picks a fresh batch of 10 coconuts and adds them to one side of his stockpile. During the day, he eats the oldest 10 coconuts from the other side of his stockpile. With this rotation, Crusoe still enjoys a full 10 coconuts (which still taste pretty good) per day, but he also has a savings fund of 50 coconuts that he can draw down in case of emergency. For example, if Crusoe should come down with a tropical illness that makes him unable to work, he has enough saved up to eat for ten days on half-rations. Because of his willingness to put in hard work and save its fruits, Crusoe has greatly enhanced his material position compared to his original situation. Rather than living on the edge of starvation, Crusoe now has a buffer of ten days.

The simple act of saving and accumulating consumption goods is very useful, but Crusoe realizes he can do much better. After surveying the materials at his disposal, Crusoe sets out to invest his savings in a long-range venture, which he expects will permanently increase his future flow of daily income. Relying on his stockpile of 50 coconuts, Crusoe decides to take two days off from climbing trees to knock down new coconuts for the stockpile.

On the contrary, Crusoe spends the first day—all 10 hours—wandering the island, gathering branches of the appropriate length and thickness. The process is slow-going, because when Crusoe spies a good candidate, he needs to use a sharp rock to saw away at the branch, before he can safely snap it off the tree without ruining it.[8] During this day, Crusoe eats 10 coconuts, reducing his stockpile down to 40. Even though he has worked all day, he has no new coconuts to show for it. Instead, he has only a collection of sturdy and long branches, which he has transformed from their original shape and location.

During the second day, Crusoe spends another 5 hours using sharp rocks to further prepare the branches. Then he spends 2 hours cutting down vines and bringing them back to camp. Finally, in the remaining 3 hours of the second workday, Crusoe lays the branches on the ground, end-to-end but with a large degree of overlap. Then he uses the vines to tie the branches snugly to each other. At the end of the second day, Crusoe's stockpile has dwindled to 30 coconuts. But in addition to this (shrinking) stockpile of savings, Crusoe has a new capital good: A long and sturdy pole.

The next day Crusoe takes his capital good out for a spin. He discovers with great satisfaction that in a single hour, his labor power—aided by the new capital good—can yield 5 coconuts. This is such a tremendous boon to his productivity that Crusoe now decides he's been working too much! Rather than working 10 hours per day gathering food, Crusoe now spends only 4 hours per day knocking them down. This brings in a daily flow of 20 coconuts per day, twice what he was "earning" with his bare hands. Wanting to replenish his stockpile to the fullest amount that still allows for tasty coconuts, Crusoe saves some of his new earnings for a few weeks, until his stockpile has grown to 100 coconuts.[9] He once again has five days' worth of full-rations, except now a "full-ration" means 20 coconuts per day. In the new equilibrium, Crusoe spends 4 hours per day knocking down 20 new coconuts, which he adds to the stockpile. During that same day, he eats the 20 oldest (ripest) coconuts in the stockpile.

Things are obviously looking up for Mr. Crusoe. Before, he had to put in 10 hours per day of fairly intensive work; it's hard to climb trees all day. In exchange for all that toil, Crusoe enjoyed 10 coconuts each day. But after his wise investment in the construction of a capital good, Crusoe finds that he only needs to spend 4 hours per day knocking down coconuts with the pole—a much easier task than climbing a tree and grabbing them with his bare hands. He also gets to enjoy twice as many coconuts per day as before.

There is one more important detail. If Crusoe wants to permanently maintain his new, higher standard of living, he can't enjoy 20 hours of leisure per day. No, in addition to spending 4 hours per day laboring in the collection of new coconuts, Crusoe must also devote some of his scarce time to the maintenance of his pole. For example, suppose that after using the pole for a full week, the component branches wriggle out of their tight knots, and each end of the pole is quite battered. What this means is that after the seventh day of using his brand new capital good, Crusoe will need to devote some time to replacing the two end branches, as well as re-wrapping the entire pole with new vines.

Now if Crusoe only works the minimum 4 hours per day, collecting coconuts, he can only get away with this slacking for seven days. On the morning of the eighth day, Crusoe would find himself with a useless pole, and he would have to spend (let's say) 7 hours on that day, working to collect new vines and two new branches, and to assemble the new pole. Moreover, in addition to working so many hours, Crusoe would have to draw down on his coconut stockpile, since he wouldn't be able to gather any new coconuts that day.

Rather than engage in this volatile schedule—seven days of light work with many coconuts, with an eighth day of intense work and no coconuts— Crusoe can smooth things out. In a typical day in the new equilibrium, he can spend 4 hours knocking down 20 new coconuts to add to his stockpile (while of course eating the ripest 20 from the same stockpile of 100). But then he also spends a fifth hour each day working on the preservation of his capital good. This way, after seven days have passed in a typical week, Crusoe will have performed the 7 hours' worth of labor necessary to restore the pole after it has been worn down from a week of usage.

In the jargon of economics, we can step back and describe what Crusoe has done. By consuming less than his daily income—by living below his means—Crusoe saved coconuts in order to build up a fund to guard against sudden disruptions in his future income. Moreover, Crusoe then invested his resources into the creation of a capital good that greatly augmented his labor productivity. After the completion of the pole, Crusoe only consumed his net income each day, because he invested enough of his gross income to just balance the depreciation of his capital good.

Measurement of National Income

National income is the sum of a country's final output of all new final goods and services produced in one year by the productive system of an economy.

Factors affecting National Income

- Resource Allocation: This is based on the physical capacity of factors of production and the given technology. The more efficient and effective factors of production leads to better National Income as the total productivity of the nation increases. Hence every nation strives to get better factors of production.
- Land Resources: The geographical location of the natural resources also affects the level of National income. That is the areas rich in coal, iron and other such essential items affect the level of GNP of the nation.
- Labor: The quality of human resource today affects the standard of a nation today. The productivity of labor is more important than quantity.
- Technology: In addition to natural resources and labour the level of invention and innovation in production affect the productivity of the factors of production. Thus, the per capita output grows with the help of technology.
- Government: Government is the key resource to provide a favorable business environment and hence it affects the productivity of the nation and in turn affects the National Income of an economy. Although, Classical's believe that the government is an impediment to growth in output.
- Political Stability: The political system of a nation affects the stability of an economy. A stable economy in turn increases the productivity and the national income of a nation. Unfavorable business environment encourages problems like wars, strikes and other social unrests which discourage economic development.

National Income Accounting

Gross Domestic Product

GDP is the total value of goods and services produced within the country during a year. This is calculated at market price and is known as GDP at market prices. There are 3 methods to calculate GDP at market price:

- The income method, under this method all incomes received by the factors of production generated in the economy during a year are added together. It includes payment for wages on both employment and self-employment, profits, interest to lenders on capital or rents to owners of land.
- The output method/product method, under this method the combined amount of the new and final output produced in different sectors of the economy, including manufacturing, financial services, transport, leisure and agriculture is taken into account.
- The expenditure method, under this method all spending of the economy by households and firms on new and final goods and services by households and firms are added together to calculate the national income of an economy.

National Income Aggregates

Value of Gross output = Price * Quantity of all goods and services produced in the country (not adjusted for bought out inputs)

Since prices differ:

Gross output = $\sum_{i=1}^{n} P_i Q_i$

Net output = Gross output – Value of bought out input (like value of raw materials purchased)

Net output = Gross output. Therefore, Net National Output = Gross national product.

If GNP is adjusted for income earned from abroad:

GNP – Net income earned from abroad = Gross domestic Product (measured at market prices = GDP_{mp}

Gross Domestic Product at Factor Cost (GDP_{fc})

GDP at factor cost is the net value added by all producers within the country.

GDP at Factor Cost = GDP_{mp} - Indirect taxes + subsidies = GDP_{fc}.

Net Domestic Product

NDP is the net output of the nation during the year. Capital assets wears out or becomes obsolete each year during the production process. Thus,

$$\text{Net Domestic Product} = \text{GDP at Factor cost} - \text{Depreciation} = \text{NDP}_{fc}$$

Nominal and Real GDP

When GDP calculated on current price, is called GDP at current prices or nominal GDP. While, when GDP is calculated on the basis of fixed prices in some previous year, it is called GDP at constant prices or real GDP. It measures the value of goods and services by ignoring the changes in the price level.

To find out the real GDP, a base year is chosen when the general price level is normal, i.e., it is neither too high nor too low. The prices are adjusted on 100 (or 1) in the base year.

$$\text{Real GDP (at base year prices)} = \text{GDP for the current year} * \frac{\text{Base year index}(100)}{\text{current year index}}$$

Suppose 2000-01 is the base year and GDP for 2014-15 is \$6, 00,000 crores and the price index for this year is 300 (2014-15 index).

Thus, Real GDP for 2000-01 = \$6, 00,000 x 100/300 = \$2, 00,000 crores. Thus, real GDP (at constant prices) = GDP (at current prices)/GDP Deflator.

GDP Deflator

GDP deflator is a barometer of price changes of goods and services included in GDP. It is a price index which is calculated as follows:

$$\text{GDP Deflator} = \frac{\text{Nominal (or current prices) GDP}}{\text{Real (or constant prices) GDP}} * 100$$

Gross National Product

GNP is the total difference in the flow of goods and services at market value resulting from current year's production of a country. It also includes the net income from abroad.

GNP includes the following final goods and services:

- Consumers' goods and services which satisfies the wants and demand of people.
- Gross investment in capital goods consisting of total capital formation, household construction and inventories of finished and unfinished goods.

- Goods and services manufactured by the government and its organizations.
- Net exports of goods and services, i.e., the difference between value of exports and value of imports of goods and services, known as Net Income from abroad (NIA).

National Income Estimation

There is a difference between National Income Accounting and National Income Estimation. Accounting tells us how to derive one NI aggregate from the other. National Income Estimation tells us how to calculate NI. But we do not use the term calculation because very often the enumerators who calculate national income have to use methods of estimation (or even guess estimates) for assessing the production or income generated during one year.

Precautions in National Income Estimation

The factors to be taken into consideration while estimating National Income:

- Money value considered: GNP is the sum of money, in which all kinds of goods and services manufactured in a country during one year are measured in terms of money at current prices and then added together. But in this manner, due to the fluctuations in the prices, the GNP is increased or declined, which may not be real. To guard against erring on this account, a particular year (base year) when prices are normal is taken and the GNP is adjusted in accordance with the index number for that year.
- Avoid double counting: In estimating GNP, the market price of only the final products should be considered. Many of the products pass through different number of stages before they are ultimately purchased by consumers. If these products are counted and calculated at every stage, they would be included many a time in the national product. Consequently, the GNP would increase too much. To avoid double counting, therefore, only the final products and not the intermediary goods should be taken into account.
- Avoid non-market value: Goods and services given free of cost are not included in the GNP, because it is not difficult to have a correct estimation of their market value or price. For example, the bringing up of a child by the mother, giving instructions to his son by a teacher, recitals to his friends by a musician, etc.
- The transactions which do not arise in the current year or which do not contribute in any way to production are not included in the GNP. The sale and purchase of second hand goods, and shares, bonds and assets of existing companies are not included in GNP because these do not make any addition to the national product, and the goods are simply transferred.
- The payments received under social security, e.g., unemployment insurance

allowance, old age pension, and interest on public loans are also not included in GNP, because the recipients do not provide any service in lieu of them. But the depreciation on machinery, other capital goods is not deducted from GNP.

- The profits earned or losses incurred due to fluctuations in market prices in the value of capital assets are not included in the GNP if they are not responsible for current production or economic activity.

  For example, if the price of a building or of a bare land increases due to inflation, the profit earned by selling it will not be a part of GNP. But if, during the current year, a portion of a house is constructed anew, the increase in the value of the house (after subtracting the cost of the newly constructed portion) will be adjusted in the GNP. Similarly, variations in the value of assets, that can be ascertained beforehand and are insured against flood or fire, are not included in the GNP.

- The income earned in restricted activities is not to be included in the GNP. Though the goods sold in the black market are priced and fulfill the needs of the people, but as they are not useful from the social point of view, the income received from their sale and purchase is always excluded from the GNP.

GNP at Market Prices

To covert gross domestic product into national product, we must add the total income from abroad in to a nation.

GNP at Market Prices = GDP at Market Prices + Net Income from Abroad

GNP at Factor Cost

GNP at factor cost is the sum of the money value of the income produced by and accruing to the various factors of production in one year in a country.

GNP at Factor Cost = GNP at Market Prices – Indirect Taxes + Subsidies

Net National Product

NNP is sum total of output on consumption goods and investment goods. But this process of production uses certain amount of fixed capital and the fixed equipment wears out with time, or other components are damaged or destroyed, and still others are rendered obsolete through technological changes.

NNP = GNP—Depreciation

NNP at Market Prices

Net National Product at market prices is the sum total of final goods and services evaluated at market price in a country. Value of final goods and services evaluated at market prices in a country.

NNP at Market Prices = GNP at Market Prices—Depreciation

NNP at Factor Cost

Net National Product at factor cost is the total output evaluated at factor prices. It includes income earned by factors of production through participation in the production process such as wages and salaries, rents, profits, etc. It is also called National Income.

NNP at Factor Cost/ National Income = NNP at Market Prices – Indirect taxes+ Subsidies

Uses of National Income Statistics

- Standard of living: One can easily compare the standard of living of different nations with the help of GNP. Hence National income statistics can be used for analyzing the standard of living of a nation.
- Policy Formulation: The National income statistics are used to compile GNP statistics of the economy. The Government then uses this data for policy formulation.
- International comparison: The standard of living of different nations can be compared with national income statistics which in turn helps to show the rate of growth or development of different nations.
- Business Decisions: The level of development of different industries and sectors respectively of an economy is analyzed with national income statistics. It in turn helps the business to plan for production and planning.

References

- Classical-Macroeconomic-Theory- and-Economic-Growth: swlearning.com, Retrieved 22, July 2020
- Robinson-crusoe-economics: lumenlearning.com, Retrieved 10, February 2020

2

Aggregate Demand and Supply

The total amount of goods and services which a company desires to sell at a specified price within a particular economy is known as the aggregate supply. The aggregate demand refers to the total amounts of goods and services that will be purchased at all the price levels possible. This chapter discusses in detail the different aspects of aggregate demand and supply such as aggregate demand curve and aggregate supply curve.

Aggregate Demand Curve

Aggregate demand (AD) is defined as the total demand for final goods and services in a given economy at a specific time. Unlike other illustrations of demand, it is inclusive of all amounts of the product or service purchased at any possible price level. Simply put, AD is the sum of all demand in an economy. It is often called the effective demand or aggregate expenditure (AE), and is the demand of all gross domestic product (GDP).

Demand Sources

- Consumption (C): This is the simplest and largest component of aggregate demand (usually 40-60% of all demand), and is often what is intuitively thought of as demand. Consumption is just the amount of consumer spending executed in an economy. Taxes play a role in this exchange as well (i.e. sales tax).
- Investment (I): Investment is a relatively large portion of demand as well, and is referred to as Gross Domestic Fixed Capital Formation. This is the money spent by firms on capital investment (new machinery, factories, stocks, etc.). Investment equates to about 10% of GDP in most economies.
- Government Spending (G): This is referred to as General Government Final Consumption, and is the expenditure by the government. This can include welfare, social services, education, military, etc. Fiscal policy is the way in which governments can alter this spending to drive economic change.
- Net Export (NX): This can be put simply as the sale of goods to foreign countries subtracted by the purchase of goods from other countries (X-M). Trade surpluses and deficits can occur based on whether or not exports or imports are higher.

In summary, the calculation of aggregate demand can be represented as follows: AD = C + I + G + (X-M). The full sum of all demand in an economy takes into account each of these factors in a quantitative way. This curve is illustrated in the figure.

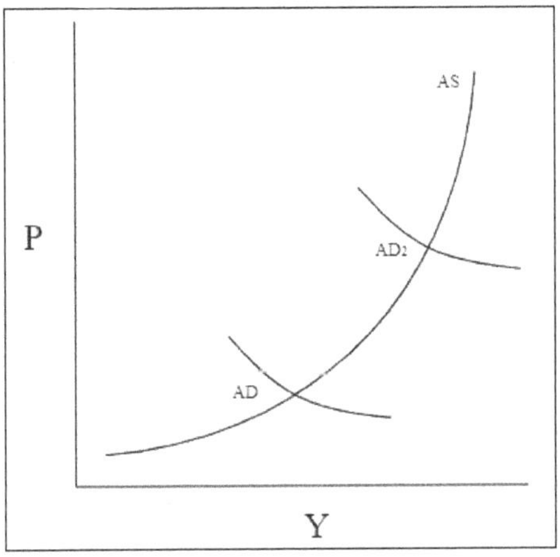

Aggregate Demand and Supply: This graph demonstrates the basic relationship between aggregate demand and aggregate supply. The aggregate demand curve is derived via the consumption, investment, government spending, and net export.

The Role of Debt

Many societies have increasingly adopted debt and credit as an integral part of their economic system. This has justified the incorporation of debt (also called the credit impulse) into the larger framework of aggregate demand. From a quantitative perspective this is simply expressed as: Spending = Income + Net Increase in Debt. Spending capital prior to the receipt of capital is an important consideration at both the consumer level and the government level (deficit spending).

The Aggregation Problem

There are some limitations to the aggregation perspective, generally summarized as the aggregation problem. The difficulty arises in treating all consumer preferences (and thus their respective demands) as homogeneous and continuous. As the numbers of consumers, the tastes of consumers and the distribution levels of incomes will alter, so too will the demand curve. This can create inaccurate assumptions in AD inputs. Simply, there is some loss of accuracy in combining such a diverse array of economic inputs.

The Slope of the Aggregate Demand Curve

Due to Pigou's Wealth Effect, the Keynes' Interest Rate Effect, and the Mundell-Fleming Exchange Rate Effect, the AD curve slopes downward. Aggregate demand (AD) is the total demand for all goods within a given market at a given time, or the summation of demand curves within a system. Understanding the basic graphical representation of this curve is useful in grasping the implications of AD on an economic system, as well as the distinct effects which drive it. As a result of Keynes' interest rate effect, Pigou's wealth effect, and the Mundell-Fleming exchange rate effect, the AD curve is downward sloping.

Keynes' Interest Rate Effect

The critical point from Keynes's perspective on the slope of the aggregate demand curve is that interest rates affect expenditures more than they affect savings. If prices fall, a given amount of money will increase in value. This will drive up interest rates and investments. It is important to note that insufficient demand in a market will not go on forever.

In understanding this fully, it is useful to look at an IS-LM graph. There are only two times when the Keynes observation on the interest rate effect will be inaccurate, and that is if the IS (investment savings) curve were to be vertical or if the LM (liquidity preference money supply) curve were to be horizontal. This makes sense if you think about it, it would basically equate to a liquidity trap. A vertical IS curve or a horizontal LM curve would essentially negate the way in which interest rates could affect aggregate demand.

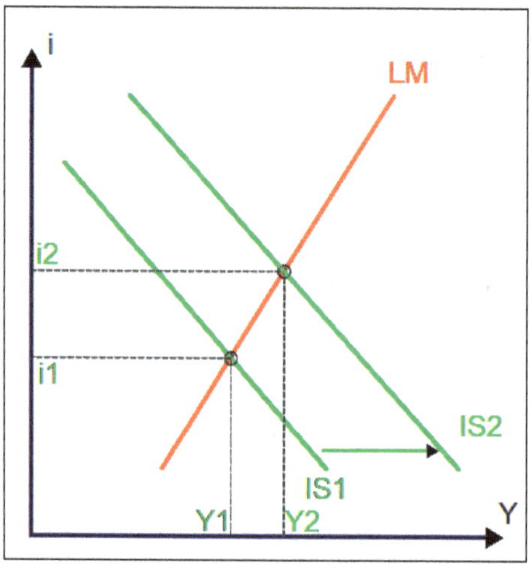

IS-LM Model: The IS-LM model takes investments and savings and compares that to liquidity and the overall money supply. It is highly useful in understanding macroeconomics from a Keynesian perspective. Interest rates (i) are on the vertical axis, and output (y) is on the horizontal axis.

Pigou's Wealth Effect

Pigou's Wealth Effect underlines the fact that liquidity traps are not sustainable. The simplest way to explain the Wealth Effect is that an increase in spending will denote an increase in wealth. In many ways, what Pigou is putting forward is the idea that downwards spiral on the IS-LM model, as predicted by Keynes due to deflation, will be counterbalanced by an increase in real wages and thus an increase in expenditure. In other words, a decrease in employment and prices will eventually see higher purchasing power and an increase in spending, creating wealth.

Mundell-Fleming Exchange Rate Effect

Perhaps the most complex of the three inputs underlined in deriving aggregate demand is the Mundell-Fleming Exchange Rate Effect. This builds off of the IS-LM model in a way that discusses it in the context of an open economy (as opposed to a closed system). It essentially takes into account a new factor (in addition to interest rates and outputs, as the traditional IS-LM model incorporates). This new factor is the exchange rates, as the name implies. Incorporating the nominal exchange rate into the mix makes it impossible to maintain free capital movement, a fixed exchange rate and independent monetary policy. This is sometimes referred to as the 'impossible trinity,' implying that trade-offs must be made. This concept is illustrated fairly well in this figure, where 'FE' is fixed expenditure.

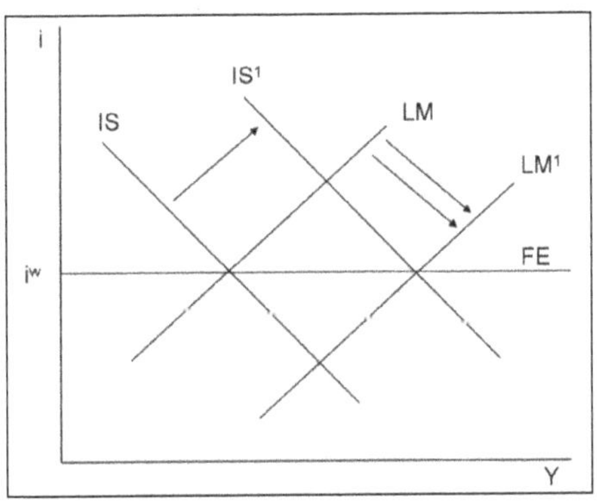

Mundell-Fleming Fixed Exchange Rate Illustration.

An increase in government spending forces the monetary authority to supply the market with local currency to keep the exchange rate unchanged. Shown here is the case of perfect capital mobility, in which the BoP curve (or, as denoted here, the FE curve) is horizontal.

Reasons for and Consequences of Shifts in the Aggregate Demand Curve

An increase in any of the four inputs into AD will result in higher real output or an increase in prices. Aggregate demand (AD) is the summation of all demand within a given economy at a given time.

Inputs

There are four inputs to consider in calculating AD (and deriving the graphical curve which represents it): consumption (C), investment (I), government spending (G), and net exports (NX, which is exports (X) – imports (I)). Changes in these inputs will have some influence on the AD curve. For example, an increase in total expenditures will result in a shift rightwards, while a decrease in expenditure will result in a shift to the left.

Aggregate Demand Curves

Two specific AD representations are useful to consider:

- Keynesian Cross: The Keynesian Cross is a simple illustration of the relationship between aggregate demand and desired total spending (linear at 45 degrees). The intersecting AD line will generally have an upwards slope, under the assumption that increased national output should result in increased disposable income.
- Aggregate Demand/Aggregate Supply Model (AD/AS): The x-axis represents the overall output, while the y-axis represents the price level. The aggregate quantity demanded (Y = C + I + G + NX) is calculated at every given aggregate average price level.

Exogenous Effects

There are a variety of direct and indirect consequences to AD shifts. The key consequences to keep in mind are changes in output and price. Some of the driving forces that will shift aggregate demand to the right:

- An exogenous increase in consumer spending.
- An exogenous increase in investment spending on physical capital.
- An exogenous increase in intended inventory investment.
- An exogenous increase in government spending on goods and services.
- An exogenous increase in transfer payments from the government to the people.
- An exogenous decrease in taxes levied.
- An exogenous increase in purchases of the country's exports by people in other countries.
- An exogenous decrease in imports from other countries.

Short-term Implications

Any increase in the overall AD will result in an outwards (right-ward) shift of the AD curve. (Conversely, a decrease in aggregate demand will cause a leftward shift of the AD curve.) This means that an increase in any of the four inputs to AD will result in a higher quantity of real output or an increase in prices across the board (this is also known as inflation). However, different levels of economic activity will result in different combinations of output and price increases.

It is useful for understanding the distribution between price increases and output increases that will result in a given economy when AD increases. To put simply, the lower the utilization of available resources in a system, the more an increase in AD will result in higher output and thus higher employment and GDP growth. However, as the system evolves and aligns itself closer to the highest potential output (optimal utilization of resources or Y), scarcity will naturally cause the prices to increase more than the overall output in a system. This is somewhat intuitive economically when scarcity and utilization are taken into account. The more difficult it is to generate a supply increase the more likely a shift in AD will drive up prices.

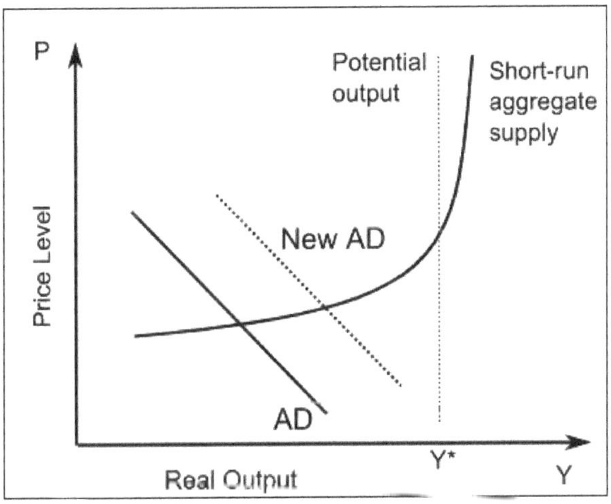

Aggregate Supply/Aggregate Demand: This graph illustrates the relationship between price and output within a given economic system in the context of aggregate demand and supply.

Other Factors Affecting Demand Curve

Changes in Aggregate Demand

Aggregate demand changes in response to a change in any of its components. An increase in the total quantity of consumer goods and services demanded at every price level, for example, would shift the aggregate demand curve to the right. A change in the aggregate quantity of goods and services demanded at every price level is a change in aggregate demand, which shifts the aggregate demand curve. Increases and decreases in aggregate demand are shown in figure "Changes in Aggregate Demand".

What factors might cause the aggregate demand curve to shift? Each of the components of aggregate demand is a possible aggregate demand shifter. We shall look at some of the events that can trigger changes in the components of aggregate demand and thus shift the aggregate demand curve.

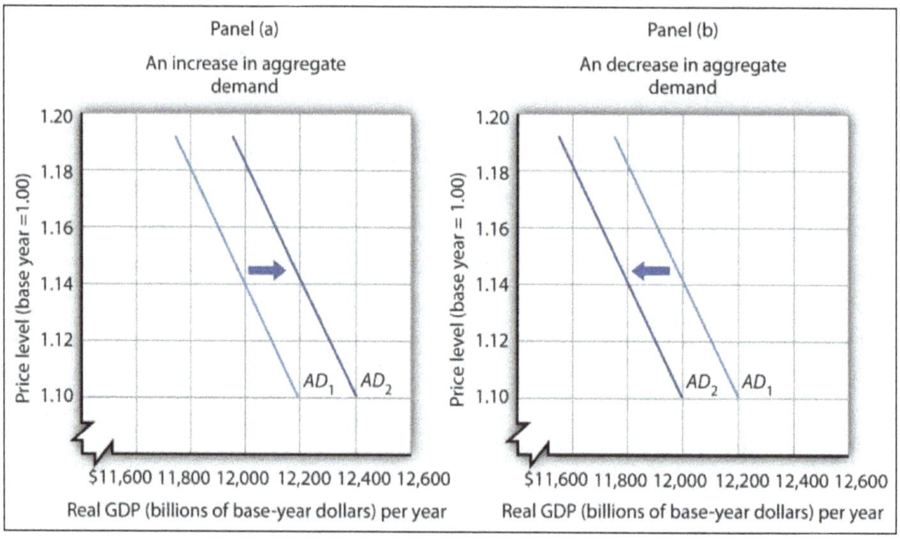

An increase in consumption, investment, government purchases, or net exports shifts the aggregate demand curve AD1 to the right as shown in Panel (a). A reduction in one of the components of aggregate demand shifts the curve to the left, as shown in Panel (b).

Changes in Consumption

Several events could change the quantity of consumption at each price level and thus shift aggregate demand. One determinant of consumption is consumer confidence. If consumers expect good economic conditions and are optimistic about their economic prospects, they are more likely to buy major items such as cars or furniture. The result would be an increase in the real value of consumption at each price level and an increase in aggregate demand. In the second half of the 1990s, sustained economic growth and low unemployment fuelled high expectations and consumer optimism. Surveys revealed consumer confidence to be very high. That consumer confidence translated into increased consumption and increased aggregate demand. In contrast, a decrease in consumption would accompany diminished consumer expectations and a decrease in consumer confidence, as happened after the stock market crash of 1929. The same problem has plagued the economies of most Western nations in 2008 as declining consumer confidence has tended to reduce consumption. A survey of 2008 showed that just 13.5% of consumers surveyed expected economic conditions in the United States to improve in the next six months. Similarly pessimistic views prevailed in the previous two months. That contributed to the decline in consumption that occurred in the third quarter of the year.

Another factor that can change consumption and shift aggregate demand is tax policy. A cut in personal income taxes leaves people with more after-tax income, which may induce them to increase their consumption. The federal government in the United States cut taxes in 1964, 1981, 1986, 1997, and 2003; each of those tax cuts tended to increase consumption and aggregate demand at each price level.

In the United States, another government policy aimed at increasing consumption and thus aggregate demand has been the use of rebates in which taxpayers are simply sent checks in hopes that those checks will be used for consumption. Rebates have been used in 1975, 2001, and 2008. In each case the rebate was a one-time payment. Careful studies by economists of the 1975 and 2001 rebates showed little impact on consumption. Final evidence on the impact of the 2008 rebates is not yet in, but early results suggest a similar outcome. Transfer payments such as welfare and Social Security also affect the income people have available to spend. At any given price level, an increase in transfer payments raises consumption and aggregate demand, and a reduction lowers consumption and aggregate demand.

Changes in Investment

Investment is the production of new capital that will be used for future production of goods and services. Firms make investment choices based on what they think they will be producing in the future. The expectations of firms thus play a critical role in determining investment. If firms expect their sales to go up, they are likely to increase their investment so that they can increase production and meet consumer demand. Such an increase in investment raises the aggregate quantity of goods and services demanded at each price level; it increases aggregate demand.

Changes in interest rates also affect investment and thus affect aggregate demand. We must be careful to distinguish such changes from the interest rate effect, which causes a movement along the aggregate demand curve. A change in interest rates that results from a change in the price level affects investment in a way that is already captured in the downward slope of the aggregate demand curve; it causes a movement along the curve. A change in interest rates for some other reason shifts the curve.

Investment can also be affected by tax policy. One provision of the Job and Growth Tax Relief Reconciliation Act of 2003 was a reduction in the tax rate on certain capital gains. Capital gains result when the owner of an asset, such as a house or a factory, sells the asset for more than its purchase price (less any depreciation claimed in earlier years). The lower capital gains tax could stimulate investment, because the owners of such assets know that they will lose less to taxes when they sell those assets, thus making assets subject to the tax more attractive.

Changes in Government Purchases

Any change in government purchases, all other things unchanged, will affect aggregate demand. An increase in government purchases increases aggregate demand; a decrease in government purchases decreases aggregate demand.

Many economists argued that reductions in defense spending in the wake of the collapse of the Soviet Union in 1991 tended to reduce aggregate demand. Similarly, increased defense spending for the wars in Afghanistan and Iraq increased aggregate demand. Dramatic increases in defense spending to fight World War II accounted in large part for the rapid recovery from the Great Depression.

Changes in Net Exports

A change in the value of net exports at each price level shifts the aggregate demand curve. A major determinant of net exports is foreign demand for a country's goods and services; that demand will vary with foreign incomes. An increase in foreign incomes increases a country's net exports and aggregate demand; a slump in foreign incomes reduces net exports and aggregate demand. For example, several major U.S. trading partners in Asia suffered recessions in 1997 and 1998. Lower real incomes in those countries reduced U.S. exports and tended to reduce aggregate demand.

Exchange rates also influence net exports, all other things unchanged. A country's exchange rate is the price of its currency in terms of another currency or currencies. A rise in the U.S. exchange rate means that it takes more Japanese yen, for example, to purchase one dollar. That also means that U.S. traders get more yen per dollar. Since prices of goods produced in Japan are given in yen and prices of goods produced in the United States are given in dollars, a rise in the U.S. exchange rate increases the price to foreigners for goods and services produced in the United States, thus reducing U.S. exports; it reduces the price of foreign-produced goods and services for U.S. consumers, thus increasing imports to the United States. A higher exchange rate tends to reduce net exports, reducing aggregate demand. A lower exchange rate tends to increase net exports, increasing aggregate demand.

Foreign price levels can affect aggregate demand in the same way as exchange rates. For example, when foreign price levels fall relative to the price level in the United States, U.S. goods and services become relatively more expensive, reducing exports and boosting imports in the United States. Such a reduction in net exports reduces aggregate demand. An increase in foreign prices relative to U.S. prices has the opposite effect. The trade policies of various countries can also affect net exports. A policy by Japan to increase its imports of goods and services from India, for example, would increase net exports in India.

The Multiplier

A change in any component of aggregate demand shifts the aggregate demand curve. Generally, the aggregate demand curve shifts by more than the amount by which the component initially causing it to shift changes.

Suppose that net exports increase due to an increase in foreign incomes. As foreign demand for domestically made products rises, a country's firms will hire additional workers or perhaps increase the average number of hours that their employees work. In either case, incomes will rise, and higher incomes will lead to an increase in consumption. Taking into account these other increases in the components of aggregate demand, the aggregate demand curve will shift by more than the initial shift caused by the initial increase in net exports.

The ratio of the change in the quantity of real GDP demanded at each price level to the initial change in one or more components of aggregate demand that produced it. is the ratio of the change in the quantity of real GDP demanded at each price level to the initial change in one or more components of aggregate demand that produced it:

$$\text{Multiplier} = \frac{\Delta(\text{real GDP demanded at each price level})}{\text{initial } \Delta(\text{component of AD})}$$

We use the capital Greek letter delta (Δ) to mean "change in." In the aggregate demand–aggregate supply model it is the number by which we multiply an initial change in aggregate demand to obtain the amount by which the aggregate demand curve shifts as a result of the initial change. In other words, we can use Equation above to solve for the change in real GDP demanded at each price level:

$$\Delta(\text{real GDP demanded at each price level}) = \text{multiplier} \times \text{initial } \Delta(\text{component of AD})$$

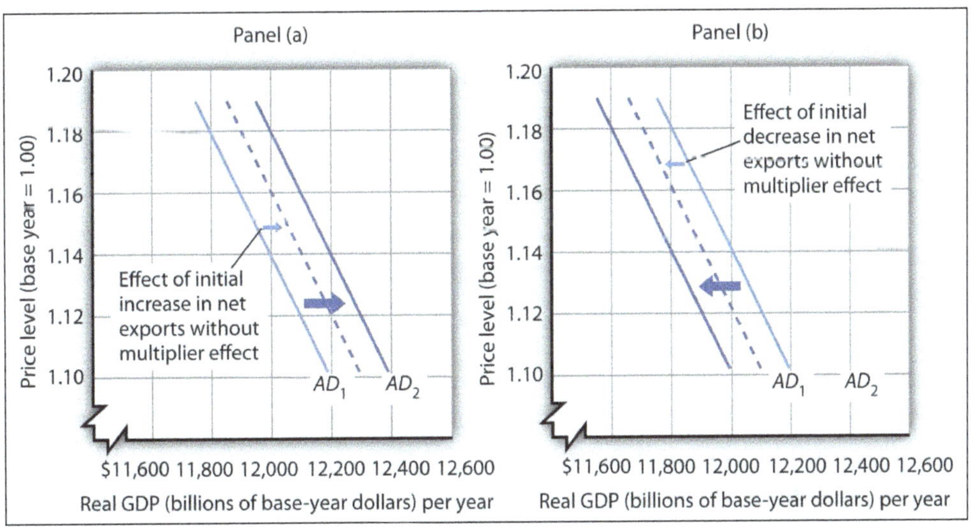

A change in one component of aggregate demand shifts the aggregate demand curve by more than the initial change. In Panel (a), an initial increase of $100 billion of net exports shifts the aggregate demand curve to the right by $200 billion at each price level. In Panel (b), a decrease of net exports of $100 billion shifts the aggregate demand curve to the left by $200 billion. In this example, the multiplier is 2.

Suppose that the initial increase in net exports is $100 billion and that the initial $100-billion increase generates additional consumption of $100 billion at each price level. In Panel (a) of figure "The Multiplier", the aggregate demand curve shifts to the right by $200 billion—the amount of the initial increase in net exports times the multiplier of 2. We obtained the value for the multiplier in this example by plugging $200 billion (the initial $100-billion increase in net exports plus the $100-billion increase that it generated in consumption) into the numerator of Equation $\text{Multiplier} = \frac{\Delta(\text{real GDP demanded at each price level})}{\text{initial } \Delta(\text{component of AD})}$ and $100 billion into the denominator. Similarly, a decrease in net exports of $100 billion leads to a decrease in aggregate demand of $200 billion at each price level, as shown in Panel (b).

Aggregate Supply Curve

An economy is in equilibrium when the quantity of goods produced in the economy is equal to demand for these goods. In other words, in output-price or output-inflation space when aggregate demand (AD) curve intersects Aggregate Supply (AS) curve, we get equilibrium level of output produced, or equilibrium level of income and spending, and the equilibrium price level.

With the objective of profit maximization, the amount of output that the firms are willing to supply at the given price level in the economy constitute aggregate supply. The amount of output that the firms are willing to supply depends on two things: (i) prices that they receive for their output, and (ii) the cost of factors of production. The cost of factors of production depends on the (i) level of inputs available, and (ii) level of technology. Thus, aggregate supply in turn reflects the condition that prevail in the factors markets. Assuming that there are two main factors of production, labour (L) and capital (K), aggregate supply curve will reflect the equilibrium in the labour market and capital market. Labour is sup-plied by the households at the going wage rate in the economy. Labour supply is affected by the population growth in the economy. Capital is supplied by the firms. An increase in investment by firms in machineries, building, equipments, and materials increases the supply of capital stock in the economy. Thus, cost of labour input is the wage rate, while the cost of capital inputs is the interest rates, the return to investment, v/s savings.

Construction of aggregate supply curve is different from the construction of the simple supply curve of a firm that is studied in microeconomics. At an individual firm level, an increase in price level is not associated with the increase in the cost of factors of production. Hence, the firms are willing to supply more at higher prices, leading to upward sloping supply curve. At the aggregate level, an increase in price means an increase in the general price level in the economy, which also increases the price of factors of production. As a result, the cost of production to the firm also increases. In such a situation, firms may not find it worth their while to increase their production. Thus, aggregate supply may not increase with increase in the price level. There is uncertainty on what will be the shape of the aggregate supply curve.

The two main solutions that are provided for this uncertainty in the construction of aggregate supply come from the classical school of thought and from the Keynesian school of thought, respectively. The shape of aggregate supply curve and its slope differ in terms of which school of thought we are studying.

Aggregate Supply Curve in Classical Approach and in Keynesian Approach

Classical economists assumed that the aggregate supply curve is vertical, indicating that at the economy wide level, the same amount of goods are supplied, irrespective of the price level. Keynesian economists, on the other hand assumed that the aggregate supply curve is horizontal, indicating that the firms are willing to supply whatever amount of goods at the existing price level. Thus, classical and Keynesian views are completely opposite to each other in terms of aggregate supply.

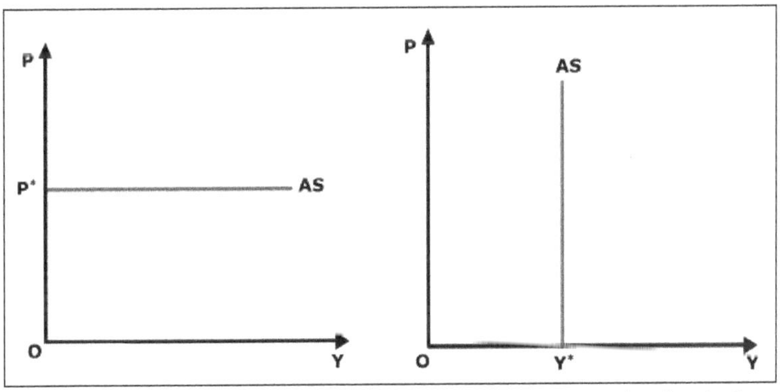

Panel (A) shows AS curve in Keynesian Case. Panel (B) shows AS curve in Classical Case. The two AS curves are completely opposite to each other.

To understand why the aggregate supply curve is different in classical and Keynesian approaches, we need to understand the time framework within which these AS curves are constructed. Basically, there are two time periods, giving rise to two aggregate supply curves: (i) short-run analysis, giving rise to Short-Run Aggregate Supply Curve (SRAS), and (ii) log-run analysis, giving rise to Long-Run Aggregate Supply Curve (LRAS).

1. Short-run Aggregate supply curve (SRAS) or the Keynesian Aggregate Supply Curve.

JM Keynes held the view that in the short-run, economy is operating below the full employment level. In other words, in the short-run, factors of production (especially labour) are not employed to their full capacity and there is unemployment. Thus, when the price level change, say it rises (due to rise in aggregate demand), firms can increase their production and hence supply, by hiring this unemployed labour force, without raising the wage rates. Thus, firms can get more labour at the current wages, and can increase its production with the same average cost of production. When the average cost of production does not change with the level of output, firms are willing to supply as much output as is demanded in the economy, at the given price level. Thus, aggregate supply curve is horizontal, as shown in Panel A of figure. The slope of AS curve approaches infinity, that is, output is highly responsive to the change in the price level.

In a nutshell, in the short-run, due to under-employment and wage –price rigidity, output will be determined by the aggregate demand. In figure below, AS curve is horizontal and AD is as usual downward sloping. Equilibrium is at point E_0, equilibrium price level is P_0 and output is Y_0. If aggregate demand increases to AD_1, price level has to go up to P_1. But due to wage-price rigidity, firms will hire more labour at the going wage rate, and produce and supply more output. New equilibrium will be attained at point E_1, where output has increased to Y_1, without any change in the price level. Thus, price level is fixed, and output is determined by AD curve.

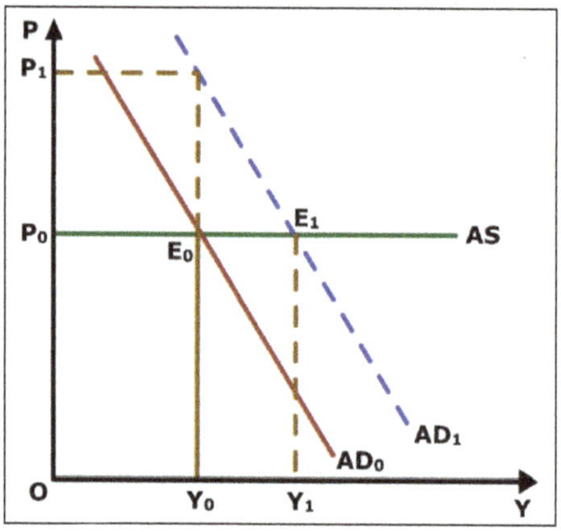

Equilibrium in short-run. Output is demand determined when AS curve is horizontal.

2. Long-run Aggregate Supply Curve (LRAS) or the Classical Aggregate Supply Curve.

Extremely opposite to Keynes view, Classical economists held the view that economy always operates at full-employment level, and any deviations from this level will be adjusted through immediate changes in the price level and the wage rates. Thus, if there are any changes in the price level, say a rise in the price level (due to increase in demand), firms cannot increase their production. In the labour market, there is no extra labour to be employed to produce extra output to meet the increased demand. Thus, nominal wages will rise in proportion to the price level, bringing the real wages back to their original level (which prevailed before the change in price level). Thus, real variables, real wages, and output will remain at their original levels, only nominal variables, nominal wages and price level will rise. Due to this dichotomy between real and nominal variables, aggregate supply curve, under classical approach is vertical, indicating the same amount of goods supplied at any price level. The slope of AS curve is zero that is output supplied in unresponsive to any changes in the price level.

In a nutshell, in the long-run, due to full employment and wage –price flexibility, output will be determined by the aggregate supply. In figure below, AS curve is vertical, and AD is as usual downward sloping. Equilibrium is at point Eo, equilibrium price level is P_0 and output is Y. If aggregate demand increases to AD_1, price level goes up to P_1, without any change in the output level. Output cannot be increased beyond Y. New equilibrium will be attained at point E_1, where price has increased to P_1, without any change in the output level. Thus, output is fixed by AS curve and price level is determined by the AD curve.

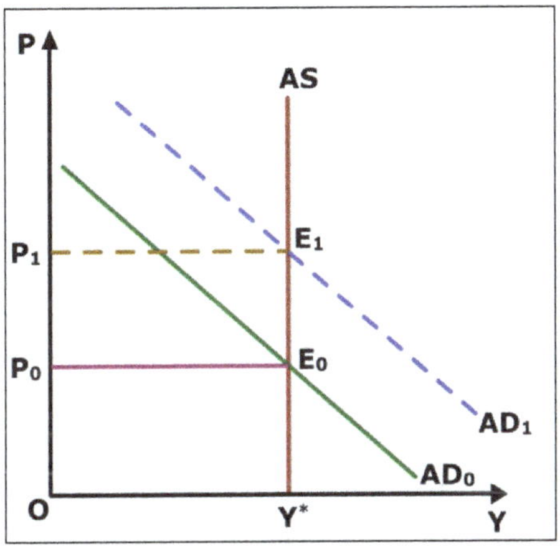

Equilibrium in long-run. Price level is demand determined when AS curve is vertical.

Intermediate Case: Medium-run Aggregate Supply Curve

Due to the differences in the two opposing explanations of the shape of aggregate supply curve, economists have come up with an intermediate case between these extreme cases. This is generally referred as the medium run case, where the economy is operating below full-employment, but close to full-employment level of output. The aggregate supply curve is upward sloping, representing positive relationship between price level and output. It is neither horizontal nor vertical. This situation arises due to wage-price stickiness, rather than rigidity or flexibility. Due to a change in the price level (due to a change in demand), wages and prices will adjust slowly to their new equilibrium levels. This is because of three reasons: sticky wages theory, sticky prices theory, and misperception theory.

1. Sticky Wage Theory: Suppose, demand increases, which results in a rise in the price level at the current output level. It is difficult for the firms to increase its supply by increasing its use of factors of production in the short-run. Generally, firms operate with some fixed factors of production (usually capital) whose quantity is difficult to change in the short-run. Even for the variable factors of production (like labour), it is not possible for the firms to increase their labour use, or to pay higher wages to their labour. For instance, if workers are hired on multi-year labour contracts with the firms, it is difficult for the firms to change the contract or to cancel the contract before the maturity period, and hence firms cannot increase the wages. Wages are sticky. In the

medium run, some of the contracts attain their maturity and are subject to change, while workers also demand higher nominal wages in response to their lower real wages. As a result, wages start adjusting to the change in the price level. But this happens only slowly, over a period of time.

2. Sticky Price Theory: When the price level increases, it is difficult for the firms to change the prices it charges, in response to the change in the general price level. For instance, consider a firm which prints its price catalogue. When price level gets changed, it is costly for the firm to change the price catalogues. If the cost of changing the prices charged in response to a change in general price level (called the menu costs) is more than the cost of raising the production and hence supply of goods, firms would prefer to continue to operate with the old prices, rather than with the new changed price level. Thus, prices are sticky. It will only be after a period of time, when the firms realize that it should charge a higher price in response to rise in the general price level, prices will start adjusting.

3. Misperception Theory: In the labour market, when nominal wages go up, in response to a rise in the price level, workers have a misperception that it is a rise in their real wages. As a result, they supply more labour, leading to higher level of employment at output. They continue to do so until they realize that the rise in wages is merely a rise in nominal wages in response to higher price level, and not a rise in real wages. Thus, output will rise and wages will adjust slowly to the changes in the price level.

Due to this sluggish adjustment of wages and prices, output will rise slowly, leading to upward sloping aggregate supply curve. Figure below shows this medium run aggregate supply curve (MRAS). Output and price level is determined by the intersection of aggregate demand and supply curves.

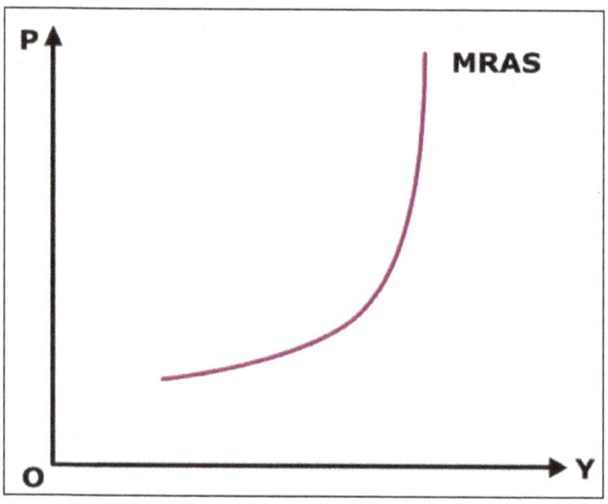

Medium run aggregate supply curve.

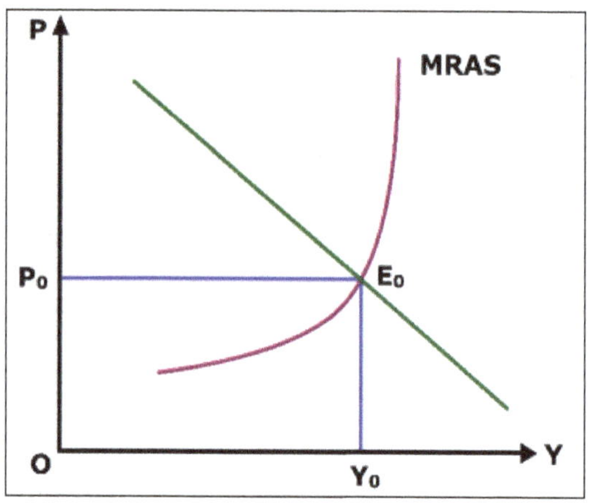

Equilibrium in medium run is attained at the intersection point of AD and AS curves at point E_0. Equilibrium level of output is Y_0, and the price level is P_0.

Synthesis of Short-run AS Curve, Long-run AS Curve and Medium-run AS Curve

The three cases for aggregate supply curves are synthesize into one single diagram, as shown in figure below. AS curve is horizontal in the short-run where wages and prices are rigid. When prices and wages start adjusting, AS curve becomes upward sloping, and it leads to a change in both real (output and real wages) and nominal variables (price level and nominal wage rate). This change in output continues until the economy reaches at full employment level of Y, where the AS curve becomes vertical.

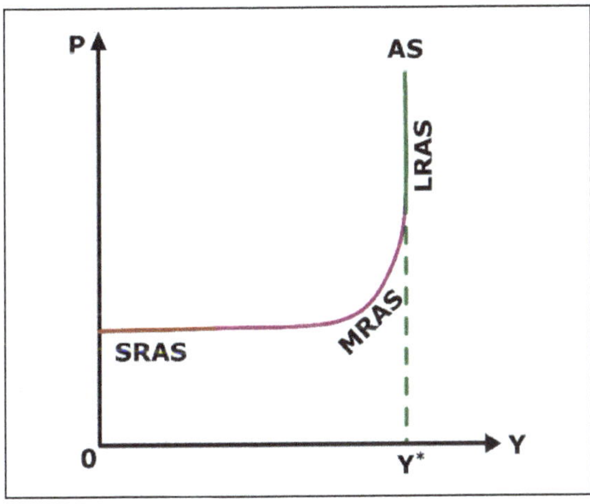

AS Curve of an economy during three different time trends.

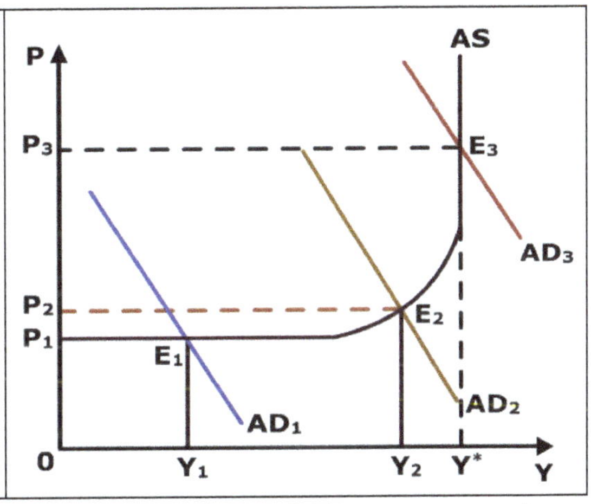

Intersection of AD and AS curves representing equilibrium in three different scenarios.

Output and price level in the economy will be determined by the intersection of aggregate demand and aggregate supply curves. The position of AD curve will determine whether the economy is operating at the full employment level, below full employment or near full employment level. In figure below, three equilibria are presented, representing the three situations. If the aggregate demand curve is represented by AD_1, the economy is operating below full-employment level, and wages and prices are rigid. If the aggregate demand is represented by AD_2, the economy is in transition phase from short run to long run. Output and price level are determined by both AS and AD curves. If the aggregate demand curve is AD_3, economy is operating at the full employment level, and nominal wages and prices are flexible to keep output full employment level of Y.

Phillips Curve

The Phillips curve shows the inverse relationship between inflation and unemployment: as unemployment decreases, inflation increases. The Phillips curve relates the rate of inflation with the rate of unemployment. The Phillips curve argues that unemployment and inflation are inversely related: as levels of unemployment decrease, inflation increases. The relationship, however, is not linear. Graphically, the short-run Phillips curve traces an L-shape when the unemployment rate is on the x-axis and the inflation rate is on the y-axis.

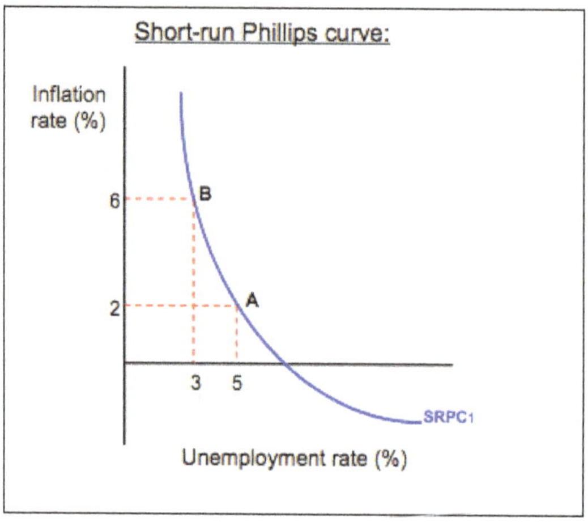

Theoretical Phillips Curve: The Phillips curve shows the inverse trade-off between inflation and unemployment. As one increases, the other must decrease. In this image, an economy can either experience 3% unemployment at the cost of 6% of inflation, or increase unemployment to 5% to bring down the inflation levels to 2%.

The early idea for the Phillips curve was proposed in 1958 by economist A.W. Phillips. In his original paper, Phillips tracked wage changes and unemployment changes in Great Britain from 1861 to 1957, and found that there was a stable, inverse relationship between wages and unemployment. This correlation between wage changes and unemployment seemed to hold for Great Britain and for other industrial countries. In 1960, economists Paul Samuelson and Robert Solow expanded this work to reflect the relationship between inflation and unemployment. Because wages are the largest components of prices, inflation (rather than wage changes) could be inversely linked to unemployment.

The theory of the Phillips curve seemed stable and predictable. Data from the 1960's modeled the trade-off between unemployment and inflation fairly well. The Phillips curve offered potential economic policy outcomes: fiscal and monetary policy could be used to achieve full employment at the cost of higher price levels, or to lower inflation at the cost of lowered employment. However, when governments attempted to use the Phillips curve to control unemployment and inflation, the relationship fell apart. Data from the 1970's and onward did not follow the trend of the classic Phillips curve. For many years, both the rate of inflation and the rate of unemployment were higher than the Phillips curve would have predicted, a phenomenon known as "stagflation." Ultimately, the Phillips curve was proved to be unstable, and therefore, not usable for policy purposes.

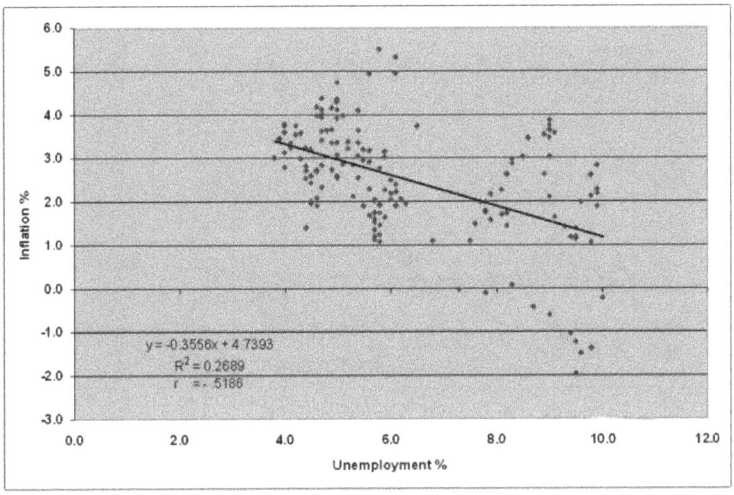

US Phillips Curve.

The data points in this graph span every month from January 2000 until April 2013. They do not form the classic L-shape the short-run Phillips curve would predict. Although it was shown to be stable from the 1860's until the 1960's, the Phillips curve relationship became unstable – and unusable for policy-making – in the 1970's.

The Relationship between the Phillips Curve and AD-AD

Changes in aggregate demand cause movements along the Phillips curve, all other variables held constant.

The Phillips Curve Related to Aggregate Demand

The Phillips curve shows the inverse trade-off between rates of inflation and rates of unemployment. If unemployment is high, inflation will be low; if unemployment is low, inflation will be high.

The Phillips curve and aggregate demand share similar components. The Phillips curve is the relationship between inflation, which affects the price level aspect of aggregate demand, and unemployment, which is dependent on the real output portion of aggregate demand. Consequently, it is not far-fetched to say that the Phillips curve and aggregate demand are actually closely related.

To see the connection more clearly, consider the example illustrated by. Let's assume that aggregate supply, AS, is stationary, and that aggregate demand starts with the curve, AD_1. There is an initial equilibrium price level and real GDP output at point A. Now, imagine there are increases in aggregate demand, causing the curve to shift right to curves AD_2 through AD_4. As aggregate demand increases, unemployment decreases as more workers are hired, real GDP output increases, and the price level increases; this situation describes a demand-pull inflation scenario.

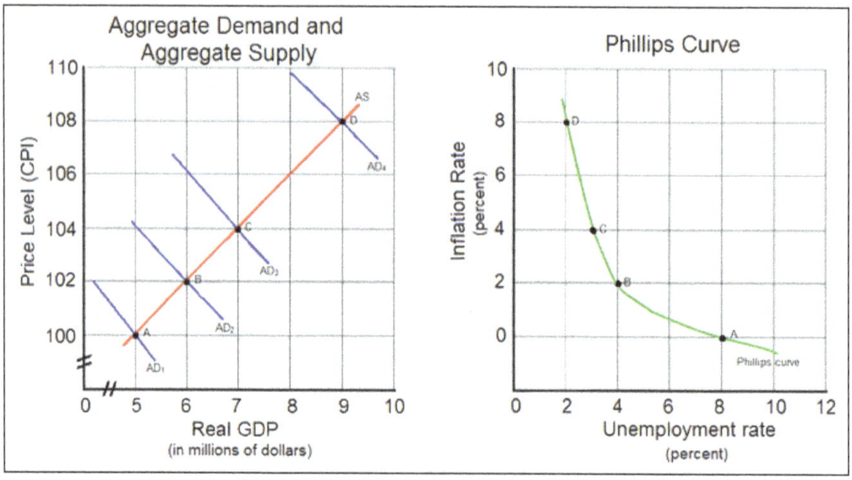

Phillips Curve and Aggregate Demand.

As aggregate demand increases from AD1 to AD4, the price level and real GDP increases. This translates to corresponding movements along the Phillips curve as inflation increases and unemployment decreases.

As more workers are hired, unemployment decreases. Moreover, the price level increases, leading to increases in inflation. These two factors are captured as equivalent movements along the Phillips curve from points A to D. At the initial equilibrium point A in the aggregate demand and supply graph, there is a corresponding inflation rate and unemployment rate represented by point A in the Phillips curve graph. For every new equilibrium point (points B, C, and D) in the aggregate graph, there is a corresponding point in the Phillips curve. This illustrates an important point: changes in aggregate demand cause movements along the Phillips curve.

The Long-Run Phillips Curve

The long-run Phillips curve is a vertical line at the natural rate of unemployment, so inflation and unemployment are unrelated in the long run. The Phillips curve shows the trade-off between inflation and unemployment, but how accurate is this relationship in the long run? According to economists, there can be no trade-off between inflation and unemployment in the long run. Decreases in unemployment can lead to increases in inflation, but only in the short run. In the long run, inflation and unemployment are unrelated. Graphically, this means the Phillips curve is vertical at the natural rate of unemployment or the hypothetical unemployment rate if aggregate production is in the long-run level. Attempts to change unemployment rates only serve to move the economy up and down this vertical line.

Natural Rate Hypothesis

The natural rate of unemployment theory, also known as the non-accelerating inflation rate of unemployment (NAIRU) theory, was developed by economists Milton Friedman and Edmund Phelps. According to NAIRU theory, expansionary economic policies will create only temporary decreases in unemployment as the economy will adjust to the natural rate. Moreover, when unemployment is below the natural rate, inflation will accelerate. When unemployment is above the natural rate, inflation will decelerate. When the unemployment rate is equal to the natural rate, inflation is stable, or non-accelerating.

An Example of Long-Run Curve

To get a better sense of the long-run Phillips curve, consider the example shown in. Assume the economy starts at point A and has an initial rate of unemployment and inflation rate. If the government decides to pursue expansionary economic policies, inflation will increase as aggregate demand shifts to the right. This is shown as a movement along the short-run Phillips curve, to point B, which is an unstable equilibrium. As aggregate demand increases, more workers will be hired by firms in order to produce more output to meet rising demand, and unemployment will decrease. However, due to the higher inflation, workers' expectations of future inflation changes, which shifts the short-run Phillips curve to the right, from unstable equilibrium point B to the stable equilibrium point C. At point C, the rate of unemployment has increased back to its natural rate, but inflation remains higher than its initial level.

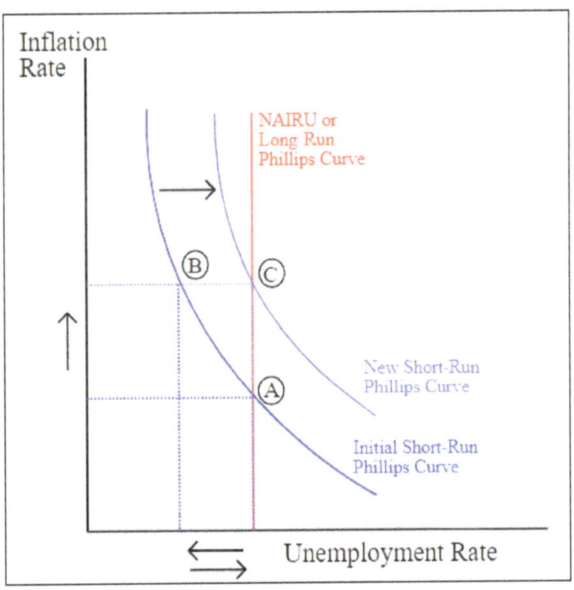

NAIRU and Phillips Curve.

Although the economy starts with an initially low level of inflation at point A, attempts to decrease the unemployment rate are futile and only increase inflation to point C. The unemployment rate cannot fall below the natural rate of unemployment, or NAIRU, without increasing inflation in the long run.

The reason the short-run Phillips curve shifts is due to the changes in inflation expectations. Workers, who are assumed to be completely rational and informed, will recognize their nominal wages have not kept pace with inflation increases (the movement from A to B), so their real wages have been decreased. As such, in the future, they will renegotiate their nominal wages to reflect the higher expected inflation rate, in order to keep their real wages the same. As nominal wages increase, production costs for the supplier increase, which diminishes profits. As profits decline, suppliers will decrease output and employ fewer workers (the movement from B to C). Consequently, an attempt to decrease unemployment at the cost of higher inflation in the short run led to higher inflation and no change in unemployment in the long run.

The NAIRU theory was used to explain the stagflation phenomenon of the 1970's, when the classic Phillips curve could not. According to the theory, the simultaneously high rates of unemployment and inflation could be explained because workers changed their inflation expectations, shifting the short-run Phillips curve, and increasing the prevailing rate of inflation in the economy. At the same time, unemployment rates were not affected, leading to high inflation and high unemployment.

The Short-Run Phillips Curve

The short-run Phillips curve depicts the inverse trade-off between inflation and unemployment. The Phillips curve depicts the relationship between inflation and unemployment rates. The long-run Phillips curve is a vertical line that illustrates that there is no permanent trade-off between inflation and unemployment in the long run. However, the short-run Phillips curve is roughly L-shaped to reflect the initial inverse relationship between the two variables. As unemployment rates increase, inflation decreases; as unemployment rates decrease, inflation increases.

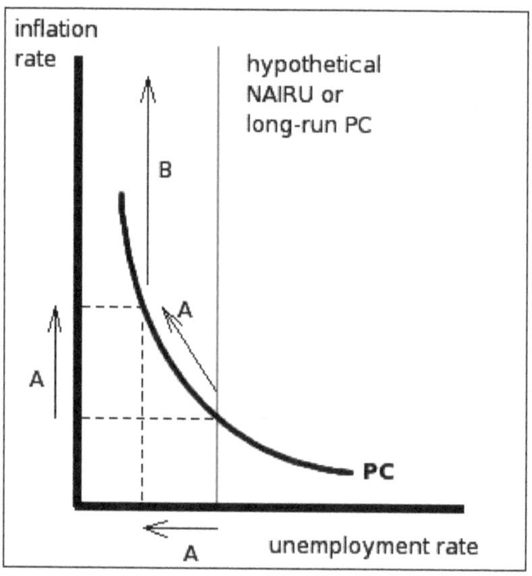

Short-Run Phillips Curve.

The short-run Phillips curve shows that in the short-term there is a tradeoff between inflation and unemployment. Contrast it with the long-run Phillips curve (in red), which shows that over the long term, unemployment rate stays more or less steady regardless of inflation rate.

Consider the example when the unemployment rate is 2%, the corresponding inflation rate is 10%. As unemployment decreases to 1%, the inflation rate increases to 15%. On the other hand when unemployment increases to 6%, the inflation rate drops to 2%.

During the 1960's, the Phillips curve rose to prominence because it seemed to accurately depict real-world macroeconomics. However, the stagflation of the 1970's shattered any illusions that the Phillips curve was a stable and predictable policy tool. Nowadays, modern economists reject the idea of a stable Phillips curve, but they agree that there is a trade-off between inflation and unemployment in the short-run. Given a stationary aggregate supply curve, increases in aggregate demand create increases in real output. As output increases, unemployment decreases. With more people employed in the workforce, spending within the economy increases, and demand-pull inflation occurs, raising price levels.

Therefore, the short-run Phillips curve illustrates a real, inverse correlation between inflation and unemployment, but this relationship can only exist in the short run. The idea of a stable trade-off between inflation and unemployment in the long run has been disproved by economic history.

Relationship between Expectations and Inflation

There are two theories of expectations (adaptive or rational) that predict how people will react to inflation. The short-run Phillips curve is said to shift because of workers' future inflation expectations. Yet, how are those expectations formed? There are two theories that explain how individuals predict future events.

Real versus Nominal Quantities

To fully appreciate theories of expectations, it is helpful to review the difference between real and nominal concepts. Anything that is nominal is a stated aspect. In contrast, anything that is real has been adjusted for inflation. To make the distinction clearer, consider this example. Suppose you are opening a savings account at a bank that promises a 5% interest rate. This is the nominal, or stated, interest rate. However, suppose inflation is at 3%. The real interest rate would only be 2% (the nominal 5% minus 3% to adjust for inflation). The difference between real and nominal extends beyond interest rates. In an earlier atom, the difference between real GDP and nominal GDP was discussed.

Adaptive Expectations

The theory of adaptive expectations states that individuals will form future expectations based on past events. For example, if inflation was lower than expected in the past, individuals will change their expectations and anticipate future inflation to be lower than expected.

To connect this to the Phillips curve, consider. Assume the economy starts at point A at the natural rate of unemployment with an initial inflation rate of 2%, which has been constant for the past few years. Accordingly, because of the adaptive expectations theory, workers will expect the 2% inflation rate to continue, so they will incorporate this expected increase into future labor bargaining agreements. This way, their nominal wages will keep up with inflation, and their real wages will stay the same.

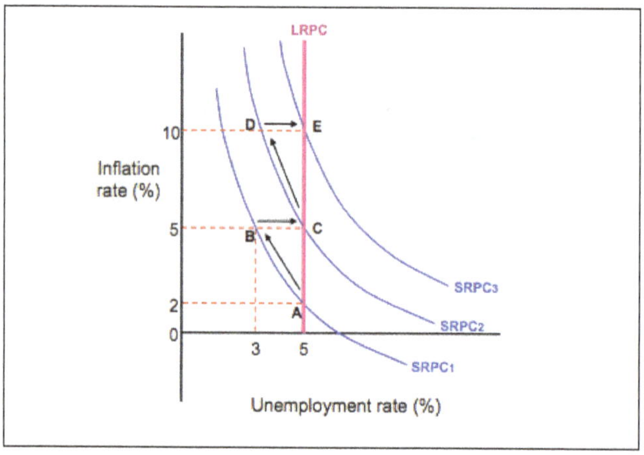

Expectations and the Phillips Curve: According to adaptive expectations theory, policies designed to lower unemployment will move the economy from point A through point B, a transition period when unemployment is temporarily lowered at the cost of higher inflation. However, eventually, the economy will move back to the natural rate of unemployment at point C, which produces a net effect of only increasing the inflation rate. According to rational expectations theory, policies designed to lower unemployment will move the economy directly from point A to point C. The transition at point B does not exist as workers are able to anticipate increased inflation and adjust their wage demands accordingly.

Now assume that the government wants to lower the unemployment rate. To do so, it engages in expansionary economic activities and increases aggregate demand. As aggregate demand increases, inflation increases. Because of the higher inflation, the real wages workers receive have decreased. For example, assume each worker receives $100, plus the 2% inflation adjustment. Each worker will make $102 in nominal wages, but $100 in real wages. Now, if the inflation level has risen to 6%. Workers will make $102 in nominal wages, but this is only $96.23 in real wages.

Although the workers' real purchasing power declines, employers are now able to hire labor for a cheaper real cost. Consequently, employers hire more workers to produce more output, lowering the unemployment rate and increasing real GDP. On, the economy moves from point A to point B.

However, workers eventually realize that inflation has grown faster than expected, their nominal wages have not kept pace, and their real wages have been diminished. They demand a 4% increase in wages to increase their real purchasing power to previous levels, which raises labor costs for employers. As labor costs increase, profits decrease, and some workers are let go, increasing the unemployment rate. Graphically, the economy moves from point B to point C.

This example highlights how the theory of adaptive expectations predicts that there are no long-run trade-offs between unemployment and inflation. In the short run, it is possible to lower unemployment at the cost of higher inflation, but, eventually, worker expectations will catch up, and the economy will correct itself to the natural rate of unemployment with higher inflation.

Rational Expectations

The theory of rational expectations states that individuals will form future expectations based on all available information, with the result that future predictions will be very close to the market equilibrium. For example, assume that inflation was lower than expected in the past. Individuals will take this past information and current information, such as the current inflation rate and current economic policies, to predict future inflation rates.

As an example of how this applies to the Phillips curve, consider again. Assume the economy starts at point A, with an initial inflation rate of 2% and the natural rate of unemployment. However, under rational expectations theory, workers are intelligent and fully aware of past and present economic variables and change their expectations accordingly. They will be able to anticipate increases in aggregate demand and the accompanying increases in inflation. As such, they will raise their nominal wage demands to match the forecasted inflation, and they will not have an adjustment period when their real wages are lower than their nominal wages. Graphically, they will move seamlessly from point A to point C, without transitioning to point B.

In essence, rational expectations theory predicts that attempts to change the unemployment rate will be automatically undermined by rational workers. They can act rationally to protect their interests, which cancels out the intended economic policy effects. Efforts to lower unemployment only raise inflation.

Shifting the Phillips Curve with a Supply Shock

Aggregate supply shocks, such as increases in the costs of resources, can cause the Phillips curve to shift. The Phillips curve shows the relationship between inflation and unemployment. In the short-run, inflation and unemployment are inversely related; as one quantity increases, the other decreases. In the long-run, there is no trade-off. In the 1960's, economists believed that the short-run Phillips curve was stable. By the 1970's, economic events dashed the idea of a predictable Phillips curve. What could have happened in the 1970's to ruin an entire theory? Stagflation caused by a aggregate supply shock.

Stagflation and Aggregate Supply Shocks

Stagflation is a combination of the words "stagnant" and "inflation," which are the characteristics of an economy experiencing stagflation: stagnating economic growth and high unemployment with simultaneously high inflation. The stagflation of the 1970's was caused by a series of aggregate supply shocks. In this case, huge increases in oil prices by the Organization of Petroleum Exporting Countries (OPEC) created a severe negative supply shock. The increased oil prices represented greatly increased resource prices for other goods, which decreased aggregate supply and shifted the curve to the left. As aggregate supply decreased, real GDP output decreased, which increased unemployment, and price level increased; in other words, the shift in aggregate supply created cost-push inflation.

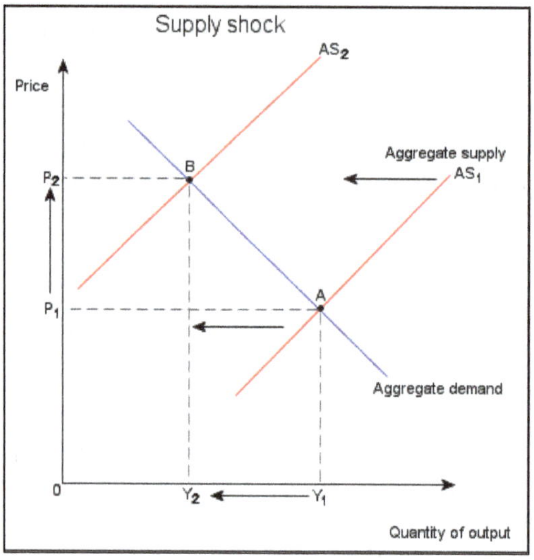

Aggregate Supply Shock.

In this example of a negative supply shock, aggregate supply decreases and shifts to the left. The resulting decrease in output and increase in inflation can cause the situation known as stagflation.

Shifting the Phillips Curve

The aggregate supply shocks caused by the rising price of oil created simultaneously high unemployment and high inflation. At the time, the dominant school of economic thought believed inflation and unemployment to be mutually exclusive; it was not possible to have high levels of both within an economy. Consequently, the Phillips curve could not model this situation. For high levels of unemployment, there were now corresponding levels of inflation that were higher than the Phillips curve predicted; the Phillips curve had shifted upwards and to the right. Thus, the Phillips curve no longer represented a predictable trade-off between unemployment and inflation.

Disinflation

Disinflation is a decline in the rate of inflation, and can be caused by declines in the money supply or recessions in the business cycle. Inflation is the persistent rise in the general price level of goods and services. Disinflation is a decline in the rate of inflation; it is a slowdown in the rise in price level. As an example, assume inflation in an economy grows from 2% to 6% in Year 1, for a growth rate of four percentage points. In Year 2, inflation grows from 6% to 8%, which is a growth rate of only two percentage points. The economy is experiencing disinflation because inflation did not increase as quickly in Year 2 as it did in Year 1, but the general price level is still rising. Disinflation is not to be confused with deflation, which is a decrease in the general price level.

Causes

Disinflation can be caused by decreases in the supply of money available in an economy. It can also be caused by contractions in the business cycle, otherwise known as recessions. The Phillips curve can illustrate this last point more closely. Consider an economy initially at point A on the long-run Phillips curve in. Suppose that during a recession, the rate that aggregate demand increases relative to increases in aggregate supply declines. This reduces price levels, which diminishes supplier profits. As profits decline, employers lay off employees, and unemployment rises, which moves the economy from point A to point B on the graph. Eventually, though, firms and workers adjust their inflation expectations, and firms experience profits once again. As profits increase, employment also increases, returning the unemployment rate to the natural rate as the economy moves from point B to point C. The expected rate of inflation has also decreased due to different inflation expectations, resulting in a shift of the short-run Phillips curve.

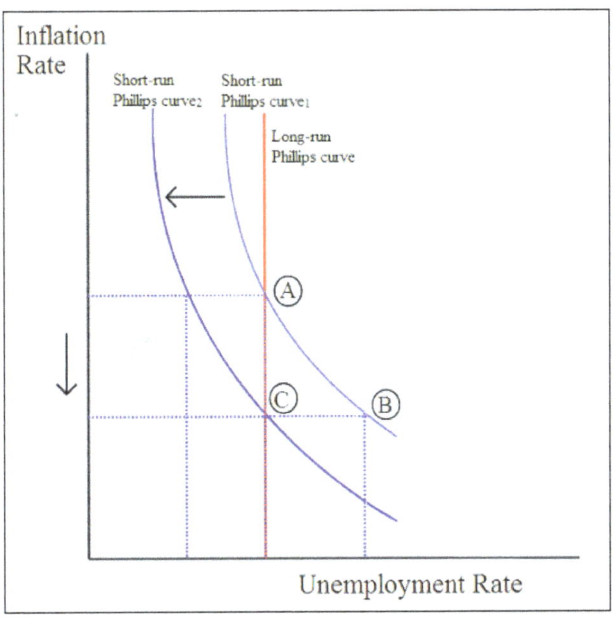

Disinflation can be illustrated as movements along the short-run and long-run Phillips curves.

Inflation vs. Deflation vs. Disinflation

To illustrate the differences between inflation, deflation, and disinflation, consider the following example. Assume the following annual price levels as compared to the prices in year 1:

- Year 1: 100% of Year 1 prices
- Year 2: 104% of Year 1 prices
- Year 3: 106% of Year 1 prices
- Year 4: 107% of Year 1 prices
- Year 5: 105% of Year 1 prices

As the economy moves through Year 1 to Year 4, there is a continued growth in the price level. This is an example of inflation; the price level is continually rising. However, between Year 2 and Year 4, the rise in price levels slows down. Between Year 2 and Year 3, the price level only increases by two percentage points, which is lower than the four percentage point increase between Years 1 and 2. The trend continues between Years 3 and 4, where there is only a one percentage point increase. This is an example of disinflation; the overall price level is rising, but it is doing so at a slower rate. Between Years 4 and 5, the price level does not increase, but decreases by two percentage points. This is an example of deflation; the price rise of previous years has reversed itself.

Deriving AD-AS Curves

Deriving Aggregate Supply

Derive the Aggregate Supply Curve by using the wage setting and price setting equations:

$$W = P^e F\underset{(-),(+)}{(u,z)}$$

$$P/W = (1+\mu) \Rightarrow P = W(1+\mu)$$

Substitute $W = P^e F\underset{(-),(+)}{(u,z)}$ into $P/W = (1+\mu) \Rightarrow P = W(1+\mu)$:

$$P = \left[P^e F(u,z)\right](1+\mu)$$

We want to re-express $P=\left[P^eF(u,z)\right](1+\mu)$ into an expression relating the price level P to output, Y. In order to do this:

$$u=\frac{U}{L}=\frac{L-N}{L}=1-\frac{N}{L}=1-\frac{Y}{L}\text{ for }Y=AN, A=1$$

Substituting this expression for u into $P=\left[P^eF(u,z)\right](1+\mu)$, one obtains:

$$P=P^e(1+\mu)F\left(1-\frac{Y}{L},z\right)$$

z, μ, are shift variables. P^e is the vertical intercept of the line at Y_n.

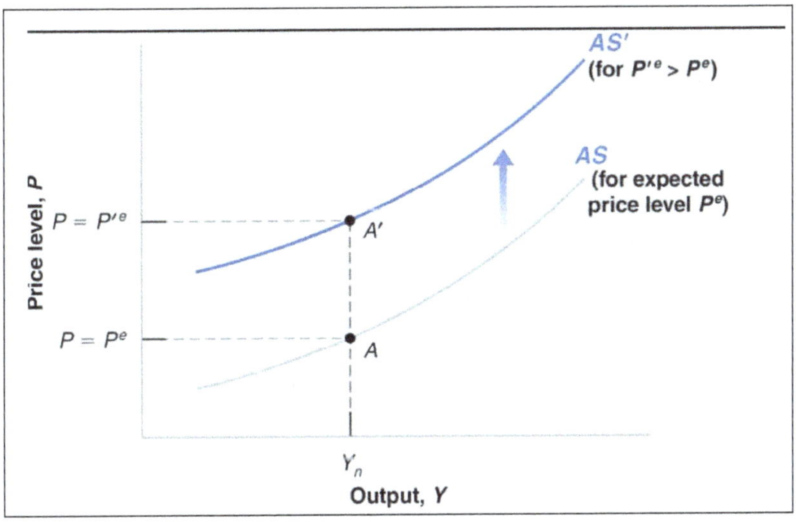

If the expected price level rises, then the AS curve shifts.

Deriving Aggregate Demand

Now, let's move to the demand side, to obtain an expression called the Aggregate Demand equation in P-Y space. This involves the IS and LM curves, which we will write in a non-parametric – or functional – form:

$$Y = C(Y - T) + I(Y, i) + G \qquad \text{<IS schedule>}$$

$$\qquad (+) \qquad (+),(-)$$

$$M / P = YL(i) \qquad \text{<LM schedule>}$$

$$(-)$$

Recall, changes in the autonomous components of T, C, I, or in G, will shift the IS curve, and changes in the money supply will shift the LM curve.

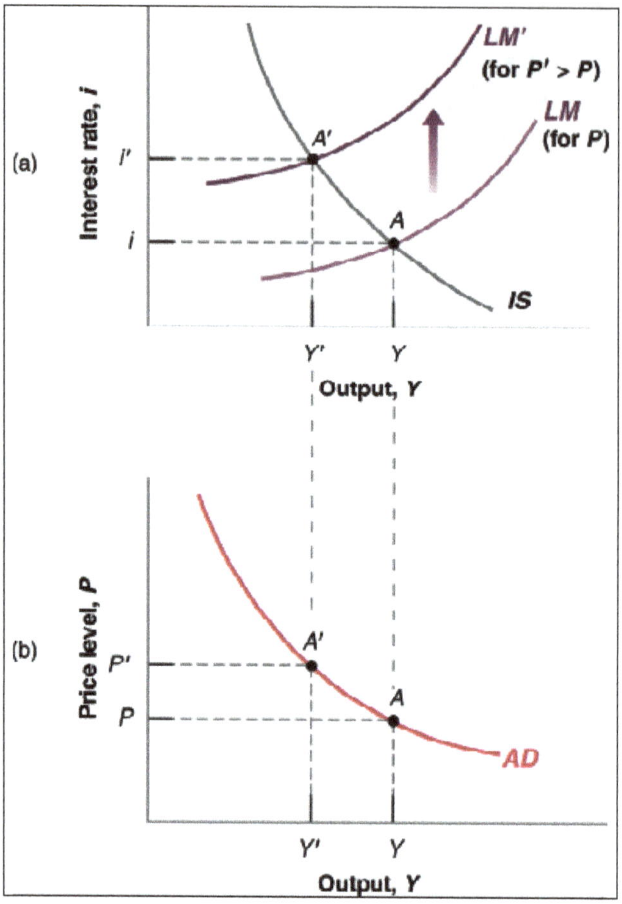

If one holds constant all terms in the IS curve, and holds the nominal money supply (M) constant, considering differing price levels will imply differing income levels, thereby tracing out a line.

One way to think of this graph is that, we solved for equilibrium income, at point A, because we held the price level constant. Instead of keeping track of separate IS and LM curves in P-Y space, we can solve for the aggregate demand curve:

$$Y = Y\left(\frac{M}{P}, G, T\right)$$ <Aggregate Demand schedule>

If we used the parametric expressions for the IS and LM curves, the aggregate demand curve would be written as:

$$Y = \hat{\gamma}\left[\Lambda_0 + \frac{b_2}{h}\left(\frac{M_0}{P}\right) - \frac{b_2\mu_0}{h}\right] \text{ for } \hat{\gamma} \equiv \frac{1}{1 - c_1(1-t_1) - b_1 + \frac{b_2}{h}}$$

Changes in the real money stock, G, or the autonomous component of T would shift the AD curve.

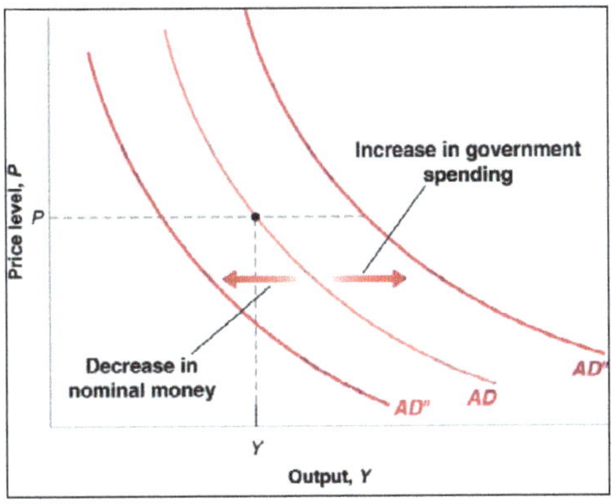

Putting AD and AS Together

In the short run, equilibrium output and the price level are given by the intersection of the two curves.

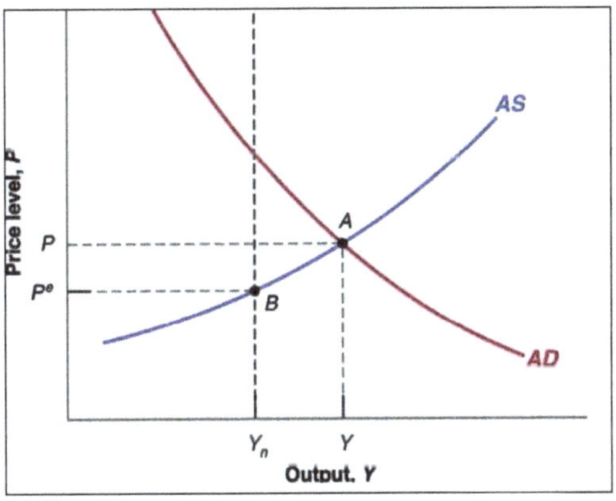

When the price level exceeds the expected price level, the expected price level is re-set at a higher level; the wage setters raise the wage they set, pushing up the price level. This is represented as an upward shift in the AS.

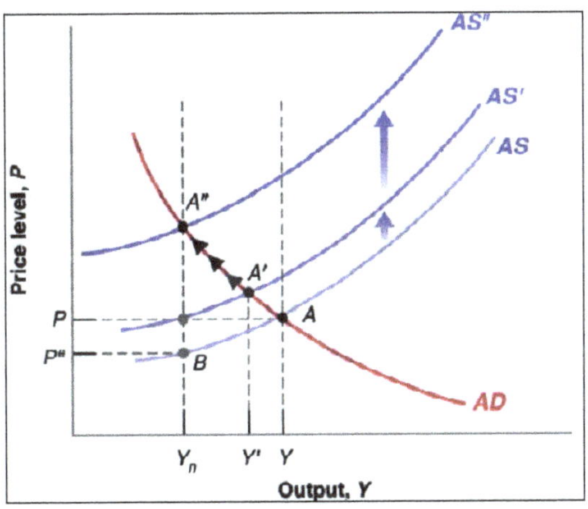

This process repeats as long as output exceeds the natural level of output (potential GDP). Only when the expected price level equals the actual will this process cease.

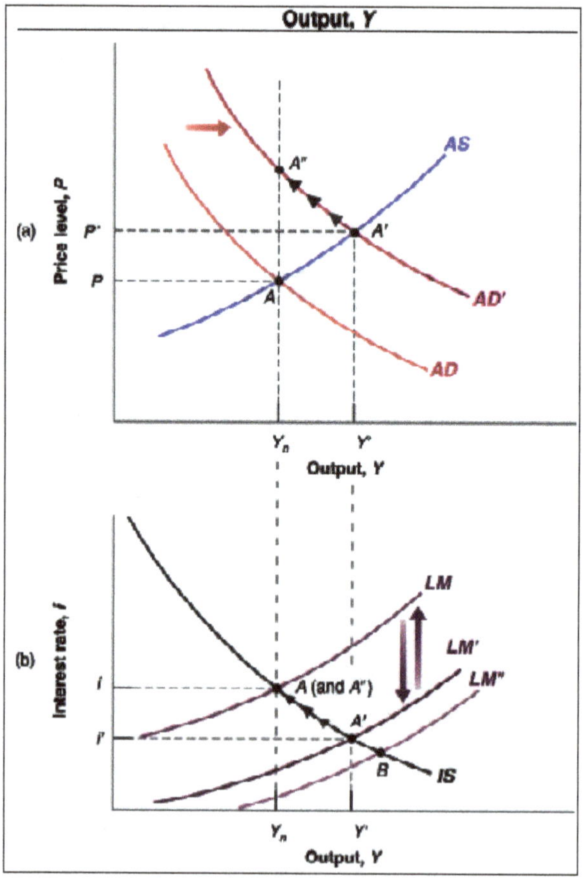

It is of interest to consider the short, medium, and long term implications of a monetary expansion. If the price level stayed constant, the LM would have shifted out as in the IS-LM analysis; but as output rises to Y', the price level rises, so the LM shifts to only LM'. Eventually as the price level rises sufficiently high that $Y = Y_n$, and the economy reaches A", then the price level is proportionately higher – that is, if the money supply were increased by 10%, then the price level would be 10% higher in the end. This phenomenon is called long run money neutrality.

Application of AD-AS Curves

Consider the model of aggregate supply and aggregate demand. In this economy,

$K = 100$

$L = 25$

$M = 200$

$V = 25$

LRAS:

$$Y = F(K,L) = K^{\frac{1}{2}}L^{\frac{1}{2}}$$

SRAS:

$$P = 25 + 1.5Y$$

1. Write an equation for the AD curve.

$$MV = PY \Rightarrow P = \frac{MV}{Y} = \frac{(200)(25)}{Y} = \frac{5000}{Y}$$

2. In the long-run, identify P_{LR} and Y_{LR}.

Aggregate demand:

$$P = \frac{5000}{Y} \Rightarrow Y_{LR} = \frac{5000}{P_{LR}}$$

Long-run equilibrium:

$$LRAS = AD \Rightarrow Y_{LR} = K^{\frac{1}{2}}L^{\frac{1}{2}} = \frac{5000}{P_{LR}}$$

$$Y_{LR} = (100)^{\frac{1}{2}}(25)^{\frac{1}{2}} = 50 = \frac{5000}{P_{LR}} \Rightarrow P_{LR} = \frac{5000}{50} = 100$$

$$(P_{LR}, Y_{LR}) = (100, 50)$$

3. Check that your long-run equilibrium satisfies the SRAS curve.

Substitute (P_{LR}, Y_{LR}) into the equation for the short-run aggregate supply curve:

$$P_{LR} = 25 + 1.5\ Y_{LR}$$
$$100 = 25 + 1.5(50) = 100$$

Which is a true statement. Therefore, the SRAS curve is consistent with long-run equilibrium at (P_{LR}, Y_{LR}) = (100, 50).

4. Suppose that V increases to 30 in this economy; this only affects the AD curve. Derive the new AD curve.

$$P = \frac{MV}{Y} = \frac{(200)(30)}{Y} = \frac{6000}{Y}$$

5. Find the new short-run equilibrium (P_{SR}, Y_{SR}).

Short-run aggregate supply:

$$P = 25 + 1.5Y \Rightarrow Y_{SR} = \frac{P_{SR} - 25}{1.5} = \frac{2P_{SR} - 50}{3}$$

Short-run equilibrium:

$$SRAS = AD \Rightarrow \frac{2P_{SR} - 50}{3} = \frac{6000}{P_{SR}}$$
$$2P_{SR}^2 - 50P_{SR} = 18000 \Rightarrow 2P_{SR}^2 - 50P_{SR} - 18000 = 0$$
$$P_{SR} = 108.188 \Rightarrow Y_{SR} = \frac{2(108.188) - 50}{3} = 55.459$$
$$(P_{SR}, Y_{SR}) = (108.188, 55.459)$$

6. Find the new long-run equilibrium (P_{LR}, Y_{LR}).

Long-run equilibrium:

$$LRAS = AD \Rightarrow Y_{LR} = K^{\frac{1}{2}}L^{\frac{1}{2}} = \frac{6000}{P_{LR}}$$
$$Y_{LR} = (100)^{\frac{1}{2}}(25)^{\frac{1}{2}} = 50 = \frac{6000}{P_{LR}} \Rightarrow P_{LR} = \frac{6000}{50} = 120$$
$$(P_{LR}, Y_{LR}) = (120, 50)$$

7. Let's say that the long-run adjustment mechanism shifts the SRAS curve up to meet the new intersection of the AD and LRAS curves. Solve for the SRAS curve that will prevail in long-run equilibrium. Solve for y-intercept b in the equation for the new SRAS curve:

$$P = b + 1.5Y \Rightarrow P_{LR} = b + 1.4Y_{LR}$$
$$120 = b + 1.5(50) \Rightarrow b = 120 - 75 = 45$$

The SRAS curve has shifted up by 20 units, which matches the long-run price increase due to the AD shift $(V \uparrow)$.

8. Draw a graph in P vs. Y space that represents the AD shift. Label equilibrium points (P_{SR}, Y_{SR}) and (P_{LR}, Y_{LR}). Draw arrows indicating the adjustment path from short-run to long-run equilibrium. Why does the SRAS curve shift during long-run adjustment?

- (P_{SR}, Y_{SR}) = (108.188, 55.459) is at the intersection point of the AD_2 and $SRAS_1$ curves.
- (P_{LR}, Y_{LR}) = (120, 50) is at the intersection point of the AD_2, $SRAS_2$, and LRAS curves.

- Arrows indicating the adjustment path would start at the $SRAS_1$ curve and end at the $SRAS_2$ curve. If you want, you can place them along the AD_2 curve from $SRAS_1$ to $SRAS_2$.
- With output above the full employment level in the short-run, unemployment declines below its natural rate, resulting in a leftward shift of the labor supply curve (S_1^L to S_2^L; workers are scarce). This results in an increase in wages $\left(w_1^* \text{ to } w_2^*\right)$. The SRAS curve shifts up during long-run adjustment because of higher labor costs due to a supply-constrained labor market; the unit cost of output has increased.

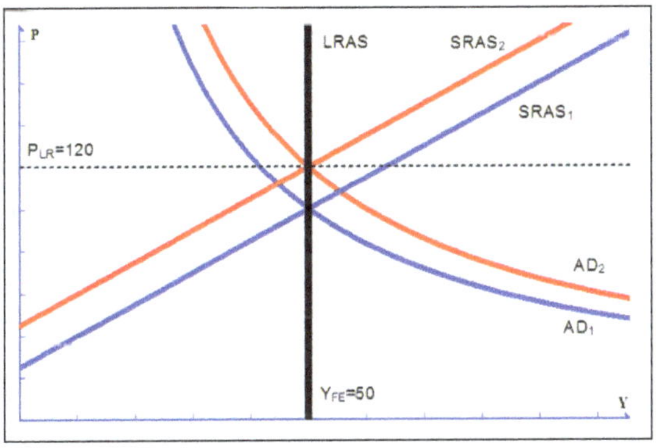

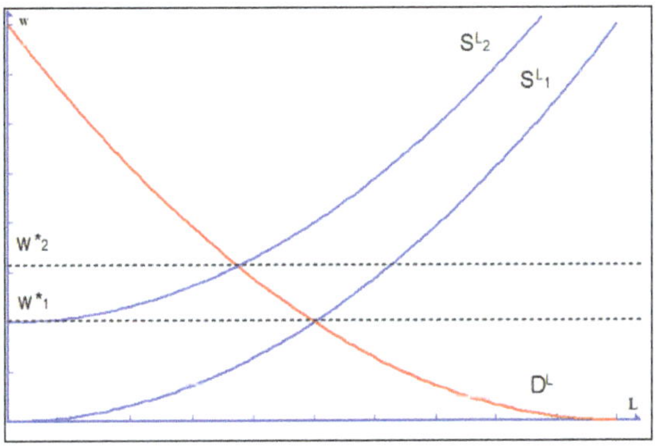

Money Market Equilibrium

At any given point of time, an individual decides, how much wealth is to be held in the form of money and how much in the form of non-monetary assets (let us say, bonds). Money holdings pay no interest but provide liquidity to the holder. However, holding wealth in non-monetary assets like bonds gives return in the form of interest. Higher wealth induces a person to hold more money and more non-monetary assets.

The magnitude of money demanded is influenced by the volume of transactions being made by the individuals, which in turn depends upon the level of income. Money is held as it facilitates making transactions. We would expect that the higher the level of income, the greater the real stock of money people and organizations will choose to hold. The demand for real money holdings also depends on the cost of holding money instead of other assets. If the interest rate is high, it makes holding wealth in the form of other assets more attractive. The higher the rate of interest on non-monetary assets, therefore, the smaller will be the quantity of money demanded. The extent of interest that one can earn by investing money in an interest-earning bond, its cost will be reduced. However, holding bonds may incur a cost in terms of losing liquidity at hand. This is because by holding a smaller inventory of money balances and an individual runs the risk of not having enough cash to pay bills. A deficit in cash holding generates the need of temporarily borrowing funds which comes with the interest costs associated with it. But if the interest foregone by holding cash is large enough, it will be worth risking and bearing these transactions costs.

At this point we should differentiate between real and nominal demand for money. The nominal demand for money is the number of units of a currency that are demanded. Correspondingly, the nominal demand for bonds is the demand for a given number of Dollars' worth of bonds. The real demand for money on the other hand is expressed in terms of quantity of goods the money will buy. So, this real demand constitutes the demand for real balances, what real balances are worth in terms of their purchasing power. The real demand for bonds is the nominal demand for bonds adjusted for prices. The reason why we are considering real rather than nominal money holdings is that the usefulness of any given stock of money balances for making transactions will be less; the higher are the prices that have to be paid to buy and sell the items which are to be exchanged. So an increase in the price level will reduce the usefulness of money in proportion. Thus, what matters is the stock of money measured in units of output, not in terms of currency units.

It should be noted that it is the nominal interest rate on other assets, not the real rate, which represents the cost of holding money. The nominal interest rate is equal to the real rate of interest plus the expected rate of inflation. Since high inflation eats away the real value of money holdings by reducing the quantity of goods which can be bought by those money balances in future, so the expected rate of inflation must be added to the real interest rate that can be earned on non-monetary assets in calculating the cost of holding money.

The wealth budget constraint in the assets market states that the real financial wealth of an individual is the sum of demand for real balances (L) and demand for real bond holdings (DB). Real financial wealth is the sum of nominal wealth (NW) divided by the price level (P).

$$L + DB = NW / P$$

The above wealth budget constraint implies that, given the real wealth of an individual, there exists a trade-off between demand for bonds and demand for money holdings. It means that a decision to hold more money balances must be accompanied by the decision to hold lesser bonds in order to maintain the real wealth. Therefore, given the real wealth, an equilibrium in money market implies an equilibrium in bonds market also. It means the asset market is in equilibrium and the state of equilibrium and disequilibrium in this market can be assessed in terms of money market or bond market. From the perspective of the economy as a whole, the total real financial wealth in the economy comprises:

$$NW / P = M / P + SB$$

This equation says that the total real financial wealth of an economy (NW/P) takes the form of real money supply (M/P) or stock of nominal balances divided by price level and the real value of the supply of bonds. The supply of money in circulation is determined by the government's monetary policy. The earlier wealth budget constraint was based on the real financial wealth and its composition of an individual, while this financial wealth represents the financial wealth that is there in the economy. If we insert individual's constraint in the economy's wealth relationship, we get:

$$L + DB = M/P + SB$$

$$(L - M/P) = (SB - DB)$$

$$(L - M/P) + (DB - SB) = 0$$

The above equation implies that if there is excess demand in money market then there will be a corresponding excess supply in bond market. If demand for money (L) is equal to the supply of money (M/P), then in that case supply of bonds (SB) must also equate with the demand for bonds (DB).

Given that there is free exchange of all capital assets, the aggregate quantity of money demanded equals the quantity in circulation. This also implies that given one's overall level of wealth, which is fixed by previous decisions to save rather than consume the willingness to hold one's existing stock of money is equivalent to the willingness to hold the same stock of non-monetary assets too. An excess demand for money must be accompanied by an excess supply of non-monetary assets and vice versa.

The pre-condition to asset market equilibrium or aggregate portfolio equilibrium is that the demand for and supply of real money balances must be equal. That in turn means that the existing set of non-monetary assets held must equal to what the asset holders desire to hold.

The wealth budget constraint implies that when the money market is in equilibrium i.e. L = M/P, the bond market too is in equilibrium i.e. DB = SB. Therefore the whole asset market can be analysed by focusing on the money market. The equilibrium in money market in turn leads to the derivation of LM curve, which shows different combinations of interest rate and income such that money market or the whole asset market is in equilibrium.

Demand for Money

An individual holds his wealth as money and other non-monetary assets. The decision of the division of wealth into money and other assets depends upon the relative costs and benefits of holding money versus other assets. The benefit of holding idle money is associated with its property of liquidity i.e. it can be spent easily. The cost of holding money is the difference between the interest rates paid on money deposits (i.e zero) and the interest return available from non-monetary assets like bonds. The demand for money is the relationship b/w the quantity of money people wants to hold and the factors that determine that quantity.

There are 3 motives for holding money.

Transactionary Motive

Money is needed in order to purchase day to day goods and services, such as buying groceries or paying the rent, etc. The transactions demand for money is the money that people hold to pay for goods & services which they anticipate buying. Whatever money balances are held in cash form in the wallet or in the form of checking account balance constitutes the transactions demand for money.

Contingency/Precautionary Motive

Money may also be kept on hand for contingencies such as having the funds available to pay to have the car repair or home repair or to pay for a trip to the doctor. The money people hold for contingencies represents their precautionary demand for money.

Speculative Motive

Money balances held for the purpose of hedging against the risk of fluctuations in the prices of financial assets are called speculative balances. Speculative demand for money is determined by the rate of interest that can be earned by holding money in the form of bonds. The market price of a bond and its yield (i.e. the rate of return) are inversely related. In holding bonds there is a risk-return trade off. Bonds are risky as their prices fluctuate. The decision of holding wealth in the form of money or bonds is taken after balancing the extra interest income that can be earned by holding bonds with the risk that bonds carry.

$$Md = M_1 + M_2$$

M_1 depends on Transactions and precautionary Motives

Therefore, $M_1 = f(y)$, which is positive

$M_2 = f(r)$ and not of income

$M_1 = kY$ and $M_2 = hi$

$h = M^d = kY + hi$

Higher income induces demand for all these purposes. We make a distinction between money held for different motives in order to understand how interest rate will affect the quantity of money demanded. There are other factors also like money income, wealth, prices, etc. which determine the quantity of money demanded.

Interest Rates and the Demand for Money

The quantity of money people hold for transactionary, precautionary and speculative purposes, varies with the interest rates that can be earned from alternative assets such as bonds. When interest rates rise on bonds rise, it becomes costly to hold money deposits, so they hold less money. When interest rates falls, people hold more money.

$$r^o \uparrow \Rightarrow P_B^o \downarrow \Rightarrow P_B^1 \uparrow \Rightarrow \pi_e^o \uparrow \Rightarrow D_B^o \uparrow$$

Where, r^o = rate of interest in current period.

P_B^o – Price of Bond in current period.

P_B^1 – Price of Bond in future period.

π_e^o – Expected profit in current period.

D_B^o – Demand of bond in current period.

This equation implies people buy bonds in current period and therefore money holding for speculative purpose decreases. This implies that when rate of interest is high M_2 is low (negative relationship). Similarly, when rate of interest is low M_2 is high. This gives us the function $M_2 = h_1$.

The quantity of money households wants to hold varies according to their income and the interest rate. It must be noted that the speculative demand for money is all the more affected by the changes in interest rates, than the precautionary and transactionary demand. When financial investors believe that the prices of bonds and other assets will fall, their speculative demand for money goes up. The speculative motive encourages individuals and firms to hold their wealth in money until the reduction in risk by holding money is perfectly balanced by the cost in terms of interest foregone for those money balances. Bonds are risky as their prices fluctuate. Rate of return on bonds is a major determinant for deciding the division of wealth between money and bonds. A fall in rate of return on bonds, risk remaining the same, leads people to hold larger proportion of wealth in the form of money rather than bonds. A rise in rate of return for a given level of risk will push more wealth towards bonds. Thus the speculative motive results in an inverse relationship between demand for money and rate of interest.

Thus, the demand curve for money is drawn showing the quantity of money demanded (transactions, precautionary, and speculative demands) at each interest rate, all other things unchanged. The demand for real balances demanded thus depends on two things, the rate of interest and the level of real income. The demand for real balances (L) can be written as:

$$L = kY - hi$$

The coefficients k and h reflect the income sensitivity and interest rate sensitivity of the demand for real balances, respectively. This implies that real balance demand is inversely related to the interest rate and positively related to the income level. The demand curve for real balances is shown in figure. It is drawn as a function of interest rate while income remains constant.

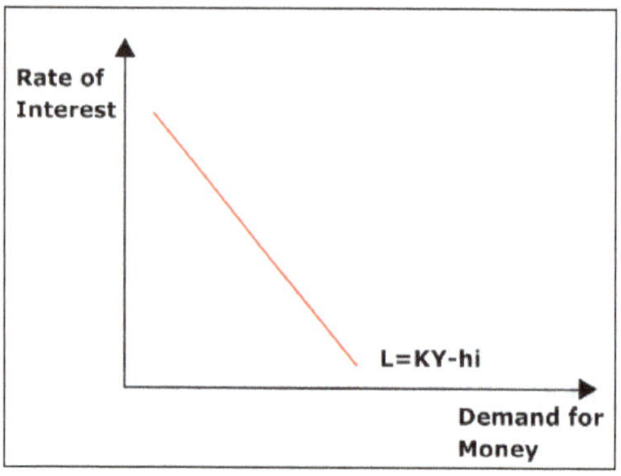

Demand for Money Curve.

The demand curve for money shows the quantity of money demanded at each interest rate with income level remain fixed. It is downward sloping expressing the negative relationship between the quantity of money demanded and the interest rate.

Supply of Money

The supply curve of money shows the relationship between the quantity of money supplied and the market interest rate, all other determinants of supply unchanged. The level of money supply is determined by the monetary authority. It regulates the supply of money through its open-market operations and reserve requirements. So, we assume the supply of money to be exogenously given by the monetary authority and it is unrelated to the prevailing interest rate in the market. Therefore, the supply curve of money is drawn as a vertical line, determined by the monetary policies. This is shown in Fig 2. The money supply curve shifts only when the monetary authority raises the supply of money through its monetary policy. In figure, the supply curve of money is a vertical line at that quantity of money supply which is determined by the monetary authority.

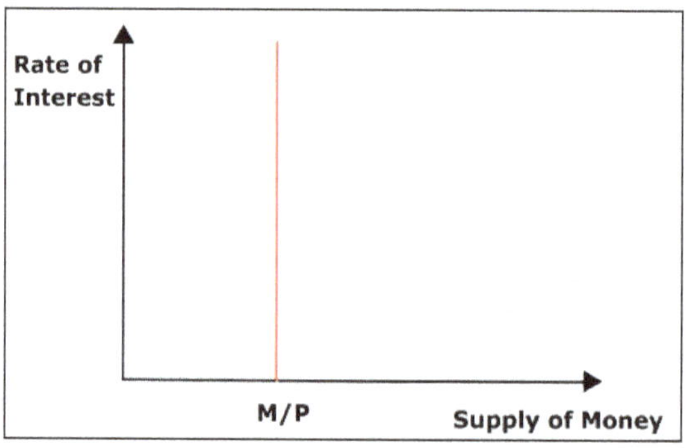

Supply of Money Curve.

Money Market Equilibrium

Money market equilibrium combines demand and supply curves for money to illustrate equilibrium in the market for money. In the money market the demand for money by individuals, firms, and other institutions is met by the quantity of money supplied by the monetary authority. The market for money is in equilibrium if the quantity of money demanded is equal to the quantity of money supplied. In figure, money market equilibrium occurs at the interest rate at which the quantity of money demanded is equal to the quantity of money supplied. The quantity of real balances is M/P and the interest rate is r.

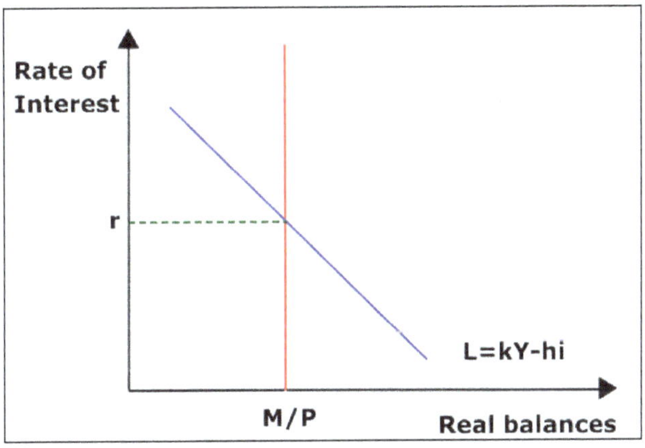

Derivation of the LM Curve

The demand curve for money is drawn to show the quantity of money people will hold at each interest rate, all other determinants of money demand remaining unchanged. A change in any of those "other determinants" will shift the demand for money. Among the most important variables that can shift the demand for money are the level of income and real GDP, the price level, expectations, transfer costs, and preferences. Suppose that the money market is initially in equilibrium at r_0 with the supply of money, M/P and the demand for money curve, L_0 as shown in Panel (a) of figure.

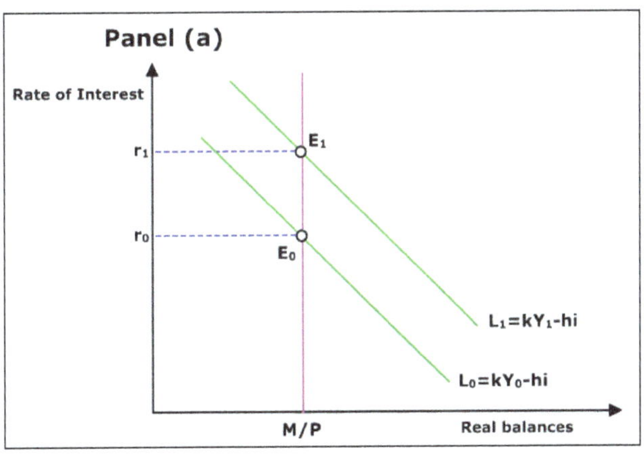

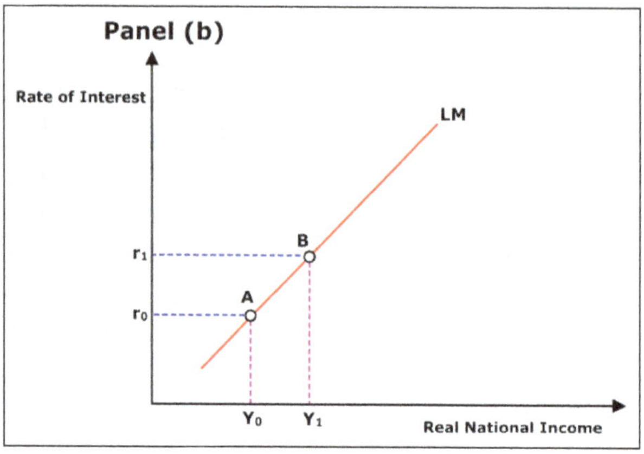

In panel A of figure, the initial equilibrium in the economy is at point E_0 where $M/P = L_0$ and rate of interest is r_0 and at this point the level of income is Y_0. In panel B, the point corresponding to E_0 is recorded as point (a) where interest rate is r_0 and income at Y_0. As a result of increase in income from Y_0 to Y_1, the demand for real balances rises from L_0 to L_1. This increase in demand leads to an increase in the interest rate as the supply for money is held constant. The interest rate adjustment causes the money market equilibrium to establish again at E_1. At this new equilibrium point E_1, the level of income is Y_1. The point corresponding to this new equilibrium is point B at interest r_1 and income Y_1. When points A and B are joined, we obtain the LM curve. Thus, LM curve is the combination of interest rates and income at which the money market clears. All points on the LM curve represent the money market equilibrium. LM curve is positively sloped as an increase in interest rate is accompanied by an increase in the level of income. This condition of money market equilibrium can also be represented in the form of LM curve equation:

$$M/P = L$$

$$M/P = kY - hi$$

$$\text{Or } i = 1/h\,[kY - M/P]$$

Shift in the LM Curve

In the money market equilibrium and in the derivation of LM curve, the supply of money is held constant, i.e. exogenously given by the monetary authorities. Any change in the real supply of money will shift the LM curve. Suppose the market for money is in equilibrium and the monetary authority changes the money supply by raising the nominal money balances (M). The impact of this change in supply of money is illustrated in Panel (a) of figure. The initial equilibrium in the economy is at point Eo where $M/P = L_0$ and rate of interest is r_0. In panel (b), the point corresponding to E_0 is recorded as point A where interest rate is ro and income at Yo. An Increase in the money supply when nominal balances increase, shifts the supply curve for money rightwards from M/P to M'/P, as shown in panel (a). At the original interest rate r_0, people do not wish to hold the newly supplied money; they would prefer to hold non-money assets. To restore equilibrium in money market at the income level Yo, the interest rate declines from r_0 to r_1. This is shown by the shift in the LM curve with the lower interest rate at the same level of income Y_0. So, the interest rate adjustment causes the money market equilibrium to establish again at E_1. The point corresponding to this new equilibrium is point B at interest r_1 and income Y_0.

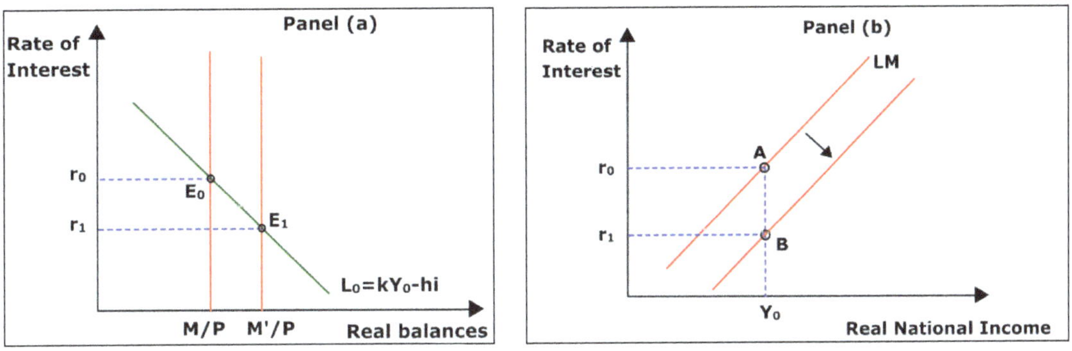

Shift in the LM Curve.

Slope of the LM Curve

The LM curve positively sloped. An increase in the interest rate reduces the demand for real balances. In order to maintain the demand for real balances equal to the fixed supply, the income level rises. So, money market equilibrium implies that an increase in the interest rate is accompanied by an increase in the level income. The slope of LM curve i.e. how flat or steep it is, depends upon two things:

1. Responsiveness of demand for money to income (k): The coefficient k in the demand for money function measures the responsiveness of demand for money to income. When demand for money is very sensitive to income, i.e. when k is high, LM curve is steeper.

2. Responsiveness of demand for money to interest rate (h): The steepness or flatness of LM curve is also determined by the sensitivity of demand for money to changes in interest rate. As the interest rate is the coat of holding money, a higher rate will induce less money holdings if the coefficient h is high. Lower h implies a steep LM curve, while a flat LM is due to high value of h. However, the slope of LM curve is equally determined by k and h.

This implies that greater the responsiveness of the demand for money to income as measured by k, and lower the responsiveness of the demand for money to the interest rate, h, the steeper the LM curve will be. Consider the LM curve equation:

$$i = 1/h\ [kY - M/P]$$

It can be seen from this equation that a given change in income Y, has a larger effect on the interest rate (i), if k is higher and h is smaller. If the demand for money is relatively insensitive to the interest rate, so that h is close to zero, the LM curve is nearly vertical. If the demand for money is very sensitive to the interest rate, so that h is large then the LM curve is close to horizontal. A large h implies that a small change in the interest rate must be accompanied by a large change in the level of income in order to maintain money market equilibrium. Thus, two coefficients, k and h, together determine the slope of LM curve.

Positions of the LM Curve

The points on the LM curve represent the points of equilibrium in the money market. All the points off the LM curve i.e. to its right and left represent money market disequilibrium. A disequilibrium is characterised by excess demand or excess supply of money. In figure, consider the points off the LM curve.

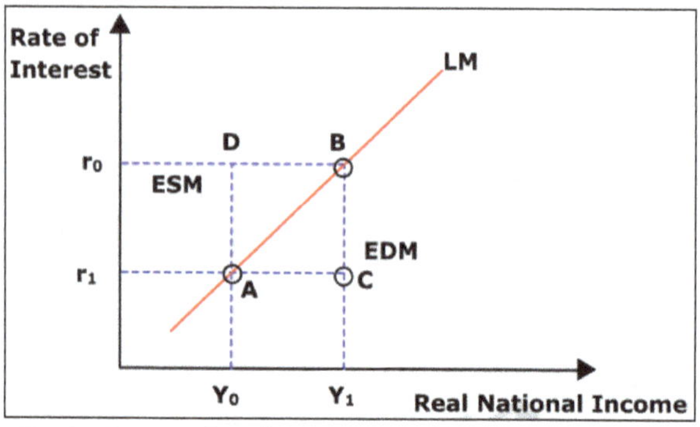

Excess Demand and Excess Supply in money market.

In figure, points A and B on the LM curve are the points of money market equilibrium. Suppose if the equilibrium is at point A and there is an increase in income from Y_0 to Y_1, which leads us to point Y1, then at the same rate of interest, r_1, it generates excess demand for money. Thus point C is the point of excess demand for money. Similarly, if we are initially at point B on the LM curve and income level falls to Y_0. Then at the same interest rate r_0 people will demand less real balances which will lead to excess supply of money. Thus, point D represents the excess supply of money in the money market.

This implies that all points above and to the left of the LM curve like D are the points of excess supply of money (ESM) and all points below and to the right of the LM curve like C are points of excess demand for money (EDM).

References

- Aggregate-demand, boundless-economics: lumenlearning.com, Retrieved 06, August 2020
- The-relationship-between-inflation-and-unemployment, boundless-economics: lumenlearning.com, Retrieved 15, January 2020

3

Keynesian Economics: An Integrated Study

The different theories and models within macroeconomics which show the ways in which aggregate demand has a significant effect on the economic output and inflation fall under Keynesian economics. The diverse theories and concepts which are studied under Keynesian economics such as Keynes's general theory of employment, interest and money, and Keynesian cross diagram have been thoroughly discussed in this chapter.

Keynesian economics is an economic theory of total spending in the economy and its effects on output and inflation. Keynesian economics was developed by the British economist John Maynard Keynes during the 1930s in an attempt to understand the Great Depression. Keynes advocated increased government expenditures and lower taxes to stimulate demand and pull the global economy out of the depression. Subsequently, Keynesian economics was used to refer to the concept that optimal economic performance could be achieved -- and economic slumps prevented – by influencing aggregate demand through activist stabilization and economic intervention policies by the government. Keynesian economics is considered a "demand-side" theory that focuses on changes in the economy over the short run.

Keynesian economics represented a new way of looking at spending, output and inflation. Previously, classical economic thinking held that cyclical swings in employment and economic output would be modest and self-adjusting. According to this classical theory, if aggregate demand in the economy fell, the resulting weakness in production and jobs would precipitate a decline in prices and wages. A lower level of inflation and wages would induce employers to make capital investments and employ more people, stimulating employment and restoring economic growth. The depth and severity of the Great Depression, however, severely tested this hypothesis.

Keynes maintained in his seminal book, "General Theory of Employment, Interest and Money," and other works, that structural rigidities and certain characteristics of market economies would exacerbate economic weakness and cause aggregate demand to plunge further.

For example, Keynesian economics refutes the notion held by some economists that lower wages can restore full employment, by arguing that employers will not add employees to produce goods that cannot be sold because demand is weak. Similarly, poor business conditions may cause companies to reduce capital investment, rather than take advantage of lower prices to invest in new plants and equipment. This would also have the effect of reducing overall expenditures and employment.

There are three principal tenets in the Keynesian description of how the economy works:

- Aggregate demand is influenced by many economic decisions—public and private. Private sector decisions can sometimes lead to adverse macroeconomic outcomes, such as reduction in consumer spending during a recession. These market failures sometimes call for active policies by the government, such as a fiscal stimulus package. Therefore, Keynesian economics supports a mixed economy guided mainly by the private sector but partly operated by the government.

- Prices, and especially wages, respond slowly to changes in supply and demand, resulting in periodic shortages and surpluses, especially of labor.

- Changes in aggregate demand, whether anticipated or unanticipated, have their greatest short-run effect on real output and employment, not on prices. Keynesians believe that, because prices are somewhat rigid, fluctuations in any component of spending—consumption, investment, or government expenditures—cause output to change. If government spending increases, for example, and all other spending components remain constant, then output will increase. Keynesian models of economic activity also include a multiplier effect; that is, output changes by some multiple of the increase or decrease in spending that caused the change. If the fiscal multiplier is greater than one, then a one dollar increase in government spending would result in an increase in output greater than one dollar.

Stabilizing the Economy

No policy prescriptions follow from these three tenets alone. What distinguishes Keynesians from other economists is their belief in activist policies to reduce the amplitude of the business cycle, which they rank among the most important of all economic problems.

Rather than seeing unbalanced government budgets as wrong, Keynes advocated so-called countercyclical fiscal policies that act against the direction of the business cycle. For example, Keynesian economists would advocate deficit spending on labor-intensive infrastructure projects to stimulate employment and stabilize wages during economic downturns. They would raise taxes to cool the economy and prevent inflation when there is abundant demand-side growth. Monetary policy could also be used to stimulate the economy—for example, by reducing interest rates to encourage investment. The exception occurs during a liquidity trap, when increases in the money stock fail to lower interest rates and, therefore, do not boost output and employment.

Keynes argued that governments should solve problems in the short run rather than wait for market forces to fix things over the long run, because, as he wrote, "In the long run, we are all dead." This does not mean that Keynesians advocate adjusting policies every few months to keep the economy at full employment. In fact, they believe that governments cannot know enough to fine-tune successfully.

Policy Implications of Keynesianism

Governments should Provide Counter-cyclical Demand Management

Keynes was critical of the UK 1931 budget, which cut wages for hospital workers, and cut back spending on roads and new houses. He argued this would depress demand further and make the recession worse. Instead, he advocated higher government spending financed by higher borrowing.

In '*A Treatise on Money*' (1930) Keynes wrote:

> "For the engine which drives enterprise is not thrift, but profit."

Keynes' policy recommendations went against classical orthodoxy. Classical orthodoxy argued higher government spending would crowd out private sector investment. Higher government borrowing would push in interest rates on bonds and reduce the quantity of private sector investment. The Treasury view was to try and balance the budget, but Keynes' criticism was this only reduced overall aggregate demand.

The Great Depression only ended in the UK and US, when government spending on military caused sufficient demand. Though there is evidence partial stimulus (e.g. in 1936, helped stimulate demand) The problem with Keynesianism is that governments are often too timid – unless there is a war.

Keynes defended his policy of expansionary fiscal policy and criticised the classical idea of crowding out.

1. Accelerator effect: This stated that investment was highly volatile. If the rate of GDP growth fell, private sector investment fell. However, if government spending increased the growth rate – this would encourage the private sector to also invest. Thus government investment could complement private sector investment – not crowd it out.

2. Multiplier effect: Government spending could have a bigger final impact on real GDP. the Multiplier is likely to be higher in a recession because there are unused resources.

3. Ending the glut: Keynes' strongest argument is that in a recession, private sector saving rises sharply leading to unused saving. Therefore, the government spending is merely making use of unemployed resources. Bond yields on government borrowing won't rise because the private sector want to buy government bonds.

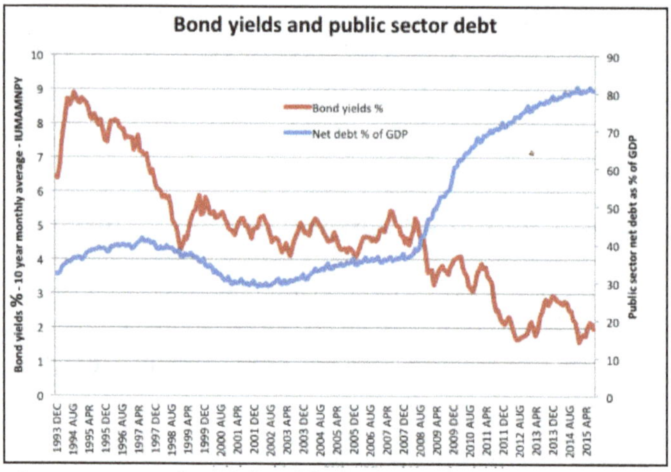

During great recession higher debt in the UK led to lower bond yields.

Counter Inflation Policy

Often ignored in a study of Keynesianism is the fact he also argued for government intervention if the economy was overheating and experiencing inflationary growth. Keynes, didn't per se, argue for higher government spending. He argued for counter-cyclical demand management. For example, in 1940, Keynes advocated higher compulsory saving to avoid the inflation of the First World War. (Out of interest, Keynes supported the Beveridge welfare state, though encouraged Beveridge to delay higher pension spendings until contributions had been collected).

The justification for government borrowing and higher spending only occurs at certain times of recession and evidence of a liquidity trap. Keynes would agree during normal growth, higher borrowing does cause crowding out.

Phillips Curve

Keynes didn't specify the Phillips curve, but later it was tacked onto Keynesianism. The Phillips Curve suggests the government faces a trade-off between unemployment and inflation – with Keynesians typically giving greater importance to reducing unemployment.

IS/LM Model

Another development from Keynesian theory. The modelling of national output to money, government budget and business expectations.

Keynesian Economics and the Great Depression

Keynesian economics is sometimes referred to as "depression economics," as Keynes' famous book, "The General Theory of Employment, Interest and Money," was written during a time of deep depression, not only in his native land of the United Kingdom but worldwide. The famous 1936 book was informed by directly observable economic phenomena arising during the Great Depression, which could not be explained by classical economic theory.

In classical economy theory, it is assumed that output and prices will eventually return to a state of equilibrium, but the Great Depression seemed to counter this assumption. Output was low and unemployment remained high during this time. The Great Depression inspired Keynes to think differently about the nature of the economy. From these theories, he established real-world applications that could have implications for a society in economic crisis.

Keynes rejected the idea that the economy would return to a natural state of equilibrium. Instead, he envisaged economies as being constantly in flux, both contracting and expanding. This natural cycle is referred to as boom and bust. In response to this, Keynes advocated a countercyclical fiscal policy in which, during the boom periods, the government ought to increase taxes or cut spending, and during periods of economic woe, the government should undertake deficit spending.

Keynes was highly critical of the British government at the time. The government cut welfare spending and raised taxes to balance the national books. Keynes said this would not encourage people to spend their money, thereby leaving the economy unstimulated and unable to recover and return to a successful state. Instead, he proposed that the government spend more money, which would increase consumer demand in the economy. This would in turn lead to an increase in overall economic activity, the natural result of which would be deflation and a reduction in unemployment.

Keynes also criticized the idea of excessive saving, unless it was for a specific purpose such as retirement or education. He saw it as dangerous for the economy because the more money sitting stagnant, the less money in the economy stimulating growth. This was another of Keynes' theories geared toward preventing deep economic depressions.

Both classical economists and free-market advocates have criticized Keynes' approach. These two schools of thought assume that the market is self-regulating and natural forces will inevitably return it to a state of equilibrium. On the other hand, Keynes, who was writing while mired in a period of deep economic depression, was not as optimistic about the natural equilibrium of the market. He believed the government was in a better position than market forces when it came to creating a robust economy.

Keynesian Economics and the Multiplier Effect

The multiplier effect is one of the chief components of Keynesian economic models. According to Keynes' theory of fiscal stimulus, an injection of government spending eventually leads to added business activity and even more spending. This theory proposes that spending boosts aggregate output and generates more income. If workers are willing to spend their extra income, the resulting growth in gross domestic product (GDP) could be even greater than the initial stimulus amount.

The magnitude of the Keynesian multiplier is directly related to the marginal propensity to consume. Its concept is simple: Spending from one consumer becomes income for another worker. That worker's income can then be spent and the cycle continues. Keynes and his followers believed individuals should save less and spend more, raising their marginal propensity to consume, to effect full employment and economic growth.

In this way, one dollar spent in fiscal stimulus eventually creates more than one dollar in growth. This appeared to be a coup for government economists, who could provide justification for politically popular spending projects on a national scale.

This theory was the dominant paradigm in academic economics for decades. Eventually, other economists, such as Milton Friedman and Murray Rothbard, showed that the Keynesian model misrepresented the relationship between savings, investment and economic growth. Many economists still rely on multiplier-generated models, although most acknowledge that fiscal stimulus is far less effective than the original multiplier model suggests.

The fiscal multiplier commonly associated with Keynesian theory is one of two broad multipliers in macroeconomics. The other multiplier is known as the money multiplier. This multiplier refers to the money-creation process that results from a system of fractional reserve banking. The money multiplier is less controversial than its Keynesian fiscal counterpart.

Keynesian Economics and Interest Rates

Keynesian economics focuses on demand-side solutions to recessionary periods. The intervention of government in economic processes is an important part of the Keynesian arsenal for battling unemployment, underemployment and low economic demand. The emphasis on direct government intervention in the economy places Keynesian theorists at odds with those who argue for limited government involvement in the markets. Lowering interest rates is one way governments can meaningfully intervene in economic systems, thereby generating active economic demand. Keynesian theorists argue that economies do not stabilize themselves very quickly and require active intervention that boosts short-term demand in the economy. Wages and employment, they argue, are slower to respond to the needs of the market and require governmental intervention to stay on track.

Prices also do not react quickly, and only gradually change when monetary policy interventions are made. This slow change in prices, then, makes it possible to use money supply as a tool and change interest rates to encourage borrowing and lending. Short-term demand increases initiated by the government reinvigorate the economic system and restore employment and demand for services. The new economic activity feeds a circular, cyclical growth that maintains continued growth and employment. Without intervention, Keynesian theorists believe, this cycle is disrupted and market growth becomes more unstable and prone to excessive fluctuation. Keeping interest rates low is an attempt to stimulate the economic cycle by encouraging businesses and individuals to borrow more money. When borrowing is encouraged, businesses and individuals often increase their spending. This new spending stimulates the economy. Lowering interest rates, however, does not always lead directly to economic improvement.

Keynesian economists focus on lower interest rates as a solution to economic woes, but they generally try to avoid the zero-bound problem. As interest rates approach zero, stimulating the economy by lowering interest rates becomes more difficult. Interest rate manipulation may no longer be enough to generate new economic activity, and the attempt at generating economic recovery may stall completely.

Japan's Lost Decade during the 1990s is believed by many to be an example of this liquidity trap. During this period, Japan's interest rates remained close to zero but failed to stimulate the economy.

The lower boundary of interest rates, then, is not necessarily an aspiration of Keynesian economists, but is rather a means to an end. When this method fails to deliver results, other strategies must be appropriated. Other interventionist policies include direct control of the labor supply, changing tax rates to increase or decrease the money supply indirectly, changing monetary policy, or placing controls on the supply of goods and services until employment and demand are restored. Keynesian theorists believe in interventionist methods, but are occasionally forced to look beyond interest rates.

Criticisms of Keynesianism

- Keynes argued that Monetary policy was relatively ineffective in in influencing demand. Many economists now see that monetary policy can play a role. There is less debate about fiscal vs. monetary policy.
- Fiscal fine-tuning is very difficult: A criticism of Keynesianism is that it is hard to make minor changes to fiscal policy to influence demand sufficiently to ensure stable growth.
- Political costs: A major criticism of Keynesianism is that it invariably leads to the growth of the state, and higher inefficient, corrupt spending. To 'pump prime' the economy, the government end up spending money on projects which creates vested interests and after the recession proves impossible to cut back. Therefore, Keynesianism has a tendency to increase the size of the state, which some see as a major drawback.
- Rational expectations: Some economists argue that people look to the future and see a tax cut as only temporary, and therefore don't spend. Instead, they

save the tax cut in anticipation of future tax rises. (Permanent life-cycle hypothesis) This means expansionary fiscal policy is ineffective.

- Break down of Phillips curve in 1970: In the 1970s, Keynesianism fell out of favour as stagflation showed rising unemployment and inflation. Instead, a new strand of economists suggested the importance of supply-side economics.

Keynes's General Theory of Employment, Interest and Money

When most countries of the world were experiencing the gravest depression of the last two hundred years – that is, the so-called Great Depression of 1929-36-economists of the time faced a challenge in the problem of increasing unemployment, shrinking national income, falling prices and failing firms.

It was a man-made calamity, a situation of poverty amidst plenty. Machines, workers and raw materials were available for production but were not being used simply because the employers feared losses in the production of goods. It seemed clear that there was something seriously wrong with the capitalist way of economic organisation. Most governments were helpless spectators to the deepening economic crisis because the economic advisers would not suggest any economic measures of state intervention in the economy.

The conservative economists liked to wait for the free-economic system to correct its ailment itself but they could not specify for how long. It was in this type of situation that Keynes was provoked to bring out his 'General Theory' (So nicknamed popularly) to justify taking up some new economic measures to tackle the situation. The policy recommendations he made were not entirely new but the theoretical justification he gave for them was remarkable. He advocated the policy of starting public works and financing them with fiat money with an unbalanced budget.

Wherever these policies were adopted, recovery was remarkably rapid. Keynes' economic thinking and economic policy at once became popular. It was a passion with the young economists and a problem with the traditional economists. The book has proved revolutionary in the sense that it has left its imprint on all branches of economic theory. We shall study, in a summary form, the main ideas of the theory.

National Income

The most important difficulty which Keynes faced in building a Theory of Employment for the economy as a whole was the definition of national income which could be related to national employment. He solved this problem in his own way.

Keynes wanted to choose the most suitable definition for this particular purpose. Dr. Marshall in his Principles of Economics had defined national income as follows: "The labor and capital of a country, acting on its natural resources, produce annually a certain net aggregate of commodities, material and immaterial, including services of all kinds and net income due on account of foreign investments must be added in this is the true net annual income or revenue of the country, or the national dividend."

No doubt Dr. Marshall's definition was theoretically sound, simple and comprehensive; even then it had serious practical limitations; for example, it is not easy to make statistically correct estimates of the total production of goods and services in a country, besides the difficulties of double counting and the portion of the produce that is retained for personal consumption. A.C. Pigou has tried to limit down the concept so as to make it practicable.

According to Prof. Pigou:" the national dividend is that part of the objective income of the community including, of course, income derived from abroad, which can be measured in money." According to Prof. Pigou, only those goods and services should be included (double counting being avoided) that are actually sold for money.

Pigou's definition is precise, convenient, elastic and workable because it did away with the difficulty of measuring the national dividend inherent in Marshall's definition. But Pigou's definition made an artificial distinction between goods that are exchanged for money and goods that are not so exchanged. The bought and the un bought do not differ in kind from one another in any fundamental respect. Again, in Pigou's definition, one could find the total amount of national dividend because we are to include where most of the goods and services are not exchanged for money.

In a country where most of the goods and services are not exchanged for money, i.e. they are simply bartered away; Pigou's definition was of no use. Fisher adopted consumption instead of production as the basis of measuring the national dividend.

According to Prof. Fisher, " the national dividend or income consists solely of services received by ultimate consumers, whether from their material or from their human environment. Thus, a piano or an overcoat made for me this year is not part of this year's income, but an addition to capital. Only the services, rendered to use during this year by these things are income."

Prof. Fisher's definition was better than both Dr. Marshall's and Prof. Pigou's in as much as it was nearer the concept of economic welfare because welfare depends upon the goods and services made available to the individuals of the community. But it is more difficult to have an idea of net consumption than net production. Moreover, the lives of durable goods which last beyond one year are very difficult to measure. Estimates are at best estimates and they can at times differ from the actual.

None of these definitions suited Keynes as he wanted to know the factors that go to determine the level of income and employment in an economy at a particular time. He wanted to know the considerations that weigh with entrepreneurs when they decide to employ certain number of men.

However, it may be noted that the suitability of any particular definition depends upon the purpose for which it is to be used. Keynes defined income in such a manner as enabled him to determine employment in the community. It is in this respect that his definition differed from those of his predecessors. Earlier definitions did not throw any light on the factors which go to determine income or its relation with employment; this purpose was amply achieved in the definition adopted by Keynes.

Keynes's Concept of National Income

Keynes' concept of national income lies somewhat between the Gross National Product and the Net National Product. Keynes does not deduct the whole of depreciation from the Gross National Product, he subtracts a little less than the whole amount of depreciation called 'User Cost'.

It is the cost of using capital equipment rather than of leaving it idle. User Cost is the difference between the depreciation in the value of the machine when it is put to use and the depreciation which would occur if not in use plus the expenditure incurred on its maintenance and upkeep. For example, a machine worth Rs. 1,000 in the beginning of the year remains worth Rs. 750 at the end of the year having suffered a reduction in the value worth Rs. 250 as a result of depreciation.

Even if the machine were not put to use, it would have suffered a loss of value on account of say rusting etc. But in this case the value of the machine has been maintained at Rs. 900 at the end of the year by incurring a small maintenance cost of Rs. 10. Thus, the user cost would be Rs. 250 (Rs. 100 + Rs. 10) = Rs. 140. In this way by adding the user costs of all the firms in the whole economy, we get the aggregate user cost of the whole economy.

When we deduct the aggregate user cost from the Gross National Product, we shall get national income of the economy in the Keynesian sense represented by A-U (where A is the Gross National Product, being the total product or value of goods and services obtained in a year and U represents the total user cost). According to Keynes, number of people to be employed (N) depends upon income in this sense.

Keynes, however, felt that the concept of income in terms of A-U is of little use when the community has to decide how much to spend on consumption. Here, the idea of 'net Income' assumes special significance. Net income is found by deducting supplementary costs V from the income (A-U). Thus, net income = A – U – V. In other words, both user costs (U) and supplementary costs (V) have to be subtracted from Gross National Product (A) to obtain the net national income.

Supplementary costs are those costs which cannot be foreseen or are beyond the control of entrepreneurs, i.e. these are contingent costs like plant becoming obsolete, catching fire. etc. Even if the entrepreneurs wished he could not avoid this loss. Such costs have to be deducted from gross income to get net income on which the consumption of the community depends. Since consumption depends upon net income, it is necessary that net income be calculated as accurately as possible.

To conclude, Keynes uses the term income in two senses:

- Gross Income (A-U) on which the volume of employment depends.
- Net Income (A-U-V) on which Consumption of the community depends.

Use of the Wage Unit

Besides the concept of income, another concept which continued to bother Keynes was the choice of units for the purpose of macroeconomic analysis and measurement in the absence of which he could never go along conveniently.

It is very necessary to measure the aggregative quantities like saving, investment, consumption, income output etc. In fact, monetary unit (money) had been employed usually as the standard of measurement. Keyncs himself measured these quantities in terms of money but found it rather unsatisfactory because with changes in prices, money does not depict true changes in the economic aggregate. Keynes, therefore, adopted a new unit for measuring the changes in the national output, that is, the unit of the employment of labor.

All industries employ labor and their outputs can be expressed in terms of employment that they offer. Keynes expressed employmcnt in terms of labor units. A labor unit may be taken to mean one hour of work by ordinary, unskilled or common worker. Thus, if volume of employment (labor units) in the economy is increasing, it is clear that there is an increase in the national output. Further, the amount of wages received by ordinary labor for an hour's work, Keynes called-wage unit.

More efficient and skilled labor, he observed, can be evaluated at a higher rate and the wage unit in this case can also be higher. In this way, Keynes reduced the magnitude of employment to wage units and measured the various types of aggregative magnitudes in terms of wage units. Most of the analysis of the General Theory is conducted in terms of relatively stable wage units (though the analysis of the theory of prices and inflation is not done in terms of constant wage units because with the rise in price, wages alone cannot remain constant).

Assumptions of Keynes's General Theory

To simplify his theory considerably, Keynes employed a few assumptions which must be noted to avoid any confusion or misunderstanding.

These assumptions are as mentioned below:

The Short Period

Keynes was writing about the short-period problem of depression. Therefore, he made the specific assumption of short-period so as to concentrate on the problem at hand. Keynes assumed that the techniques of production and the amount of fixed capital used remain constant in the model of his theory. In his view, short period is that in which new investments do not change the technique, the organisation and equipment. This considerably simplified his analysis, for he could thereby take employment and output as moving together in the same direction.

Perfect Competition

He assumed that there is a fairly high degree of competition in the markets. Or if there is some monopoly clement somewhere, then its degree remains unchanged.

Operation of the Law of Diminishing Returns

Further, directly flowing from his assumption of unchanging techniques was his assumption of the operation of diminishing returns to productive resources or increasing cost.

Absence of Governmental Part in Economic Activity

The government is assumed to play no (significant) part either as a taxer or as a spender. He ignored the fiscal operations of the government in his analysis to highlight the causes of and remedies for the instability of the pure capitalist economy.

A Closed Economy

Keynes further assumed that the economy under analysis is a closed one; that is, he did not explicitly recognise in his analysis the influence of exports and imports. This considerably simplified his work.

Heroic Aggregation

Keynes in his general theory dealt with aggregates like the national income, saving, investment, etc. and measured them in wage units to be able to ignore the questions arising out of changes in relative prices of resources.

Static Analysis

The 'General Theory' does not trace out the effect of the future on the present economic events clearly. Its analysis remains comparatively static, though at times Keynes introduced expectations in his analysis.

Apparatus of Keynes's General Theory

His theory is built up on the basic idea that 'Effective Demand' determines employment.

The effective demand in turn depends upon:

- Consumption, and
- Investment, which depends upon marginal efficiency of capital and the rate of interest.

Consumption (C) and Investment (I) further depend on a large number of other influences in the economy. Some of these are controllable by policy, others are not so. We have to select the more easily manageable factors influencing aggregate income and employment. All this requires detailed study of Keynes's General Theory. Before we do so, it will help us to know the general framework or apparatus of Keynes's theory.

The general apparatus of the Keynesian theory of employment can be briefly summarised in the following form:

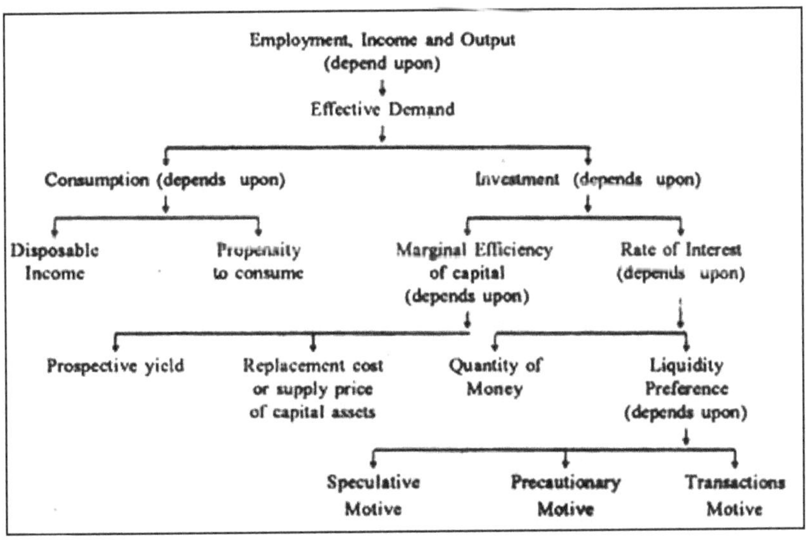

We start explaining the concepts from the top of the format given above. It conveys the impression that there are several factors on which employment depends. In the short period, employment, income and aggregate output are interrelated.

Keynes's first proposition was that total income depends upon the volume of total employment, which depends upon effective demand (D), which in turn, depends upon consumption expenditure (D_1) and investment expenditure (D_2): therefore, Effective Demand $D = D_1 + D_2$. Consumption depends upon the size of income and the propensity to consume while investment depends upon marginal efficiency of capital and the rate of interest.

The rate of interest depends upon the quantity of money and liquidity preference while the marginal efficiency of capital depends upon the expected profitability (M.E.C.) and replacement cost of capital assets. These propositions contain the essentials of the general theory' of employment. Let us study the concepts and relations one by one.

Effective Demand

Effective demand manifests itself in the spending of income. It is judged from the total expenditure in the economy. The demand in the economy is ordinarily for two types of goods – consumption goods and investment goods. The demand for consumption goods forms a major part of the total demand and it goes on increasing with increase in income and employment. At various levels of income and employment, there will be different levels of aggregate demand, but all the levels of demand are not effective.

Effective demand is the demand for goods and services in the economy as a whole which is fully satisfied by the supply of the output as a whole. It was this theory of demand and supply of output as a whole which was neglected for more than 100 years and which Keynes analysed. He divided effective demand into two components – consumption and investment. Consumption depends upon propensity to consume and investment is determined by inducement to invest.

Propensity to Consume

Propensity to consume, also called the consumption function, is a key concept to Keynesian theory of employment. The equation Y= C+I, expresses the relationship between C and Y. We can write this relation as C=f(Y). It tells us that there is a direct relation between income and consumption. Consumption function is written as a schedule of various amounts of consumption expenditure that consumers will incur at different levels of income.

It simply lays down that as our incomes increase; consumption will also increase though not in the same proportion as the increase in income. Propensity to consume refers to the actual consumption that takes place at different levels of income. An important fact about the consumption function is that it is stable in the short run because the consumption habits of the community remain more or less stable in the short run. According to Prof. Hansen, Consumption Function is the most important contribution of J.M. Keynes.

Saving (S)

In Keynesian Economics saving is defined as the excess of income over consumption, i.e., S = Y – C. The fundamental fact about saving is that its volume depends upon income. A man's saving is that part of his money income that is not spent on consumption goods. Generally speaking, saving is done in the form of cash or in buying shares and stocks, bonds etc. Community saving is simply an aggregate of individual saving. Classical economists believed that saving was a great private and social virtue.

Keynes, however, called it a social vice, as more saving on the part of an individual will mean less saving on the part of another individual, leaving the total savings of the community unaffected. Thus, according to Keynes, during a period of depression or recession encourage spending more to increase effective demand.

Investment (I)

In Keynesian economics, investment does not mean financial investment i.e., investing money in buying existing stocks and shares, bonds or equities. Here, it means real investment in new capital goods Investment in Keynesian economics is that expenditure which should result in an increase of employment of the factors of production in new factories and consumption.

In practical life the exact line of demarcation between investment and consumption is easily drawn; for example, expenditures on food and clothing are clearly consumption while those on buildings, factories and transportation facilities are easily investment.

Investment also includes additions to stocks of manufactured and semi-manufactured goods (inventories) as well as in fixed capital. Production in excess of what is currently-consumed is called investment. The distinction between consumption and investment is fundamental to Keynes' General Theory.

Since consumption expenditures in the short run remain stable, Keynes's theory stated in simple terms maintains that employment depends upon investment. This may be great simplification of facts but it brings forth the crucial importance of investment in Keynesian theory of employment. The fact of the matter is that employment fluctuates on account of the fluctuations in investment. Therefore, it is important to understand what determines the amount of investment.

Marginal Efficiency of Capital (MEC)

Investment depends upon the marginal efficiency of capital on the one hand and the rate of interest on the other. Marginal efficiency of capital refers to the expected profitability of an additional capital asset; it may be defined as the highest rate of return over cost accruing from an additional unit of a capital asset. In other words, it is the highest rate of return over cost expected from producing one more unit (marginal unit) of a particular type of capital asset.

In Keynes's view, fluctuations in the marginal efficiency of capital are the fundamental cause of the business cycle. Its importance lies in the fact that in a private enterprise economy investment depends upon it. If the expected rate of profitability (MEC) of an additional unit of capital asset is high, private investors would be prepared to invest, otherwise not. There are a large number of short-run and long-run influences which affect the marginal efficiency of capital.

Liquidity Preference (LP)

Liquidity preference is a new concept used by Keynes. His theory of interest depends upon it. Interest, in turn, affects investment and employment. Liquidity preference means preference for liquidity or cash. Keynes's view was that money offers ready purchasing power for commodities and bonds. To guard against the risks of uncertain and vague future, people want to hold some of their assets in cash. In order to carry daily transactions, to meet unforeseen contingencies and in order to take advantage of the market movements of bond prices, people want to hold cash; this constitutes the demand side of the Keynesian theory of the rate of interest.

The desire to hold cash, however, is not an absolute desire; it can be easily overcome by offering sufficiently high reward in the form of interest. The higher the liquidity preference i.e., the desire of the people to hold cash, the higher the rate of interest which must be offered to overcome their liquidity preference. Keynes considered government as the sole supplier of money in the short period.

Multiplier (K)

Multiplier is the key concept of Keynes. Keynes' multiplier is investment multiplier in the sense that a small increase in investment (A1) is expected to lead to a much higher increase in income (Ay). Investment multiplier (Income multiplier) expresses the relationship between an initial investment and the ultimate increase in national income.

It shows that an initial increase in investment increases the national income by a multiple of it. Keynes believed that whenever an investment is made in an economy, the national income increases not only by the amount of investment, but by something much more than the original investment.

Suppose in order to cure unemployment an investment of Rs. 5 crores is made in public works, the effect of this original investment would be to increase the national income several fold. If the national income is increased by an amount of say Rs. 15 crores then investment multiplier is 15/5 = 3. In the analysis of trade cycle, theory of multiplier is an important tool Keynes's policy of public works was based on his belief in the working of the multiplier vigorously in the depression phase.

Underemployment Equilibrium

The concept of underemployment equilibrium is the most revolutionary idea put forth by Keynes. Classical economists always believed that the economy was in equilibrium at full employment level only, but in his general theory Keynes could show successfully that the free enterprise market economy could be in equilibrium at less than full employment-to this, he gave the name of underemployment equilibrium.

According to Keynes, this was the normal situation of a free-enterprise market economy and economists hailed this idea of Keynes as the most significant gift to economics. Keynes disputed the classical assumption of automaticity of full employment and the classical prescription that in the event of an economic depression wage cuts would bring about full employment in the economy.

According to him what actually existed in the capitalist society was under-employment and not full employment. Underemployment equilibrium was the result of private under-investment in relation to the savings available in the capitalist economy at the given income level.

Simple Income Determination

Having discussed the factors which determine the level of economic activity (income, output and employment) in the economy, Keynes went on to build a simple model of income determination at a particular time. He did not draw any diagram in his 'General Theory' but his ideas can be better understood with the help of such a simple diagram as is given below. It shows the simple process of income determination in an economy.

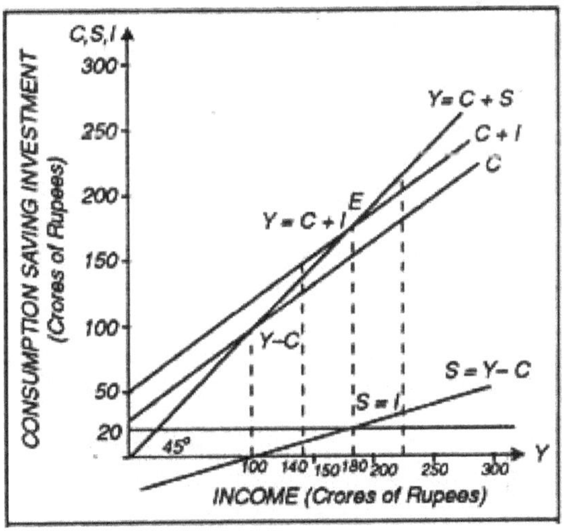

Simple Income Determination.

The horizontal axis of figure above shows the levels of income and the vertical axis shows the levels of consumption, saving and investment in the economy. The straight line through the origin (Y = C + S) makes an angle of 45° with the two axes. Therefore, the various points on this line are equidistant from the horizontal and the vertical axis.

The points on this line fulfill the equilibrium condition in the economy: i.e. at different points on this line total income is equal to total expenditure. The equilibrium level of income in the economy can be determined only with reference to a point on this line. It may be called 'Income = Expenditure' line.

The straight line labelled C shows the behavior of consumption expenditure with respect to income. It is straight line rising upwards to the right intersecting the 45° line where the whole of income is spent on consumption. It has a constant slope and therefore shows a functional relation between income and consumption.

As such it is called Consumption Function. Let us presume (with Keynes) that the level of investment is not related to income. Let investment be 20 crores of rupees whatever the level of income. We can add it to the various levels of consumption shown by the consumption function and get the C +I (total expenditure) line. The C +I line lies parallel to and above C, the vertical distance between them showing investment For determining the equilibrium level of income we need the total expenditure (C + 7) line and the 45° line (Y= C+S).

The point E where the aggregate expenditure line intersects the 45° line shows that income is equal to total expenditure, Y= C + I. In other words, it shows that whatever people earn is being spent either on consumption or on investment. Therefore, point E shows equilibrium in the economy. The equilibrium level of income is determined at Rs. 180 crores.

The Two Approaches to Income Determination

In his 'General Theory' Keynes used two approaches to the determination of income

- The Income-Expenditure Approach and
- The Saving Investment Approach.

Both these approaches lead to the determination of the same level of income. It will be useful for us to understand the two approaches at the outset.

The Income-Expenditure Approach (Y = C + I)

Keynes defined the equilibrium of the economy as that situation in which total income (Y) equals the total expenditure (C + I). This is to say that total expenditure constitutes aggregate demand while total income is the aggregate supply. Table is meant to illustrate the income expenditure approach to macro equilibrium. Column 1 in the table shows the various levels of income while column 2 shows the levels of consumption associated with it.

As income increases, consumption also increases but not so much as the increase in income. The result is that saving, which is income not spent on consumption, goes on increasing. Column 3 in the table shows that at the level of income of 50 crores, saving is negative, that is, minus 10 crores. This is because people spend on consumption to the extent of Rs. 70 crores while their income is only Rs. 60 crores.

It means disserving or accumulated-wealth consumption. At the income level of Rs. 100 crores consumption is also Rs. 100 crores and this means zero saving. Further as income rises, saving also rises. Consumption is only one, though major, component of expenditure. The other component is investment.

Table Y=C+I is the same as S=1 (Rupees Crores)					
1 Income	2 Consumption	3 Saving	4 Investment	5 Expenditure	6 Unintended investment
Y	C	S	I	C+1	I_m
60	70	10	20	90	-30
100	100	0	20	120	-20
160	150	10	20	170	-10
180	160	20	20	170	0
220	190	30	20	210	10
260	220	40	20	240	20

The Saving-Investment Approaches (S=I)

The second approach to income determination given in the 'General Theory' is based on the Keynesian definitions of Saving and Investment. Keynes defined saving as that part of income which is not spent on consumption, S = Y – C. He defined investment as expenditure on goods and services not meant for consumption, i.e., I = Y = C. When equilibrium prevails in the economy, income equals expenditure and since S and I are both equal to Y- C, saving must equal investment.

Saving in that case equals intended or planned investment. In ease of disequilibrium, planned or intended or ex-ante saving is more than or less than planned investment. Planned saving at the levels of income of Rs. 180 crores equals planned investment. At income levels less than this, planned saving is much less than planned investment. As there is disequilibrium, income will have to rise. At levels of income greater than Rs. 180 crores, planned saving is more than planned investment so that income falls to correct the disequilibrium. When the economy is having an equilibrium level of income, saving and investment are equal. Not only is income equal to expenditure, Y = C +I, but saving also equals investment, S = I.

The values of income, consumption and saving, have been plotted in the figure. We find that the S and I curves intersect vertically down the point E at which C + I line intersects the 45° line. The same level of income gets determined whether we have the Y = C +I approach or the S=I approach.

Since the former is a direct approach while the latter is an indirect approach, the two approaches are called the Front- Door Approach and the Back-Door Approach respectively. This dual approach to income determination has proved of great help in theoretical model building on the one side and national income accounting on the other.

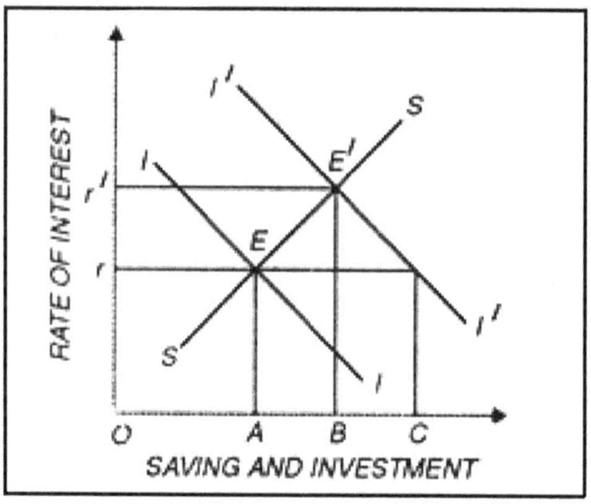

Role of interest equates S and I.

Policy Recommendations of Keynes's Theory

There were a few direct policy implications of Keynes' theory.

Firstly, it was clear that a laissez-faire capitalist economy will not be able to maintain full employment even if it is attained. Therefore, Keynes justified state intervention in economic affairs to fight instability.

Secondly, he could very nicely provide reasons for departures from the policy of balanced budgets. During depression he would advocate a deficit budget to stimulate effective demand and in times of inflation, he wanted the government to have a surplus budget to restrict effective demand. Professor A.P. Lerner, a disciple of Keynes, called it the policy of Functional Finance.

Thirdly, Keynes spelt out the specific form which state intervention has to take to counter economic depression. He laid down the policy of starting public works financed from deficit financing through direct throw of additional currency or via credit creation. Such public investment, he said, best achieves the multiplier effects.

He observed that public works need to be undertaken only as long as private investment is deficient. As soon as private investment is stimulated and the economy is well on its way to recovery, public works need no more be carried on. Thus, through his theoretical contribution Keynes not only shook the Classical Theory in its roots but also demolished its policy implications completely. He gave practically useful policy.

Limitations of the Keynesian Theory

The limitations of Keynes's theory and policy became obvious when the policies advocated by the Keynesians were implemented after the Second World War. Keynesian demand management policies were used by the governments of most Western countries in the attempt to keep the unemployment levels down.

Generally these policies were successful in preventing heavy unemployment like that experienced during the days of the Great Depression. But unfortunately they tended to give rise to the phenomenon known as 'stop-go'. That means, Keynesians wanted the government to go on raising aggregate demand to reduce unemployment to the acceptable level.

But it was found that Keynes's policies tended to create inflationary pressures to control which the government had to reduce aggregate spending. Thus all 'go' periods tended to be followed by 'stop' periods and it became difficult to achieve long-term economic growth. The main problem with the Keynesian model was that it was meant for the short run. It is not always possible to predict the effects of policy changes adopted in the short run.

Secondly, the Keynesian model failed to adequately take into account the problem of stagnation with inflation. Indeed, the basic model assumed that wages and prices are fixed as long as the government is reducing unemployment. Prices in Keynes's model use only after full employment. Experience in the 1970's in particular has shown that high rates of inflation can co-exist with high rates of unemployment. This is known as stagflation. No explanation of this is provided by the Keynesian Theory.

Thirdly, the coincidence of inflation and unemployment makes the Keynesian policy recommendation very questionable. For example, if the economy is in a deflationary gap situation but is also suffering from a 15 per cent rate of inflation, an increase in government spending or a cut in taxation designed to reduce the unemployment is likely to worsen the rate of inflation.

Fourthly, Keynesian model has been criticised on the ground that it tends to understate the influence of money on the real variables (like consumption and investment) in the economy. In the Keynesian model, a change in money supply only affects national income through its effect on the rate of interest. It is because of this that Keynesians have put more faith in fiscal rather than monetary policy.

We conclude by observing that the nature of economic problems of more developed economies has changed so much that Keynesian policies alone are not so much relevant. These policies needed modification and moderation. Nevertheless, the way in which modern economists view macro-economic problems owes much to the Keynesian framework. Keynes's work has left a deep mark on modern macro-economics.

Liquidity Preference

According to Liquidity Preference Theory, the rate of interest is the payment for parting with liquidity.

Liquidity refers to the convenience of holding cash. Everyone in this world likes to have money with him for a number of purposes. This constitutes his demand for money to hold.

The sum-total of all individual demands forms the demand for money for the economy. On the other hand, we have got a supply of money consisting of coins plus bank notes plus demand deposits with banks. The demand and supply of money, between themselves, determine the rate of interest.

Motives for Liquidity

Money may be demanded to satisfy a number of motives. These are mentioned below.

Transactions Motive

We get income only periodically. We must keep some money with us till we receive income next, otherwise how can we carry on transactions? Transactions motive also includes business motive. It takes some time before the businessman can sell his product in the market. But he must pay wages to the workers, cost of raw material, etc., now. He must keep some cash for the purpose.

Precautionary Motive

Everyone lays by something for a rainy day. Some money must be kept to meet unforeseen situations and emergencies.

Speculative Motive

Future is uncertain. Rate of interest in the market continues changing. No one can guess what turn the change will take. But everybody hopes, and with confidence, that his guess is likely to be correct. It may or may not be so. Some money, therefore, is kept to speculate on these probable changes to earn profit.

Interest-rate Determination

Money demanded for all these motives or purposes constitutes demand for money, or liquidity preference. Liquidity preference means how much cash people like to keep with them at a particular time. The higher the liquidity preference, given the supply of money, the higher will be the rate of interest; and vice versa. Further, given the liquidity preference, the larger the supply of money, the lower will be the rate of interest, and the smaller the supply of money, the higher the rate of interest.

According to Keynes, the demand for money, i.e., the liquidity preference, and supply of money determine the rate of interest. It is in fact the liquidity preference for speculative motive which along with the quantity of money determines the rate of interest.

We have explained above the speculative demand for money. As for the supply of money, it is determined by the policies of the Government and the Central Bank of the country. The total supply of money consists of coins plus notes plus demand deposits with banks.

We see, thus, that according to liquidity preference theory, the rate of interest is purely a monetary phenomenon. Productivity of capital has very little, though indirect, say in determining the rate of interest. How the rate of interest is determined by the equilibrium between the liquidity preference for speculative motive and the supply of money is shown in the figure below.

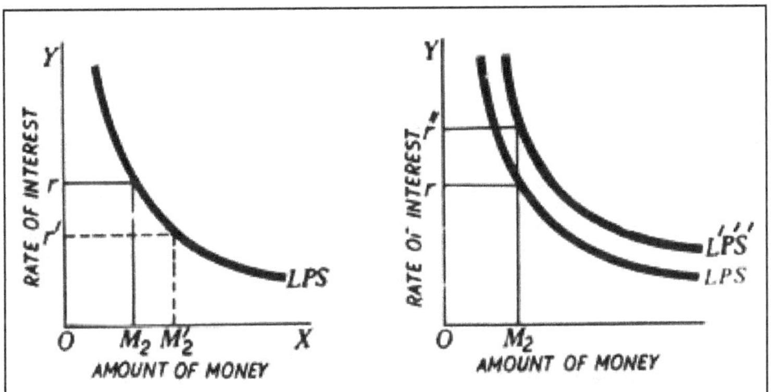

(a) Liquidity Preference Curve (b) Interest-Rate Determination

In part (a) of the figure, LPS is the cur of liquidity preference for speculative motive. In other words, LPS curve shows the demand for money for speculative motive. To begin with, OM_2 is the quantity of money available for satisfying liquidity preference for speculative motive. Rate of interest will be determined where the speculative demand for money is in balance with, or equal to, the (fixed) supply of money OM2. It is clear from the figure that speculative demand for money is equal to OM_2quantity of money at or rate of interest. Hence or is the equilibrium rate of interest.

Assuming no change in expectations, an increase in the quantity of money (via open-market operations) for the speculative motive will lower the rate of interest. In part (a) of the figure, when the quantity of money increases from OM_1 to OM_2, the rate of interest falls from Or to Or', because the new quantity of money $OM'_;$ is in balance with the speculative demand for money at Or' rate of interest. In this case, we move down the LPS curve. Thus, given the schedule or curve of liquidity preference for speculative motive, an increase in the quantity of money brings down the rate of interest.

It is worth mentioning that shifts in liquidity preference schedule or curve can be caused by many other factors which affect expectations and might take place independently of changes in the quantity of money by the Central Bank. Shifts in the liquidity preference curve may be either downward or upward, depending on the way in which the public interprets a change in events.

If some change in events leads the people on balance to expect a higher rate of interest in the future than they had previously anticipated, the liquidity preference for speculative motive will increase, which will bring about an upward shift in the curve of liquidity preference for speculative motive and will raise the rate of interest.

In part (b) of the figure, assuming that the quantity of money remains unchanged at OM_2, with the rise of the liquidity preference curve from LPS to L'P'S', the rate of interest rises from Or to Or", because at Or", the new speculative demand for money is in equilibrium with the supply of money OM_2. It is worth noting that when the liquidity preference speculative motive rises from LPS to L'P'S', the amount of money hoarded does not rise; it remains as OM; as before. Only the rate of interest rises from Or to Or" to equilibrate the new liquidity preference for speculative motive with the available quantity of money OM_2.

Thus, we see that Keynes explained interest in terms of purely monetary forces and not in terms of real forces like productivity of capital and thrift, which formed the foundation-stones of both classical and loanable fund theories. According to him, demand for money for speculative motive together with the supply of money determines the rate of interest.

Moreover, according to Keynes, interest is not a reward for saving or thriftiness or waiting, but for parting with liquidity. Keynes asserted that it is not the rate of interest which equalises saving and investment, but this equality is brought about through changes in the level of incomes.

Marginal Efficiency of Capital

The marginal efficiency of capital displays the expected rate of return on investment, at a particular given time. The marginal efficiency of capital is compared to the rate of interest.

This theory suggests investment will be influenced by:

(1) The marginal efficiency of capital.

(2) The interest rates.

Generally, a lower interest rate makes investment relatively more attractive.

If interest rates, were 3%, then firms would need an expected rate of return of at least 3% from their investment to justify the investment.

If the marginal efficiency of capital was lower than the interest rate, the firm would be better off not investing, but saving the money.

Importance of Interest Rates in Determining the Marginal Efficiency of Capital

To finance investment, firms will either borrow or reduce savings. If interest rates are lower, it's cheaper to borrow, or their savings give a lower return making investment relatively more attractive.

Marginal Efficiency of Capital

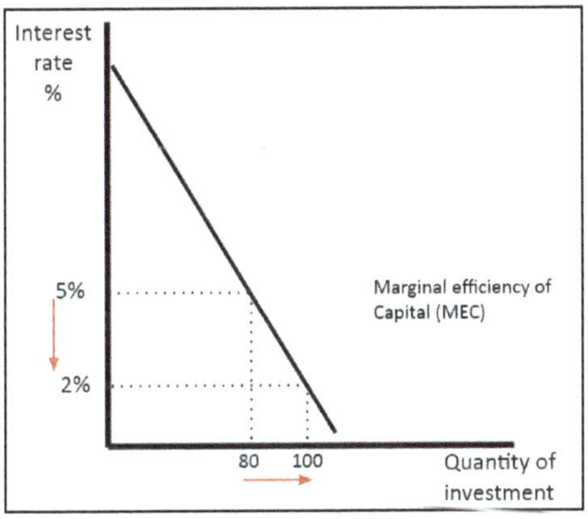

- A cut in interest rates from 5% to 2% will increase investment from 80 to 100.
- The alternative to investing is saving money in a bank; this is the opportunity cost of investment.

If the rate of interest is 5%, then only projects with a rate of return of greater than 5% will be profitable.

How responsive is Investment to Interest Rates?

In Keynesian investment theory, interest rates are one important factor. However, in a liquidity trap, investment may be unresponsive to lower interest rates. In some circumstances, demand for investment is very interest inelastic.

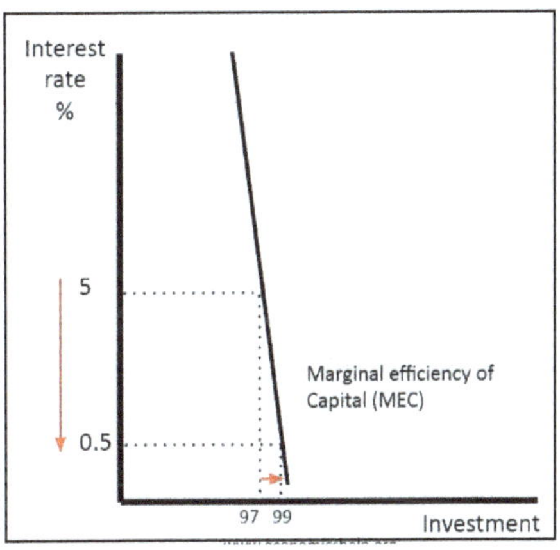

In a liquidity trap, business confidence may be very low. Therefore, despite low-interest rates, firms don't want to invest because they have low expectations of future profits.

Factors which Shift the Marginal Efficiency of Capital

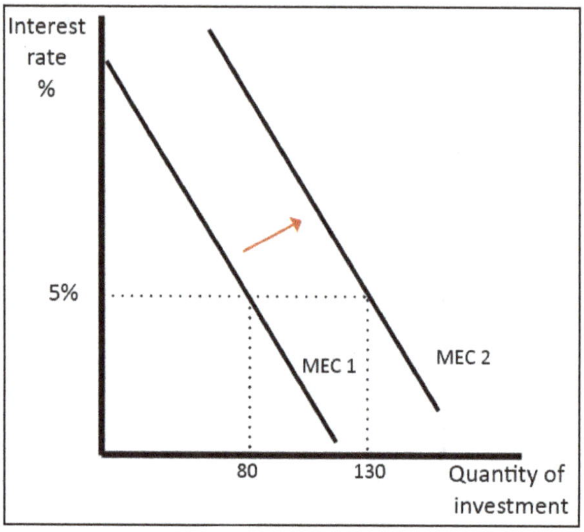

At the same rate of interest rate – more investment projects are demanded. This could reflect an improvement in economic circumstances, which encourage firms to invest.

Factors that can Affect Investment Schedule

1. The cost of capital: If capital is cheaper, then investment becomes more attractive. For example, the development of steel rails made railways cheaper and encouraged more investment.
2. Technological change:If there is an improvement in technology, it can make investment more worthwhile.
3. Expectations and business confidence: If people are optimistic about the future, they will be willing to invest because they expect higher profits. In a recession, people may become very pessimistic, so even lower interest rates don't encourage investment. (e.g. during recession 2008-12, interest rates were zero, but investment low).
4. Supply of finance: If banks are more willing to lend money investment will be easier.
5. Demand for goods: Higher demand will increase the profitability of capital investment.
6. The rate of Taxes: Higher taxes will discourage investment. Sometimes, governments offer tax breaks to encourage investment.

Keynesian Cross Diagram

Expenditure-output, or Keynesian Cross Model

The fundamental ideas of Keynesian economics were developed before the aggregate demand/aggregate supply, or AD/AS, model was popularized. From the 1930s until the 1970s, Keynesian economics was usually explained with a different model, known as the expenditure-output approach.

This approach is strongly rooted in the fundamental assumptions of Keynesian economics. It focuses on the total amount of spending in the economy, with no explicit mention of aggregate supply or of the price level. Although, it is possible to draw some inferences about aggregate supply and price levels based on the diagram.

The Axes of the Expenditure-output Diagram

The expenditure-output model determines the equilibrium level of real gross domestic product, or GDP, by the point where the total or aggregate expenditures in the economy are equal to the amount of output produced.

If you take a look at the diagram below, you'll see that the axes of the Keynesian cross diagram presented show real GDP on the horizontal axis as a measure of output and aggregate expenditure on the vertical axis as a measure of spending.

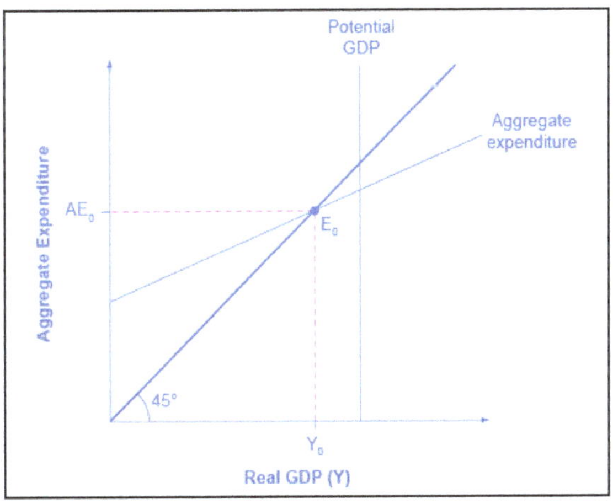

"The Expenditure-Output (or Keynesian Cross) Model".

Remember that GDP can be thought of in several equivalent ways—it measures both the value of spending on final goods and also the value of the production of final goods. All sales of the final goods and services that make up GDP will eventually end up as income for workers, managers, and investors and owners of firms. The sum of all the income received for contributing resources to GDP is called national income, Y on the diagram above. When talking about the expenditure-output model, it is sometimes useful to refer to real GDP as national income. Both axes are measured in real—inflation-adjusted—terms.

The Potential GDP Line and the 45-degree Line

The Keynesian cross diagram contains two lines that serve as conceptual guideposts to orient the discussion. The first is a vertical line showing the level of potential GDP. Potential GDP means the same thing here that it means in the AD/AS diagrams. It refers to the quantity of output that the economy can produce with full employment of its labor and physical capital.

The second conceptual line on the Keynesian cross diagram is the 45-degree line, which starts at the origin and reaches up and to the right. A line that stretches up at a 45-degree angle represents the set of points (1, 1)(1,1)left parenthesis, 1, comma, 1, right parenthesis, (2, 2)(2,2)left parenthesis, 2, comma, 2, right parenthesis, (3, 3)(3,3)left parenthesis, 3, comma, 3, right parenthesis, and so on, where the measurement on the vertical axis is equal to the measurement on the horizontal axis.

In this diagram, the 45-degree line shows the set of points where the level of aggregate expenditure in the economy, measured on the vertical axis, is equal to the level of output or national income in the economy, measured by GDP on the horizontal axis.

When the macroeconomy is in equilibrium, it must be true that the aggregate expenditures in the economy are equal to the real GDP—because by definition, GDP is the measure of what is spent on final sales of goods and services in the economy. Thus, the equilibrium calculated with a Keynesian cross diagram will always end up where aggregate expenditure and output are equal—which will only occur along the 45-degree line.

The Aggregate Expenditure Schedule

The final ingredient of the Keynesian cross or expenditure-output diagram is the aggregate expenditure schedule, which shows the total expenditures in the economy for each level of real GDP. The intersection of the aggregate expenditure line with the 45-degree line—at point E_0 in the diagram above—shows the equilibrium for the economy because it is the point where aggregate expenditure is equal to output or real GDP.

Equilibrium in the Keynesian Cross Model

With the aggregate expenditure line in place, the next step is to relate it to the two other elements of the Keynesian cross diagram.

The point where the aggregate expenditure line crosses the 45-degree line will be the equilibrium for the economy. It is the only point on the aggregate expenditure line where the total amount being spent on aggregate demand equals the total level of production. In the diagram, this point of equilibrium, E_0, happens at 6,000.

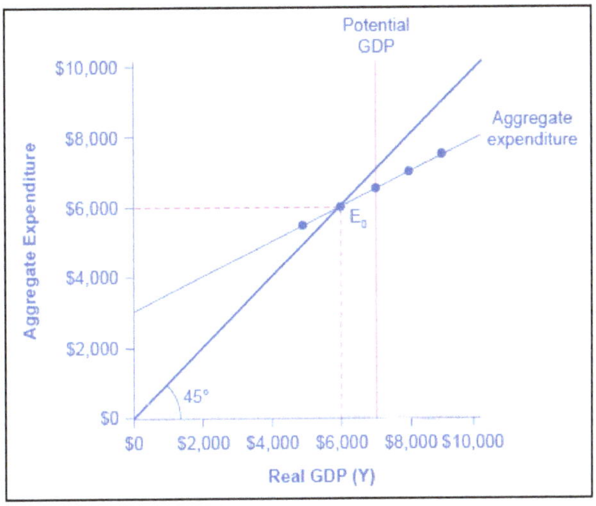

Equilibrium is a point of balance where no incentive exists to shift away from that outcome. To understand why the point of intersection between the aggregate expenditure function and the 45-degree line is a macroeconomic equilibrium, let's take a look at the diagram below.

Consider what would happen if an economy found itself to the right of the equilibrium point E, say at point H where output is higher than the equilibrium. At point H, the level of aggregate expenditure is below the 45-degree line, showing that the level of aggregate expenditure in the economy is less than the level of output. As a result, at point H, output is piling up unsold—not a sustainable state of affairs.

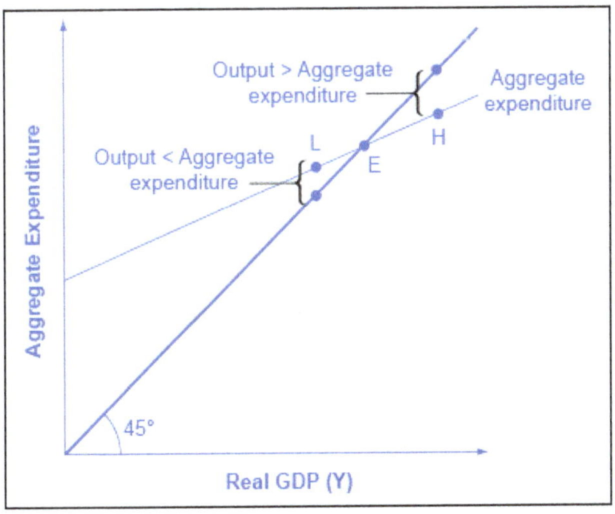

On the other hand, consider the situation where the level of output is at point L where real output is lower than the equilibrium. In this case, the level of aggregate demand in the economy is above the 45-degree line, indicating that the level of aggregate expenditure in the economy is greater than the level of output. When the level of aggregate demand has emptied the store shelves, it cannot be sustained either. Firms will respond by increasing their level of production.

So, the equilibrium must be the point where the amount produced and the amount spent are in balance, at the intersection of the aggregate expenditure function and the 45-degree line.

Liquidity Trap

Liquidity trap refers to a situation in which an increase in the money supply does not result in a fall in the interest rate but merely in an addition to idle balances: the interest elasticity of demand for money becomes infinite. Under normal conditions an increase in money supply, resulting in excess cash balances, would cause an increase in bond prices, as individuals sought to acquire assets in exchange for money, and a corresponding fall in interest rates.

In such a situation, described by Keynes as liquidity trap, individuals believe that bond prices are too high and will therefore fall, and correspondingly that interest rates are too low and must rise They, therefore, believe that to buy bonds would be to incur a capital loss and as a result they hold only money. This means that an increase in the money supply merely increases idle balances and leaves the interest rate unaffected.

Keynes pointed out that during depression when the rate of interest is very low, the demand curve for money (or the liquidity preference curve) becomes completely elastic (horizontal). The rate of interest has fallen enough. It cannot fall further.

The horizontal portion of the liquidity preference curve is referred to as the liquidity trap. In this portion of the curve, the demand for money is infinitely elastic with respect to the interest rate. Reductions in the interest rate, in this portion only, increases people's desire to hold cash balances.

The implication here is that any attempt to achieve the internal expansion through increased investment brought about by lowering the interest rates would fall, because any increase in the money supply created in order to reduce the rate of interest would be held in the form of cash balances, making it impossible to use interest rates (monetary policy) to expand the economy.

Keynes pointed out that the actual rate of interest cannot fall to zero because the expected rate cannot fall to zero. People's expectations play a very important role in altering the rate of interest. Individuals' views on the level of bond prices may be summarised in terms of their views about the interest rate.

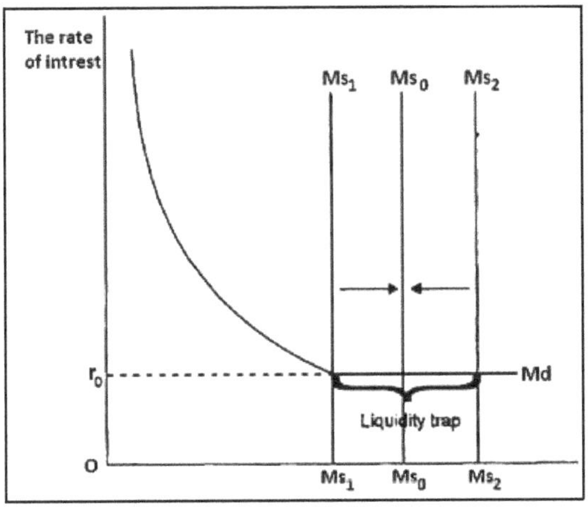

Liquidity trap

Keynes' theory assumes that each individual has his own view about the long-run equilibrium interest rate and that there corresponds to this a critical rate below which are individual holds only money and above which he holds only bonds. Clearly, if everyone is holding money as each one is in the liquidity trap then the current interest rate must be below the lowest critical rate situation.

However, in practice, there is no statistical evidence to support the existence of a liquidity trap. Furthermore, while the hypothesis rests on the view that expectations are regressive it offers no theory of precisely how these are formed.

Curing the Liquidity Trap

There are a number of ways to help the economy come out of a liquidity trap:

1. The Federal Reserve can raise interest rates, which may lead people to invest more of their money, rather than hoard it.
2. A (big) drop in prices. When this happens, people just can't help themselves from spending money.
3. Increasing government spending. When the government does so, it implies that the government is committed and confident in the national economy. This tactic also fuels job growth.

Neo-Keynesian Economics

Neo-Keynesianism is a modification of Keynesian economics to suit the historical conditions that took shape after World War II. Among the theory's most prominent advocates are R. Harrod, N. Kaldor, J. Robinson, E. Domar, and A. Hansen.

Neo-Keynesianism developed in the first half of the 1950's under the influence of the deepening general crisis of capitalism and the related transition from monopoly to state-monopoly capitalism, the scientific and technological revolution, the economic competition between the two world systems, and the collapse of imperialism's colonial system. Faced with new historical conditions that made the rate of economic growth a matter of life and death for capitalism, neo-Keynesianism could not limit itself, as had J. M. Keynes' theories, to a consideration of the problems of anticrisis economic policy. Therefore, neo-Keynesianism focuses on the quantitative relationships of extended capitalist reproduction or, in neo-Keynsian terms—the problems of economic dynamics and economic growth, which serve as the chief theoretical foundation for the economic policy of state-monopoly capitalism.

Neo-Keynesianism's point of departure is the chief premise of Keynesian economics: that capitalism has lost its spontaneous mechanism for restoring economic equilibrium and that, consequently, state regulation of the capitalist economy is necessary. However, neo-Keynesianism calls for systematic, direct influence by the bourgeois state on the capitalist economy, whereas Keynesian theory advocates periodic, indirect influence on the economy. In this respect, neo-Keynesianism reflects a more mature level in the development of state-monopoly capitalism. The maturation of state-monopoly capitalism has been accompanied by changes in the fundamental problems confronting the bourgeois conception of state regulation of the economy. The emphasis has shifted from the theory of employment, which is oriented toward anticrisis regulation of the economy, to theories of economic growth, whose goal is to find ways to ensure stable rates of economic development for the capitalist system.

Methodologically, neo-Keynesianism is characterized by a macroeconomic, national economic approach to problems of capital reproduction, using aggregate categories (for example, national income, aggregate social product, aggregate supply and demand, and aggregate investment). These categories make it possible to grasp the most general quantitative relationships of capitalist reproduction and to avoid consideration of its class essence and antagonistic character. Like Keynesian theory, neo-Keynesianism emphasizes the concrete, economic quantitative relationships of the simple process of labor in its national economic aspect, making inferences from capitalist production relationships or interpreting them on a crude, apologetic level.

Under the conditions created by the scientific and technological revolution, neo-Keynesian economics has been forced to reject the method of making inferences from change in the productive forces of capitalist society, which was characteristic of Keynesian theory, and introduce indexes of technological development into its analysis. Thus, Harrod developed the concept of the capital coefficient, which he defines as the ratio between the total capital stock and the national income, for a certain period of time. In other words, the capital coefficient is an index of the "capital-intensity" of a unit of national income.

Neo-Keynesianism also poses the question of different types of technological progress, distinguishing technological progress that results in savings of human labor from progress that ensures savings of labor embodied in the means of production ("capital," in neo-Keynesian terminology). "Neutral" technological progress, which is considered a typical phenomenon, is defined as the type of technological development in which the trends toward savings of labor and savings of capital are balanced, so that the numerical ratio of labor and capital and, consequently, the organic structure of capital do not change. At the same time, analysis shows that, owing to the contradictory character of the factors influencing the dynamics of the organic structure of capital, that structure's basic tendency is toward growth, especially under the conditions created by the present scientific and technological revolution.

Neo-Keynesianism supplemented Keynes' theory of capitalist reproduction, including his multiplier theory, with the accelerator principle. On the basis of a combination of the multiplier and accelerator theories, neo-Keynesianism interprets the expansion of capitalist reproduction not as a socioeconomic process but as a technological and economic one. The adherents of neo-Keynesian theory have worked out specific formulas for extended capitalist reproduction—models of economic growth, which generally do not represent the aggregate movement of the components of the total social product and capital, considered from the point of view of their physical and cost structure. The neo-Keynesian models of economic growth usually grasp only a few of the quantitative relationships of the reproduction of capital, particularly those related to its concrete economic aspect.

The neo-Keynesian conception of "economic growth" (measures to restructure the economy, and the acceleration of capital investment in scientific research, in new technology, and in the infrastructure by means of state financing) encounters the limitation inherent in the objective of capitalist production. That is, it runs into state-monopoly capitalism's policy of limiting and sometimes even lowering the standard of living of the working masses. (This policy includes the "wage freeze," tax increases affecting workers' incomes, and state price controls, which raise the cost of living.) As a result, neo-Keynesian measures for regulation of the economy have not eliminated and cannot eliminate the contradictions inherent in capitalism. Moreover, the policy of economic growth has led to deficit financing of the economy, inflation, the intensification of the trade war among the capitalist countries, the currency crisis, and destruction of the natural environment.

Neoclassical Synthesis

After Keynes, Keynesian analysis was combined with neoclassical economics to produce what is generally termed "the neoclassical synthesis", which dominates mainstream macroeconomic thought. Though it was widely held that there was no strong automatic tendency to full employment, many believed that if government policy were used to ensure it, the economy would behave as classical or neoclassical theory predicted.

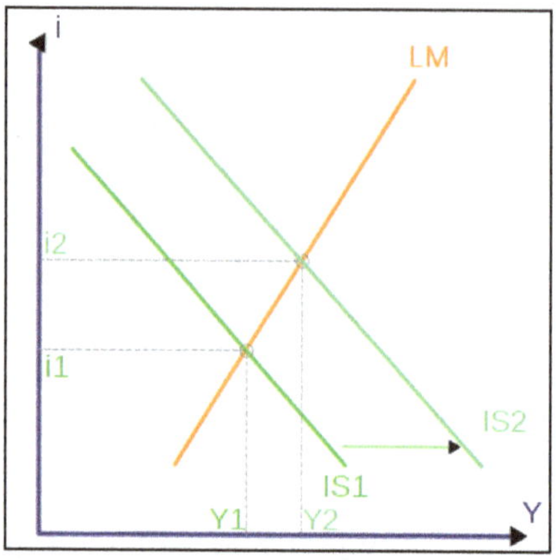

The IS–LM model is used to analyze the effect of demand shocks on the economy.

In the post-World War II years, Keynes's policy ideas were widely accepted. For the first time, governments prepared good quality economic statistics on an ongoing basis and a theory that told them what to do. In this era of New Deal liberalism and social democracy, most western capitalist countries enjoyed low, stable unemployment and modest inflation.

IS–LM Model (Investment Saving–Liquidity Preference Money Supply)

It was with John Hicks that Keynesian economics produced a clear model which policy-makers could use to attempt to understand and control economic activity. This model, the IS–LM model, is nearly as influential as Keynes' original analysis in determining actual policy and economics education.

It relates aggregate demand and employment to three exogenous quantities, i.e. the amount of money in circulation, the government budget and the state of business expectations. This model was very popular with economists after World War II because it could be understood in terms of general equilibrium theory.

Phillips Curve

The second main part of a Keynesian policy-maker's theoretical apparatus was the Phillips curve. This curve, which was more of an empirical observation than a theory, indicated that increased employment and decreased unemployment implied increased inflation. Keynes had only predicted that falling unemployment would cause a higher price, not a higher inflation rate. Thus the economist could use the IS–LM model to predict, for example, that an increase in the money supply would raise output and employment—and then use the Phillips curve to predict an increase in inflation.

The strength of Keynesianism's influence can be seen by the wave of economists which began in the late 1940s with Milton Friedman. Instead of rejecting macro-measurements and macro-models of the economy, they embraced the techniques of treating the entire economy as having a supply and demand equilibrium, but unlike the Keynesians—they argued that "crowding out" effects would hobble or deprive fiscal policy of its positive effect. Instead, the focus should be on monetary policy, which was largely ignored by early Keynesians. The monetarist critique pushed Keynesians toward a more balanced view of monetary policy and inspired a wave of revisions to Keynesian theory.

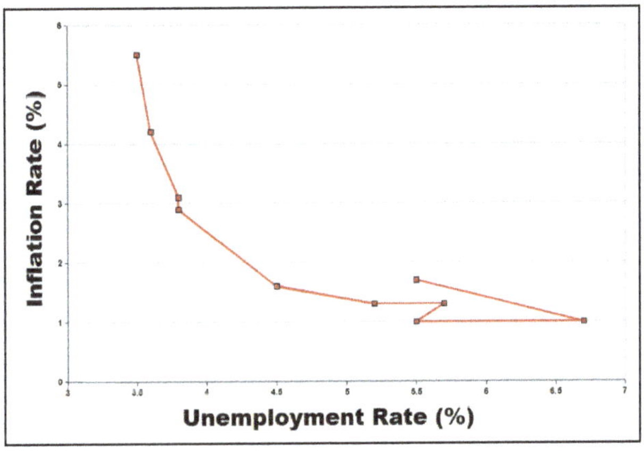

The Phillips curve in the U.S in the 1960s.

Through the 1950s, moderate degrees of government demand leading industrial development and use of fiscal and monetary counter-cyclical policies continued and reached a peak in the "go go" 1960s, where it seemed to many Keynesians that prosperity was now permanent. However, with the oil shock of 1973 and the economic problems of the 1970s, modern liberal economics began to fall out of favor. During this time, many economies experienced high and rising unemployment, coupled with high and rising inflation, contradicting the Phillips curve's prediction.

This stagflation meant that both expansionary (anti-recession) and contractionary (anti-inflation) policies had to be applied simultaneously, a clear impossibility. This dilemma led to the rise of ideas based upon more classical analysis, including monetarism, supply-side economics and new classical economics. This produced a "policy bind" and the collapse of the Keynesian consensus on the economy.

New Keynesian Economics

New Keynesianism refers to a branch of Keynesian economics which places greater stress on microeconomic foundations to explain macro-economic disequilibrium. A key element of new Keynesianism is the role of wage rigidities and price rigidities to explain the persistence of unemployment and macro economic disequilibrium.

New Keynesianism combines elements of traditional Keynesianism (sometimes referred to as old Keynesianism) with classical theory.

Elements of New Keynesianism

- Many markets are imperfectly competitive (have a degree of monopoly power). Therefore firms have the ability to set prices, and firms may often be reluctant to cut prices – leading to price rigidity.
- Many labor markets are imperfect. In particular, wages can be 'sticky downwards' e.g. both unions and firms both resist nominal wage cuts.
- If there is a shock to the economy, such as a short-term fall in demand, markets don't clear, and we end up with real wage unemployment.
- Real interest rates may depart from the 'natural interest rate'. The job of monetary authorities is to restore the correct interest rate to avoid macro-economic instability.

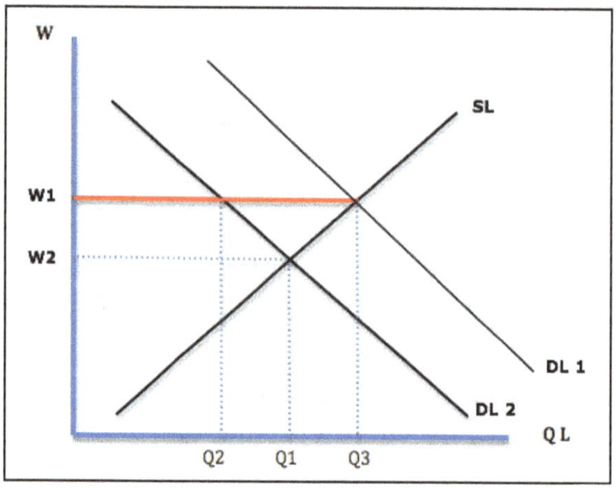

This diagram shows how a fall in demand for labor causes unemployment – if there are wage rigidities which keep wages at W1 and not fall to W2.

- New Keynesians believe there is a role for monetary and fiscal policy to play a role in stabilising the economy and reducing unemployment. However, they tend to favour monetary policy.
- New Keynesians place a greater emphasis on development models from micro-economic behavior to predict macro-economic outcomes. These models are known as Dynamic stochastic general equilibrium (DSGE).
- A very simplified understanding of these models could be gained from the basic Taylor rule – The Taylor rule suggests the optimal interest rates given the rate of inflation and the output gap.

- Some New Keynesian models, e.g. by Blanchard have stressed aiming at low inflation (e.g. optimal inflation target of 2%) These models state that targeting the optimal inflation rate also leads to an optimal rate of growth and unemployment. (This is sometimes known as the divine coincidence, though the breakdown of the great moderation has undermined the predominance of low inflation targetting.

Some of the important strands are discussed under four broad headings:

- Sticky nominal (money) wages
- Sticky nominal prices
- Sticky real wages
- Coordination failures

Sticky Nominal Wages

In the classical theory of labor market, there is always full employment in the economy and no involuntary unemployment. In case of unemployment, a cut in money wages can achieve full employment. Firms can instantly adjust the quantities of labor they employ without any cost because of the flexibility of money wages.

In the Keynesian theory, involuntary unemployment exists which can be removed by cut in real wages by increasing aggregate demand, output and employment. Keynes held that money wages are sticky. Within the Keynesian tradition, new Keynesian economists have developed the new Keynesian theory of the labor market based on nominal wages stickiness.

Assumptions

This theory is based on the following assumptions:

- Nominal wages are sticky in the labor market.
- They are set on the basis of contracts for a stipulated period.
- They are set to make the expected quantity of labor demanded equal the expected quantity of labor supplied.
- Trade unions and firms form a rational expectation of future demand and supply of labor.
- They agree on a wage that makes the expected quantity of labor demanded equal to the expected quantity supplied on the average over the period of contract.
- Firms determine the employment level.

- Workers are prepared to supply the required quantity of labor demanded at the fixed money wage over the period of the contract.
- The employment level is determined by the actual demand for labor.

Explanation

Given these assumptions, in the new Keynesian theory of the labor market, money wages are set in contracts between workers (unions) and employers (firms) which maintain money wages over an agreed period. Such contracts are made because the demand for labor increases during recoveries and decreases during recessions which require changes in wage rates. Therefore, workers and employers find such wage contracts advantageous because there are high costs of collecting information about labor and negotiating frequent wage agreements.

When unions and firms start negotiations for agreed money wage rates over a stipulated period, they take a view of the expected demand for and supply of labor on the average. They know that setting very high wages rates will lead to very low employment on the average and large unemployment.

On the other hand, setting very low wage rates will lead to a shortage of labor. Thus both parties act rationally and agree on such wage rates that make the expected quantity of labor demanded equal to the expected quantity of labor supplied.

The determination of money wage rate in the new Keynesian theory of labor market is shown in figure below. During the period of the contract, the effective supply of labor is the horizontal line W_0W which shows the agreed wage rate of OW_0. Workers agree to supply the quantity of labor which the firms demand at this contracted wage rate. In the figure, S is the expected supply curve of labor and D_0 is the expected demand curve for labor.

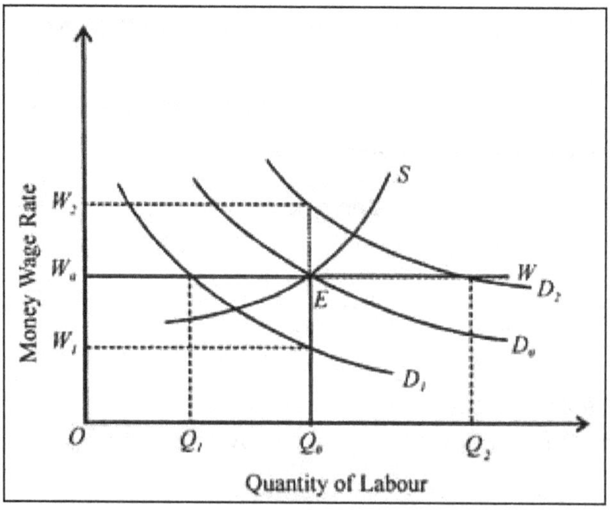

These curves meet at point E on the agreed money wage rate OW_0 where the expected labor employed is OQ_0. If the demand for labor happens to be more than expected at D_2, the quantity of labor employed increases to OQ_2. If the demand for labor happens to be D_1, the labor employed falls to OQ_1.

The above analysis shows that the quantity of labor employed depends on the expected demand for labor. The expected demand for labor is determined by the expected price level and expected forecasts about the marginal product of labor (MP_L).

MP_L, in turn, determines the quantity of labor which the firms will employ at each possible real wage rate. Similarly the expected supply of labor is also based on the expected price level and on expectations about the number of workers available for work at different real wage rates.

Suppose the price level rises or the marginal product of labor increases. These increases will shift the demand for labor curve to the right from D_0 to D_2 and equivalently the money wage rate that firms are willing to pay for that employment level.

So the quantity of labor employed increases to OQ_2 from OQ_0 and money wage rate from OW_0 to OW_2 In the opposite case with a fall in the price level or decrease in the marginal product of labor, the demand for labor, curve will shift to the left from D_0 to D_1 and equivalently the money wage rate will be reduced from OW_0 to OW_1. The firms will reduce the quantity of labor employed from OQ_0 to OQ_1.

In the above analysis, when the price level rises or falls by say 50%, the money wage rate also declines or increases by 50%, the agreed money wage rate OW_0 remains the same. It is only when the demand for labor happens to be the same as expected at D_0 that the level of employment is equal to its expected level of OQ_0.

However, under gradually increasing wage rates, workers who stick to their jobs for a long time in the same firm get less than the value of their marginal product as they approach retirement. But over the long period, they are paid wages on the average equal to the value of their marginal product.

Staggered Wage Contracts Theory

One of the theories of nominal wage rigidities in the new Keynesian analysis is of staggered contracts. In the staggered contracts approach, not all labor unions sign contracts at the same time. There is no synchronization of contracts.

Contracts are renewed at various times so that the dates on which new contracts start are staggered and they overlap. Such overlapping long-term wage contracts lead to nominal wage rigidity. During the contract period, the wage rate is fixed and linked to the expected rate of inflation by price indexing.

If prices are expected too high, workers will demand larger wage increases and firms will be willing to pay them because their own prices are expected to rise. Besides expectations of inflation, wage fixation is influenced by expectations of wages paid to other workers and the level of employment.

Taylor in his staggered contract approach takes aggregate nominal demand indexation as a source of nominal wage rigidity. He assumes the nominal wage fixed over the period of the contract at a level that depends on the expected price and expected future demand and output. A monetary disturbance affects demand and output during the period of contract until a new contract is negotiated.

Suppose the monetary authorities reduce the money supply in the economy which reduces aggregate demand and output. This requires a proportionate adjustment in nominal wages to maintain full employment. Since the wage contracts are staggered, wage adjustment is very slow in response to changes in aggregate demand and output. This makes nominal wages sticky.

Mankiw Sticky Prices Model: Menu Costs

The classical and new classical microeconomic theories are based on the assumption of flexibility of prices where prices clear markets by adjusting demand and supply quickly. New Keynesian economists, on the other hand, believe in the stickiness of prices in the short-run.

Markets do not clear quickly because adjusting prices is costly. Frequently adjusting prices of their goods involve costs to firms. A large sector of the economy is made up of price-makers who sell goods in monopolistic or imperfectly competitive markets. For them, adjusting prices is costly

The costs of adjusting prices are called the menu costs. Changing prices requires the use of resources by a firm. It has to print new price lists (menus), catalogues, and other printed material. A super market has to reliable all products and shelves with the new prices. A hotel and a restaurant have to reprint its menu with new prices. Meetings, phone calls, and trips by representatives of a firm to renegotiate with suppliers, all fall under the category of menu costs.

In the menu costs approach to sticky prices, it is profitable for firms to react to small changes in demand by keeping prices constant over a short period and responding with changes in output. Because of menu costs, firms do not change their prices every time with a change in demand conditions. Menu costs are incurred each time prices are changed periodically rather than continuously. Thus menu costs explain the short-run stickiness of prices.

In the menu cost hypothesis, prices adjust slowly because changes in prices have externalities. When one firm reduces the price of a product, it benefits other firms in the economy. When it reduces the prices it charges, it lowers the average price level slightly and thereby raises real income. The increase in real income, in turn, raises the demand for the products of all firms.

This macroeconomic impact of one firm's price adjustment on the demand for the products of all other firms is called an aggregate-demand externality by Mankiw. With aggregate demand externality, small menu costs can make prices sticky.

Assumptions

The sticky nominal price analysis of menu costs is based on the following assumptions:

1. There is an imperfectly competitive market which consists of a number of monopolistic competitive firms.
2. Firms produce standardized or differentiated products.
3. Firms are price-makers having some control over the prices of their products.
4. Price adjustments involve costs for firms.
5. The demand curves are linear.
6. The marginal cost curve is horizontal.

Explanation

Given these assumptions, we illustrate in figure below how menu costs work and affect the adjustment of price and quantity of a firm's product. Let us suppose that the firm's demand has declined so that the original demand curves D_0 shifts to the left to D_1 and correspondingly its original MR_0 curve to MR_1.

Similarly its marginal cost has also declined. It has been shown as MC_1 which remains fixed. The original marginal cost curve MC_0 has not been shown to simplify the figure. The original price is OP_0 and quantity is OQ_0 when MR_0 intersects MC_1 at E.

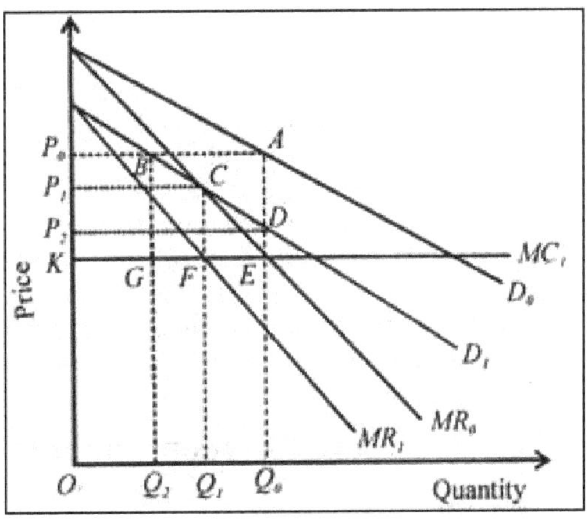

The firm's profit is $KEAP_0$. With the decline in demand, the intersection of MR_1 and MC_1 is at F and the price falls to OP_1 and quantity to OQ_1. Consequently, profit declines to $KFCP_1$. If the menu costs are high, the firm will keep the price at OP_0, reduce output to OQ_2 and earn $KGBP_0$ profit. The firm will reduce price to OP_2 only if the extra profit ($KEDP_2$-$KGBP_0$) exceeds the menu cost. The firm will not, therefore, reduce the price and there will be nominal price rigidity at OP_0.

Criticisms

The menu costs approach has been criticised on the following grounds:

1. The menu costs approach is defective in that it considers only costs of price adjustment and not costs of output adjustment.
2. This approach assumes that marginal cost moves in proportion with demand. As demand rises or falls, marginal cost also increases or declines in the same proportion. In fact, no firm can assume that its marginal cost will be perfectly correlated with its aggregate demand.
3. This hypothesis tries to explain nominal rigidities in adjustments of the level of prices. But it fails to explain rigidities in adjustments of the rate of change of prices.
4. Critics point out that menu costs are small and have become smaller as computers allow the printing of menus at a small marginal cost.
5. Economists do not agree that menu costs can explain price stickiness in the short run because they are very small. Small menu costs cannot explain recession in the economy.
6. Another flaw is that small menu costs may be important for an individual firm but they are unlikely to affect the economy as a whole.

Sticky Real Wages

In the new classical labor theory, labor market is cleared continuously at the market-clearing real wage rate but it does not explain involuntary unemployment. On the other hand, the new Keynesian theories focus on the real wage rigidity where workers are not paid market-clearing wage and involuntary unemployment exists even in the long run.

There are four main approaches to real wage rigidities. They are:

1. Asymmetric information model,
2. Implicit contract theory,
3. Insider-outsider theory, and
4. Efficiency wage theory.

Asymmetric Information Model

Asymmetric information is a situation in which some persons have more information about some things than others. This idea that each person has asymmetrical information relative to others was used to develop a labor market model by Grossman and Hart.

They assumed that managers know more about the interests of the firm than do the workers. Given this better knowledge, it is possible and profitable for managers to deceive the workers about the real position of the firm.

They enter into contracts with workers for employment commitments whereby the firm pays them rigid real wages. However, there is an employment commitment in this model that tends to increase the amount of employment in the firm.

Implicit Contract Theory

Two American economists, Baily and Azariades, have developed the implicit contract theory. Usually employment contracts between workers and firms are explicit agreements. But often there are other dimensions that are not written in the actual contracts.

These dimensions are called implicit contracts. Workers and firms enter into implicit contracts concerning job insurance and income because workers are risk-averse with respect to income. Workers dislike the risk arising from income and fluctuations of employment more than the firms.

Consequently, firms offer workers an implicit contract that is partially an income and job insurance contract and partially an employment contract. According to Baily and Azariades, such contracts lead to rigidity in real wages that are not affected by fluctuations in business conditions and employment levels during a recession.

Insider and Outsider Theory

The insider and outsider theory of labor market was developed by A. Lindback and D. Snower. This theory assumes that there are frictions and imperfections in the labor market that act to divide it in terms of employment opportunities.

Insiders are those workers who already have jobs and outsiders are those who are unemployed in the labor market. Insiders are represented by unions who have more say in wage bargaining than the outsiders. Unions negotiate the real wage with firms and set it higher than the market-clearing level so that the outsiders are excluded from jobs leading to involuntary unemployment in the presence of fall in aggregate demand.

Unions use their bargaining power to negotiate wages through turnover costs. Turnover costs relate to the costs of firing, hiring and retaining of new workers. These costs prevent the firms to employ outsiders in place of insiders.

Unions can also prevent the entry of outsiders for jobs threatening strikes and work-to-rule. Insiders can also use these costs against outsiders to achieve a higher negotiated wage than the wage at which the outsiders are prepared to work.

However, unions can raise the real wage only up to a certain level because if the real wage is higher than the capacity of the firms to pay, less insiders will be employed, if the aggregate demand falls in the economy.

This theory also explains the persistence of involuntary unemployment if the real wage is set very high above the market-clearing level. This is called hysteresis. In times of high involuntary unemployment in a recession, the insiders may use their bargaining power to prevent outsiders form entering into the labor force.

Those who become outsiders may lose their influence on wage bargaining contracts because they are no longer union members. Moreover, with persistence involuntary unemployment, it becomes difficult for the long-term unemployed workers to work because their skills have deteriorated.

Under the circumstances, a long- period of high involuntary unemployment will tend to become locked-in. This is the hysteresis effect. When outsiders cannot enter the labor market, the hysteresis effect leads to wage stickiness.

Efficiency Wage Theories

In new Keynesian economics, payment of efficiency wages leads to real wage rigidity and the failure of market-clearing mechanism. High wages increase efficiency and productivity of workers. Despite an excess supply of labor, firms do not cut wages even though such a move would increase their profits. Firms also do not cut wages because it would lower productivity and raise costs. So it is in the interest of firms to set the real wage above the market-clearing level. Such a wage is called the efficiency wage.

There are four efficiency wage theories which are explained below.

Turnover Costs Theory

According to this theory, the real wage is set to minimise turnover costs of firms. Turnover costs include the costs of firing and hiring workers, and training of new workers. It is profitable for firms of reduce such costs. By paying high real wages above the market-clearing wage, firms can prevent experienced and efficient workers from leaving the firm to join other firms. It can also reduce recruiting costs to replace such workers and costs of training new workers.

Selection Theory

Firms do not know the quality of workers at the time of selection. Firms have imperfect information about potential workers at the time of hiring them. Selection procedures being costly, firms always try to select higher quality workers. Good quality workers have a higher reservation (minimum) wage than low quality workers.

If a firm pays below the reservation wage, it will not attract good quality workers. By paying a wage higher than the reservation wage, the firm will attract better quality workers. By paying a higher wage, the firm avoids adverse selection (i.e., does not hire low quality workers and reduce productivity of the firm), improves the average quality of workers and increases its productivity. Thus it is advantageous for firms to pay the efficiency wage above the market-clearing wage.

On-the-job Efficiency or Gift Exchange Theory

Another efficiency wage theory is that a real wage above the market-clearing wage improves on-the-job efficiency of workers. A higher wage improves the physical well being of the workers. Their consumption level increases.

They can afford better nutritional food and become more healthy. This improves their efficiency and raises their productivity. Moreover, a higher wage acts as an incentive to workers to invest in skill formation so as to move in the upper ranks of the firm. Thus a higher wage is a gift to the workers which they reciprocate with higher efficiency and increased productivity.

The Shirking Theory

The shirking theory is based on the premise that firms cannot easily monitor the work effort of workers and that workers themselves decide how hard to work. Two options are available to a worker: shirking and no-shirking. Shirking workers if caught by the management are fired (dismissed).

Workers know that if fired, they are not likely to get employment immediately at the existing wage. The firm can encourage workers not to shirk work by paying a higher wage. Thus a wage at which no-shirking occurs is an efficiency wage. Such a wage is an employment cost to workers of being fired. Having a job at a higher wage is advantageous to them than being unemployed. So a higher wage is an inducement to workers not to shirk.

Assumptions

This theory is based on the following assumptions:

1. Workers either have jobs or are unemployed.
2. Those workers who shirk work are fired.
3. The fired workers do not find employment immediately and remain unemployed for some time.

4. Those workers who receive the efficiency wage do not shirk.
5. There is always unemployment in the labor market at the efficiency wage.

Explanation

Given these assumptions, this efficiency wage theory is explained in figure below where S is labor supply curve and D is the labor demand curve. These curves meet at point E where OL workers are employed in the firm who are working at OW wage rate.

The labor demand curve assumes that these workers do not shirk work. But the management finds that some workers shirk work. So they are fired and are unemployed. Since the firm has incurred cost of recruitment and training of some workers, it will ensure that they do not shirk.

For this, it pays a higher wage to them which is the no- shirking or efficiency wage. At this wage, there is always the threat of being fired and becoming unemployed. This induces workers not to shirk. In the figure Ns is the no-shirking labor supply curve which intersects the labor demand curve at point E_1. OW_1 is the efficiency wage at which OL_1 workers are employed and LL_1 workers remain unemployed who are fired for shirking. The efficiency wage OW_1 is above the market-clearing wage OW.

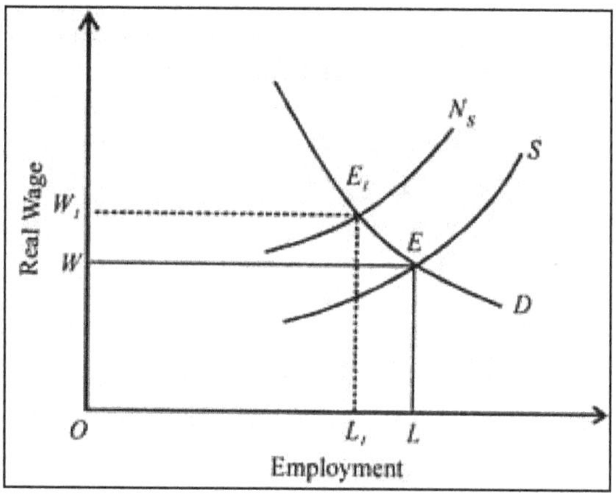

Coordination Failure

New Keynesian theories of wage and price stickiness have inconsistencies because they neglect constraints and spillovers and focus on single markets, one at a time, in a partial equilibrium framework. Cooper and John show that spillovers and strategic complementarities lead to coordination failure.

The term 'strategic complementarities' represents a situation in which the optimal decision of one firm is positively dependent on the decision of the other firm. Strategic complementarities are a necessary condition for certain kinds of multiple equilibria that lead to coordination failure and to aggregate fluctuations.

Coordination failure arises when firms and unions try to fix prices and wages to anticipate the actions of other price and wage setters. If there is a change in nominal demand, no firm will have an incentive to change its price exactly in the same proportion unless it believes that other firms will do so immediately. Similarly, unions bargaining for wages will be concerned about the wages other unions may negotiate. But such settings of prices and wages are not possible and they lead to coordination failure.

Suppose there are two firms A and B producing potentially related goods whose demand falls. Each firm has to decide how much price it should cut so as to maximise its profit. The decision to cut its price and profit more would depend on the decision made by the other firm.

But the price strategy chosen by one firm is not known to the other firm. This is a duopoly game where each firm has the option of earning more profit or less profit by a price cut or no price cut when demand falls and recession starts.

Table below shows the strategy followed by each firm in terms of expected profit when it expects the other to make a move about the price. If both firms do not cut their prices in the face of reduced demand, each makes a profit of $20 million and recession starts.

Table: Pay-off matrix in $ million

		B's Strategy	
		Price cut ↓	No Price cut ↓
A's Strategy	Price cut →	[50] 50	[10] 20
	No Price cut →	[20] 10	[20] 20

Figures in squares relate to Firm A

If both firms cut their prices, each earns a high profit of $50 million and the recession is averted. But if firm A cuts its price, it earns a low profit of $ 10 million and if firm B does not cut its price, it earns a high profit of $20 million. In this situation, by cutting its price, firm A has improved the position of firm B, which can avoid recession and earn a high profit.

This is due to an aggregate demand externality. Now suppose if firm A expects that firm B will cut its price, it will also cut its price and both will earn the highest profit of $50. Both are able to avert the recession.

But if each firm expects the other to maintain the same price, each will earn $20 million, the recession will continue. All these situations lead to multiple equilibria. However, the last outcome when each firm earns $20 million is due to coordination failure.

Post-Keynesian Economics

Core Elements

Post-Keynesian economics (PKE) is an economic paradigm that stems from the work of economists such as John Maynard Keynes (1883-1946), Michal Kalecki (1899-1970), Roy Harrod (1900-1978), Joan Robinson (1903-1983), Nicholas Kaldor (1908-1986), and many others. It is defined by the view that the principle of effective demand as developed by J. M. Keynes in the *General Theory* (1936) and M. Kalecki (1933) holds in the short, as well as in the long run. That is, that economic activity in a capitalist monetary economy is demand-driven and that there are no built-in mechanisms that guarantee full employment and full utilisation of capacities.

Post-Keynesians are united in their rejection of the different versions of neoclassical economics as inappropriate for the analysis of a monetary, capitalist economy. They are also unanimous in their joint endeavour of building an alternative economic theorythat is more suitable for analysing the inherent features of modern capitalist economies, such as unemployment, (financial) crises, business cycles, depressions, technological change, and uneven development.

They have an understanding of the economy as being structured by institutions such as firms, labor unions, wage and credit contracts, government regulation and so forth. These institutions determine economic behavior to a large extent, which is why PKE gives a certain priority to macro- and mesoeconomic analyses.

On the microeconomic level, PKE stresses that the future is fundamentally uncertain. It follows that individuals cannot act perfectly rationally as understood by mainstream economists. They rather make decisions based on rules of thumb, as they can deal better with incomplete and complex information. Rules of thumb are also very much influenced by social conventions and norms, which can lead to stability (e.g. nominal wage contracts stabilising the price level), as well as to instability (e.g. due to herd behavior in financial markets). Fundamental uncertainty also shapes behavior of firms, which operate in imperfectly competitive markets rendering them price makers and quantity takers.

PKE studies a wide array of economic fields ranging from short-run macroeconomics (unemployment, economic output and inflation), long-run macroeconomics (growth and distribution), monetary economics, finance and the international monetary system to microeconomic approaches to the theory of the firm, theory of consumption, exchange rate theory, financialisation, and much more. Correspondingly, PKE provides a rich set of policy proposals which often differ considerably from standard recipes offered by mainstream economics. Two examples are the emphasis on fiscal policy as the main tool to fight economic recessions in the short-run and the view that central banks should maintain low interest rates and regulate the banking system rather than narrowly focusing on fighting inflation. Another case in point would be the endorsement of labor market institutions that foster collective wage bargaining and establish a nominal wage anchor that no one can undercut. This compels firms to compete by quality and productivity without causing deflation by lowering wages.

Although by name they are very similar, post-Keynesianism is quite different from Old Keynesianism as well as New Keynesian economics. Post-Keynesians regard the New Keynesian approach as mainly neoclassical with some alterations that lead to market imperfections, but which do not improve their analysis of the real world. Nevertheless, New Keynesian economics not post-Keynesian economics, is usually what students learn to be modern Keynesianism.

Terms, Analysis, Conception of Economy

PKE seeks to analyse capitalist economies that are characterised by certain distinctive features. Capitalist economies are monetary production economies in which money (credit) is advanced by banks or other financial institutions to firms to invest in physical capital and labor to produce goods and services. Those are sold to obtain a profit and to repay the debt plus interest that has been incurred to finance investment. This monetary circuit establishes not only a circular flow of income between the main sectors of the economy, but also links economic units like households, firms or governments, to each other over time through their asset and liability structure. The capitalist macro-economy thus forms a system that has to be analysed in a *systemic* way — what happens in one sector of the economy has effects on other sectors, too.

Post-Keynesians conceive capitalist economies as highly productive, but unstable and conflictive systems. Economic activity is determined by effective demand, which is typically insufficient to generate full employment and full utilisation of capacity. Fluctuations in effective demand are mostly due to changes in investment expenditures, which are in turn strongly affected by expectations. Expectations of economic agents are influenced by social conventions and rules of thumb due to fundamental uncertainty about the future. In times of generally optimistic expectations, investment demand may be buoyant and set in motion a phase of strong credit growth, capital accumulation and income generation.

New credit money is created to finance investment expenditures. Then, economic output and employment is determined in the goods market according to the level of investment demand. The money spent on investment appears as income in the deposit accounts of other entrepreneurs or households. A credit-investment-income mechanism is thereby established and investment demand creates corresponding saving. The income generated through the production of new investment goods stimulates consumption demand. If everything runs well, expectations of agents become validated as payment obligations are met and the economy prospers. PKE thus assumes that there is a potential economic equilibrium that is determined by monetary and real factors. However, sudden changes in expectations may bring the economy out of equilibrium. Strong boom phases due to optimistic expectations can then be followed by drastic downturns, which are often induced by pessimistic expectations, distributional conflict or financial fragility. This depresses investment and consumption expenditures, invalidates income expectations and induces a period of debt defaults and economic crisis. These boom and bust phases are regarded as systemic features of monetary production economies that can only be mitigated by certain economic institutions and policies that help sustain economic expectations and activity and thereby reduce uncertainty about the future.

In PKE, employment is not determined in the labor market but rather labor demand is determined by aggregate demand in the goods market and not by the real wage rate. However, the labor market determines nominal wages and therefore nominal unit labor costs. These have a strong influence on the general price level and hence inflation, as well as on income distribution. In contrast to orthodox economics, the level of prices is not determined by the level of the money supply in PKE and neither is the rate of inflation determined by the growth rate of money supply. Therefore, post-Keynesians do not regard inflation as being a monetary phenomenon. Instead, inflation is regarded as the outcome of unresolved distributional conflict. This conflict is caused by conflicting claims over the distribution of income between the main social classes, wage-earners in different industries or sectors, entrepreneurs and rentiers (i.e. people who earn capital income from property or financial assets), and the foreign sector in an open economy. For example, if the real wage target of workers or unions is in conflict with the profit target of firms, firms will partly pass through increases in nominal wages to prices, which will lead to inflation if the firms have price setting power. While inflation therefore is a usual outcome of the wage bargaining process even in "normal" times, it may be accelerated by sudden increases in the costs of inputs, e.g. because of currency depreciations or commodity price shocks.

The pursuit of profit makes capitalism a dynamic system that is usually growing over time due to investment and technical change. However, growth dynamics are regarded as strongly influenced by short-run economic performance which is mainly driven by aggregate demand. The economy is developing in historical time, which means that the past has a persistent effect on the future through path dependency. Temporary adverse shocks may therefore reduce potential output permanently, just as well as a high unemployment rate might push up the non-accelerating inflation rate of unemployment (NAIRU), and the actual growth rate influences the natural rate of growth. Short-run effects, therefore, heavily influence long-run economic development.

Ideology and Political Goals

PK theory itself is in principle compatible with a wide range of ideologies or goals. To exaggerate a bit, on the one hand, PKE can be an analytical framework of a socialist politician who wants to overcome capitalism or, on the other hand, it can be a tool for a pro-capitalist investment banker to analyse the economic environment that she finds herself in. The point is that PKE lends itself to different ideologies, since its main aim is to understand the dynamics of capitalist systems from a macroeconomic point of view, regardless of whether one wants to maintain or overcome capitalism. Nevertheless, every academic has a specific ideology that he or she employs in the assessment of a theory.

Post-Keynesianism has not been strongly or uniquely associated with any major political movement. However, it is safe to say that post-Keynesians in general do not wish to eliminate capitalism, they wish to tame it and envisage an economic system which would constitute some middle way between liberalism and socialism. Therefore, some central ideological foundations and political goals of many post-Keynesian economists can also be found in the historical development of social democratic thought and corresponding emphasis on the prospects for non-zero sum game, class-cooperative capitalism. However, many post-Keynesians strongly disagree with the political programs that were put forward by social democratic parties of Western capitalist countries after the neoliberal turn to the "third way" in the 1990s.

In justifying the pursuit for socially progressive capitalism, many post-Keynesian economists claim to find historical precedence for these prospects in the Golden Age or Fordist regime of capitalism, from the 1950s to the 1970s. This period notably featured, in advanced capitalist countries, steady economic growth, a more egalitarian distribution of income, full (or close to full) employment, a stronger social security net, greater regulation of the financial sector and a more actively interventionist state engaged in aggregate demand management than that seen during the subsequent 'neoliberal era'. The features of this era can be seen as some kind of blueprint for the kind of economic system post-Keynesians advocate for. In order to get there, the overarching political objective is to change the effectiveness of the state and the political-economic system. The question of how this can be achieved in the social and political domain is not often directly answered in PK literature. While there are some attempts in PKE which investigate the question of the socio-economic and socio-political factors that can lead to certain shifts of overall economic or capitalist regimes, it can be argued that these questions are not the major concern of PK academic literature. Rather, PKE states what needs to be achieved at the macroeconomic level in order to avoid the instabilities and/or persistent structural weaknesses related to capitalism. These include stagnation, excessive inflation or deflation, recessions, financial and economic crises, among others. For example, many post-Keynesians argue that a more even distribution of income between capitalists and workers will boost aggregate demand and growth and can therefore result in increasing the gross profits of the capitalist class. This emphasises the fact that for PKE, there is no fundamental trade-off between social cohesion as a political target and growth as the economic means to maintain high levels of employment and to improve living conditions. However, as the analysis of social developments leading to political change are of minor concern relative to specific economic policy recommendations in PKE, one can easily get the impression that the PK approach to politics has a certain affinity to technocracy. This is despite many post-Keynesians being well aware of the socio-political challenges hindering their "technical" recommendations from being implemented.

Most post-Keynesian economists would subscribe to the idea of achieving a more socially just system, with full employment, low levels of income inequality and high levels of individual freedom. While today many post-Keynesian economists do recognise that infinite growth is problematic from an environmental perspective, it remains the central instrument to achieve full employment and therefore can be seen as a key goal of PKE.

PKE favours a macroeconomic policy mix with an active role for fiscal policy to stabilise the economy in the short and the long run. Monetary policy should target low interest rates to provide stability in the monetary, financial and real sector. Other policies to stabilise the economy could be achieved with strict financial market regulation via credit controls, asset-based reserve requirements, among others. Also, it is considered important that central banks act as lenders of last resort. Wage and incomes policies should lead to steady nominal unit labor cost growth in line with the desired inflation rate. PK economists are generally supportive of trade unions as they have an important influence on wage bargaining coordination and therefore price stability. Regarding international economic policies, PKE does not regard free trade as beneficial for poorer countries as long as it does not help them to build their own competitive manufacturing sectors. To achieve that post-Keynesians favour capital controls, managed exchange rates and infant industry protection.

Current Debates and Analyses

There are different areas of debates and analyses that PK research has concentrated on. The focus that is placed on different problems and research areas is strongly influenced by the developments of economies and societies, by fads and fashions, by the advancement of computer technology and, of course, by historical events.

One area where many contributions have recently been made is in the use of econometric studies trying to determine if a country is wage-led or profit-led. While in wage-led countries an increase in the wage share leads to higher aggregate demand, it reduces aggregate demand in a profit-led country. In extensions to this approach, the effects of personal income inequality, financialisation, open economy issues, fiscal policy and other factors on growth are being researched. Furthermore, the notion of financialisation has recently given rise to a rich literature that describes and analyses structural changes in many economies towards a greater importance and dominance of the financial sector. The contributions in this field range from institutional and descriptive analyses on the micro- and meso-level to econometric studies and formal macroeconomic models. PK contributions to the financialisation debate highlight its negative effects on investment, income distribution and financial stability. However, there are still puzzles to be solved such as how financialisation relates to neoliberalism.

With the historical event of the Global Financial Crisis (GFC), the interest in Hyman Minsky's financial instability hypothesis was renewed, in an attempt to better understand the complex connection of the real and the financial sector and the tendency for crises. This is being done especially with the help of dynamic models that seek to cast Minsky's ideas in a more rigorous formal framework.

The overall awareness about ecological problems and, in particular, climate change have also had an influence on PKE. However, it has to be said that traditionally, post-Keynesians did not spend a lot of time thinking about environmental issues but have focussed rather on achieving full employment by economic growth. However, the focus on environmental constraints has received a lot more attention in recent years. PK economists see ecological economics as having strong microeconomic foundations but relying too much on neoclassical macroeconomics, and so they attempt to introduce PK macroeconomics to the analysis.

Finally, there has been a strong increase in the diversity of modelling methods used by PK economists. For example, the GFC has generally reaffirmed the post-Keynesian insistence on the important role of money and finance for economic activity. This has given another boost to stock-flow consistent modelling. Large scale SFC models are being developed that describe an entire national economy, while multi-country open economy models look at international trade and finance. Another field of advancement is agent-based modelling to understand how the complex interactions on the microeconomic level can affect macroeconomic outcomes. This is still in early stages as post-Keynesians have only recently started to work with these models. Other authors focus on issues like disequilibria, instability, and how the economy moves from one equilibrium to another through time. This research area employs increasingly complex models with non-linear dynamics that often require computer techniques to numerically simulate different possible solutions to the model. These models give an insight into the sometimes chaotic adjustment processes that happen in the real world and thus have a very different flavour than the tranquil and harmonious mainstream general equilibrium models.

Keynes's Theory of Wages and Prices

The simple Classical theory of employment is based on two fundamental postulates.

The first is that "wage is equal to the marginal product of labor" Accepting the law of Diminishing Marginal Productivity as employment increases, any increase in employment is necessarily associated with lower real wage rates.

If, however, unemployment still persists, it must be due to the refusal of the workers to accept the lower real wage rate which corresponds to the reduced marginal product of their labor.

The second postulate of the Classical theory is that "the existing real wage is equal to the marginal disutility of employment". That is, "the utility of the wage when a given volume of labor is employed is equal to the marginal disutility of that amount of employment".

Keynes expressed it thus:

> "That is to say, the real wage of an employed person is that which is just sufficient (in the estimation of employee a persons themselves) to induce the volume of labor actually employed to be forthcoming. Disutility must be taken to cover every kind of reason which might lead a man, or a body of men to withhold their labor rather than accept a wage which had to them a utility below a certain minimum."

This postulate implies that workers' demand is essentially for real wage and not for money wage and the relationship between the two is direct. The second postulate gives the supply schedule for various levels of employment forthcoming at different real wage rates, while the first postulate gives the demand schedule for employment.

Given the supply and demand functions, "The amount of employment is fixed at the point where the utility of the marginal product balances the disutility of the marginal employment."

The two postulates would get simultaneously satisfied at the point of intersection of the demand schedule and the supply schedule for employment. The classical theorists would not admit the possibility of involuntary unemployment; the economy would be normally at the full employment equilibrium. There is either frictional unemployment or voluntary unemployment.

The short-run classical model can be presented diagrammatically through the following figure. It is based on the following assumptions:

- The supply of labor is an increasing function of real wage rates, i.e., more labor will be offered for higher real wage rates.
- The demand for labor is a decreasing function of real wage rates i.e., less labor will be hired for higher real wage rates and more at lower real wage rates.
- There are no imperfections or institutional rigidities in the labor market, i.e. labor is perfectly mobile.
- Aggregate demand (for goods and services) remains constant and no changes are anticipated.
- Population, tastes, technology, etc. are given.

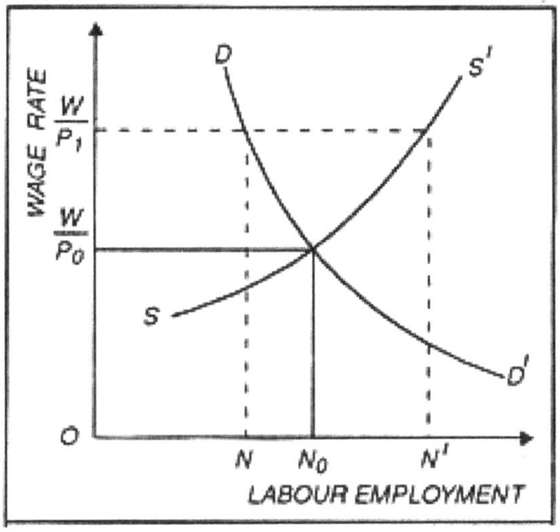

Wages and employment in classical theory.

The Demand for Labor

A firm in a competitive industry will hire workers up to the point where the value of marginal product (marginal product multiplied by the price of output) just equals the cost of the factor. The demand for labor, therefore, may be written as: N_d= D (W/P); which states that the demand for labor is a function of the real wage rate. According to the law of Diminishing Marginal Returns, the marginal product of labor declines as more workers are hired. It follows that if the level of employment is to be increased, the real wage must fall. The demand for labor is, therefore, a decreasing function of the real wage rate.

The Supply of Labor

Classicals assumed that a change in the quantity of labor supplied will take place only if the real wage changes. Consequently, the classical labor supply function may be written as: N_s = S (W/P).

The Equilibrating Mechanism

Given the supply and demand functions of labor, we can explain the equilibrating mechanism in the labor markets in the following steps:

- W/P, i.e. the average money wage deflated by price level is shown on the vertical axis, while the horizontal axis measures the various amounts of employment or N.
- DD curve represents the demand for labor indicating that more labor is hired at lower real wage rates, ON < ON_0; SS is the supply curve showing that more labor is offered at higher real wage rates ON being > ON_0.

- When the wage rate is (W/P_1) the system is in disequilibrium, so that workers bid down money wages relatively to prices to the level of W/P_0 eliminating unemployment to the extent of by NN_0. At the real wage rate (W/P_1) the quantity of labor demanded is ON, while workers offer ON' units of labor.

- It means there is excess supply of labor to the extent of AW. When more workers are willing to work at the going real wage rate than business is willing to hire, we have involuntary unemployment. Should the real wages fall to (W/P_Q), involuntary unemployment would disappear.

- (W/P_Q) is the equilibrium wage rate in the market where amount of labor demanded is equal to the amount of labor supplied and N_0 is the full employment level. Anybody unwilling to work at that wage rate is, therefore, considered voluntarily unemployed.

- Thus, demand for and supply of labor are so related to real wage rate that any discrepancy between the two will cause such a change in real wage rate that full employment is restored. In equilibrium, therefore, we have $D(W/P) - S(W/P) = o$ and $N = N_0$.

This logic was applied to all types of labor markets. Hence, on the basis of above argument unemployment was considered incompatible with equilibrium. Such is the self-adjusting classical system of automatic full employment equilibrium.

It is, therefore, clear why during the pre-Keynesian era when classical theories held sway, employment problem was never taken so seriously. The state of full employment was considered as a normal feature of the free-enterprise economy any deviation from it being taken as frictional, temporary, and originating from the imperfections of the market.

From Particular to General Wage Cut

During the Great Depression, Prof. A C. Pigou proposed the policy of general wage cutting. One finds it hard to agree with the classical reasoning that a general wage cut will remove unemployment, unless the wage cut is a particular wage cut in a single firm or industry. It may be true that wage cut in a single industry (say Toys industry) may increase employment if there is no fall in the demand for toys.

It cannot be presumed from this that the demand for the toys would not be affected at all if a general wage cut (as opposed to a particular wage cut in toy industry) is applied to the economy as a whole. If the wages of the workers employed in the toy industry only are reduced, there is no doubt that the cost of production of toys will also be reduced more than the fall in the demand for toys.

Thus, while the income of the workers employed in the toy industry has been reduced, the workers in other industries continue to enjoy the same purchasing power and with a fall in the prices of toys, the demand for toys will go up leading to more production and employment.

It may, however, be noticed that the wage cut proposed by the classicals is the general wage cut affecting the economy as a whole rather than a particular wage cut.

As such, if the general wage cut applied in the economy as a whole reduces purchasing power of the people (results in a fall in the effective demand) it is highly doubtful that the demand for toys would go up resulting in an increase of output and employment in the toy industry. This will happen only when the wage cut is a particular wage cut (in toy industry alone).

Keynes' Criticism of Wage Cuts Policy

Keynes strongly opposed the classical theory of automatic adjustment through flexible wage rates including the Pigovian formulation of Say's Law on the ground that the same had become obsolete under modern conditions.

Keynes particularly rejected the thesis that unemployment would disappear if workers accept sufficiently low wages. He regarded wage cuts to remedy unemployment as unsound both from the theoretical and practical points of view. He considered such a step as highly anti- moral and anti-social.

From the practical viewpoint also he doubted the validity of such a step. In his view, collective bargaining by labor unions, unemployment insurance, minimum wage laws, etc. had come to stay. Keynes' theory of employment does not depend upon flexibility of wage rates. He argued that employment depends upon effective demand and not on the wage bargains between employers and workers.

According to him, even if wage rates become flexible under thorough-going competition, unemployment could still exist. Keynes recognised that wages are a double-edged weapon. Reduced wages not only diminish the costs but they also reduce money incomes and purchasing power of these workers.

Classicals laid more stress on the cost aspect but Keynes emphasized the income aspect of wages. According to Keynes, wages arc a source of demand and when these are cut, general purchasing power also suffers. Total demand and total expenditure decline as a result of wage cuts. Hence, to him, this was no good method to achieve full employment.

Keynes's Break with the Classicals

Keynes rejected the classical theory of unemployment, which in his view held (i) that the wage bargains between workers and employers determine (real) wages, (ii) that the level of (real) wages thus arrived at determines the amount of employment. He agreed basically with the assumption of diminishing returns that an increase in employment can only occur to the accompaniment of a decline in the rate of real wages.

He differed with the classical theory in his argument that there was no expedient by which labor as a whole could reduce its real wage to a given figure by making revised money bargains with the entrepreneurs.

However, the extent to which Keynes' break with the classical view was less than complete was evident in his remark that "If our central control succeeds in establishing an aggregate volume of output corresponding to full employment as nearly as is practicable; the classical theory comes into its own again from this point onwards."

The volume of employment, according to Keynes is determined by effective demand. To him, unemployment is not due to the refusal of the workers to accept a wage corresponding to their marginal productivity but due to inadequate aggregate demand.

Demand determines employment and employment determines the marginal products and therefore wages. The manipulation of wage rates, Keynes thought, was not a sound way to increase employment. Manipulation of demand for labor is a far more effective policy.

Keynes vehemently opposed the classical theory of automatic adjustment because the same had become obsolete in the conditions of contemporary, capitalist world. Keynes particularly objected to the notion that unemployment would disappear if workers would just accept sufficiently low money wage rates.

According to him this classical reasoning turned out to be extremely disastrous both from the theoretical and practical points of view.

He contended that collective bargaining by trade unions, minimum wage laws, unemployment benefits, etc. have become an integral part of the modern advanced, democratic economics possessing increased productivity and technology. The classical theory of employment though quite logical and simple on account of strong basic postulates was unacceptable owing to the unrealistic nature of its assumptions.

References

- 4-most-important-features-of-new-keynesian-economics-31244: yourarticlelibrary.com, Retrieved 28,May 2020
- Liquidity-preference-theory-motives-and-criticism-with-diagram 1805:economicsdiscussion.net, Retrieved 12, July 2020
- Hayes, M.G. (2008). The Economics of Keynes: A new guide to the General Theory. Edward Elgar Publishing. pp. 2–3, 31. ISBN 978-1-84844-056-2
- Marginal-efficiency-capital: economicshelp.org, Retrieved 25, March 2020

- “The Neoclassical-Keynesian Synthesis”. The History of Economic Thought Website. The New School. Archived from the original on June 5, 2002. Retrieved 23, April 2020
- Post-keynesian-economics, orientation: exploring-economics.org, Retrieved 18, June 2020
- Classical-theory-on-wage-and-employment-with-diagram-macro-economics-14599: economics-discussion.net, Retrieved 27, May 2020

4

Types of Market Structure

There are different types of markets which are studied within the discipline of macroeconomics. A few of them are monopoly, oligopoly, duopoly, monopsony and natural monopoly. The topics elaborated in this chapter will help in gaining a better perspective about these types of markets as well as information asymmetry and income distribution.

Market Structure

In economics, market structure is best defined as the organisational and other characteristics of a market.

Types of Market Structures

1. Monopolistic competition, a type of imperfect competition such that many producers sell products or services that are differentiated from one another (e.g. by branding or quality) and hence are not perfect substitutes. In monopolistic competition, a firm takes the prices charged by its rivals as given and ignores the impact of its own prices on the prices of other. This market structure exists when there are multiple sellers who are attempting to seem different than each other.
2. Oligopoly, in which a market is run by a small number of firms that together control the majority of the market share.
    - Duopoly, a special case of an oligopoly with two firms.
    - Monopsony, when there is only a single buyer in a market.
    - Oligopsony, a market where many sellers can be present but meet only a few buyers.
3. Monopoly, where there is only one provider of a product or service.
    - Natural monopoly, a monopoly in which economies of scale cause efficiency to increase continuously with the size of the firm. A firm is a natural monopoly if it is able to serve the entire market demand at a lower cost than any combination of two or more smaller, more specialized firms.
4. Perfect competition, a theoretical market structure that features low barriers to entry, identical products with no differentiation, an unlimited number of producers and consumers, and a perfectly elastic demand curve.

Elements and Concerns

The imperfectly competitive structure is quite identical to the realistic market conditions where some monopolistic competitors, monopolists, oligopolists, and duopolists exist and dominate the market conditions. The elements of Market Structure include the number and size distribution of firms, entry conditions, and the extent of differentiation.

These somewhat abstract concerns tend to determine some but not all details of a specific concrete market system where buyers and sellers actually meet and commit to trade. Competition is useful because it reveals actual customer demand and induces the seller (operator) to provide service quality levels and price levels that buyers (customers) want, typically subject to the seller's financial need to cover its costs. In other words, competition can align the seller's interests with the buyer's interests and can cause the seller to reveal his true costs and other private information. In the absence of perfect competition, three basic approaches can be adopted to deal with problems related to the control of market power and an asymmetry between the government and the operator with respect to objectives and information: (a) subjecting the operator to competitive pressures, (b) gathering information on the operator and the market, and (c) applying incentive regulation.

Quick Reference to Basic Market Structures

Market Structure	Seller Entry Barriers	Seller Number	Buyer Entry Barriers	Buyer Number
Perfect Competition	No	Many	No	Many
Monopolistic competition	No	Many	No	Many
Oligopoly	Yes	Few	No	Many
Oligopsony	No	Many	Yes	Few
Monopoly	Yes	One	No	Many

The correct sequence of the market structure from most to least competitive is perfect competition, imperfect competition, oligopoly, and pure monopoly.

The main criteria by which one can distinguish between different market structures are: the number and size of producers and consumers in the market, the type of goods and services being traded, and the degree to which information can flow freely.

Monopoly

A monopoly ("alone" or "single" and "to sell") exists when a specific person or enterprise is the only supplier of a particular commodity (this contrasts with a monopsony which relates to a single entity's control of a market to purchase a good or service, and with oligopoly which consists of a few entities dominating an industry). Monopolies are thus characterized by a lack of economic competition to produce the good or service, a lack of viable substitute goods, and the possibility of a high monopoly price well above the firm's marginal cost that leads to a high monopoly profit. The verb *monopolise* or *monopolize* refers to the *process* by which a company gains the ability to raise prices or exclude competitors. In economics, a monopoly is a single seller. In law, a monopoly is a business entity that has significant market power, that is, the power to charge overly high prices. Although monopolies may be big businesses, size is not a characteristic of a monopoly. A small business may still have the power to raise prices in a small industry (or market).

"I Like a Little Competition"—J. P. Morgan

"I Like a Little Competition"—J. P. Morgan by Art Young. Cartoon relating to the answer J. P. Morgan gave when asked whether he disliked competition at the Pujo Committee.

A monopoly is distinguished from a monopsony, in which there is only one *buyer* of a product or service; a monopoly may also have monopsony control of a sector of a market. Likewise, a monopoly should be distinguished from a cartel (a form of oligopoly), in which several providers act together to coordinate services, prices or sale of goods. Monopolies, monopsonies and oligopolies are all situations such that one or a few of the entities have market power and therefore interact with their customers (monopoly), suppliers (monopsony) and the other companies (oligopoly) in ways that leave market interactions distorted.

Monopolies can be established by a government, form naturally, or form by integration.

In many jurisdictions, competition laws restrict monopolies. Holding a dominant position or a monopoly of a market is often not illegal in itself, however certain categories of behavior can be considered abusive and therefore incur legal sanctions when business is dominant. A government-granted monopoly or *legal monopoly*, by contrast, is sanctioned by the state, often to provide an incentive to invest in a risky venture or enrich a domestic interest group. Patents, copyrights, and trademarks are sometimes used as examples of government-granted monopolies. The government may also reserve the venture for itself, thus forming a government monopoly.

Market Structures

In economics, the idea of monopoly will be important for the study of management structures, which directly concerns normative aspects of economic competition, and provides the basis for topics such as industrial organization and economics of regulation. There are four basic types of market structures by traditional economic analysis: perfect competition, monopolistic competition, oligopoly and monopoly. A monopoly is a structure in which a single supplier produces and sells a given product. If there is a single seller in a certain industry and there are not any close substitutes for the product, then the market structure is that of a "pure monopoly". Sometimes, there are many sellers in an industry and/or there exist many close substitutes for the goods being produced, but nevertheless companies retain some market power. This is termed monopolistic competition, whereas in oligopoly the companies interact strategically.

In general, the main results from this theory compare price-fixing methods across market structures, analyze the effect of a certain structure on welfare, and vary technological/demand assumptions in order to assess the consequences for an abstract model of society. Most economic textbooks follow the practice of carefully explaining the *perfect competition* model, mainly because of its usefulness to understand "departures" from it (the so-called *imperfect competition* models).

The boundaries of what constitutes a market and what doesn't are relevant distinctions to make in economic analysis. In a general equilibrium context, a good is a specific concept entangling geographical and time-related characteristics (*grapes sold during October 2009 in Moscow* is a different good from *grapes sold during October 2009 in New York*). Most studies of market structure relax a little their definition of a good, allowing for more flexibility at the identification of substitute-goods. Therefore, one can find an economic analysis of the market of *grapes in Russia*, for example, which is not a market in the strict sense of general equilibrium theory monopoly.

Characteristics

- *Profit Maximizer*: Maximizes profits.
- *Price Maker*: Decides the price of the good or product to be sold, but does so by determining the quantity in order to demand the price desired by the firm.
- *High Barriers*: Other sellers are unable to enter the market of the monopoly.

- *Single seller*: In a monopoly, there is one seller of the good that produces all the output. Therefore, the whole market is being served by a single company, and for practical purposes, the company is the same as the industry.
- *Price Discrimination*: A monopolist can change the price and quality of the product. He or she sells higher quantities, charging a lower price for the product, in a very elastic market and sells lower quantities, charging a higher price, in a less elastic market.

Sources of Monopoly Power

Monopolies derive their market power from barriers to entry – circumstances that prevent or greatly impede a potential competitor's ability to compete in a market. There are three major types of barriers to entry: economic, legal and deliberate.

- *Economic barriers*: Economic barriers include economies of scale, capital requirements, cost advantages and technological superiority.
- *Economies of scale*: Monopolies are characterised by decreasing costs for a relatively large range of production. Decreasing costs coupled with large initial costs give monopolies an advantage over would-be competitors. Monopolies are often in a position to reduce prices below a new entrant's operating costs and thereby prevent them from continuing to compete. Furthermore, the size of the industry relative to the minimum efficient scale may limit the number of companies that can effectively compete within the industry. If for example the industry is large enough to support one company of minimum efficient scale then other companies entering the industry will operate at a size that is less than MES, meaning that these companies cannot produce at an average cost that is competitive with the dominant company. Finally, if long-term average cost is constantly decreasing, the least cost method to provide a good or service is by a single company.
- *Capital requirements*: Production processes that require large investments of capital, or large research and development costs or substantial sunk costs limit the number of companies in an industry. Large fixed costs also make it difficult for a small company to enter an industry and expand.
- *Technological superiority*: A monopoly may be better able to acquire, integrate and use the best possible technology in producing its goods while entrants do not have the size or finances to use the best available technology. One large company can sometimes produce goods cheaper than several small companies.
- *No substitute goods*: A monopoly sells a good for which there is no close substitute. The absence of substitutes makes the demand for the good relatively inelastic enabling monopolies to extract positive profits.

- *Control of natural resources*: A prime source of monopoly power is the control of resources that are critical to the production of a final good.
- *Network externalities*: The use of a product by a person can affect the value of that product to other people. This is the network effect. There is a direct relationship between the proportion of people using a product and the demand for that product. In other words, the more people who are using a product the greater the probability of any individual starting to use the product. This effect accounts for fads, fashion trends, social networks etc. It also can play a crucial role in the development or acquisition of market power. The most famous current example is the market dominance of the Microsoft office suite and operating system in personal computers.
- *Legal barriers*: Legal rights can provide opportunity to monopolise the market of a good. Intellectual property rights, including patents and copyrights, give a monopolist exclusive control of the production and selling of certain goods. Property rights may give a company exclusive control of the materials necessary to produce a good.
- *Deliberate actions*: A company wanting to monopolise a market may engage in various types of deliberate action to exclude competitors or eliminate competition. Such actions include collusion, lobbying governmental authorities, and force.

In addition to barriers to entry and competition, barriers to exit may be a source of market power. Barriers to exit are market conditions that make it difficult or expensive for a company to end its involvement with a market. Great liquidation costs are a primary barrier for exiting. Market exit and shutdown are separate events. The decision whether to shut down or operate is not affected by exit barriers. A company will shut down if price falls below minimum average variable costs.

Monopoly Versus Competitive Markets

While monopoly and perfect competition mark the extremes of market structures there is some similarity. The cost functions are the same. Both monopolies and perfectly competitive (PC) companies minimize cost and maximize profit. The shutdown decisions are the same. Both are assumed to have perfectly competitive factors markets. There are distinctions, some of the more important of which are as follows:

- *Marginal revenue and price*: In a perfectly competitive market, price equals marginal cost. In a monopolistic market, however, price is set above marginal cost.
- *Product differentiation*: There is zero product differentiation in a perfectly

competitive market. Every product is perfectly homogeneous and a perfect substitute for any other. With a monopoly, there is great to absolute product differentiation in the sense that there is no available substitute for a monopolized good. The monopolist is the sole supplier of the good in question. A customer either buys from the monopolizing entity on its terms or does without.

- *Number of competitors*: PC markets are populated by an infinite number of buyers and sellers. Monopoly involves a single seller.
- *Barriers to Entry*: Barriers to entry are factors and circumstances that prevent entry into market by would-be competitors and limit new companies from operating and expanding within the market. PC markets have free entry and exit. There are no barriers to entry, or exit competition. Monopolies have relatively high barriers to entry. The barriers must be strong enough to prevent or discourage any potential competitor from entering the market.
- *Elasticity of Demand*: The price elasticity of demand is the percentage change of demand caused by a one percent change of relative price. A successful monopoly would have a relatively inelastic demand curve. A low coefficient of elasticity is indicative of effective barriers to entry. A PC company has a perfectly elastic demand curve. The coefficient of elasticity for a perfectly competitive demand curve is infinite.
- *Excess Profits*: Excess or positive profits are profit more than the normal expected return on investment. A PC company can make excess profits in the short term but excess profits attract competitors, which can enter the market freely and decrease prices, eventually reducing excess profits to zero. A monopoly can preserve excess profits because barriers to entry prevent competitors from entering the market.
- *Profit Maximization*: A PC company maximizes profits by producing such that price equals marginal costs. A monopoly maximises profits by producing where marginal revenue equals marginal costs. The rules are not equivalent. The demand curve for a PC company is perfectly elastic – flat. The demand curve is identical to the average revenue curve and the price line. Since the average revenue curve is constant the marginal revenue curve is also constant and equals the demand curve, Average revenue is the same as price (AR = TR/Q = P x Q/Q = P). Thus the price line is also identical to the demand curve. In sum, D = AR = MR = P.
- *P-Max quantity, price and profit*: If a monopolist obtains control of a formerly perfectly competitive industry, the monopolist would increase prices, reduce production, and realise positive economic profits.
- *Supply Curve*: in a perfectly competitive market there is a well defined supply function with a one-to-one relationship between price and quantity supplied. In a monopolistic market no such supply relationship exists. A monopolist cannot

> trace a short term supply curve because for a given price there is not a unique quantity supplied. As Pindyck and Rubenfeld note, a change in demand “can lead to changes in prices with no change in output, changes in output with no change in price or both”. Monopolies produce where marginal revenue equals marginal costs. For a specific demand curve the supply “curve” would be the price/quantity combination at the point where marginal revenue equals marginal cost. If the demand curve shifted the marginal revenue curve would shift as well and a new equilibrium and supply “point” would be established. The locus of these points would not be a supply curve in any conventional sense.

The most significant distinction between a PC company and a monopoly is that the monopoly has a downward-sloping demand curve rather than the “perceived” perfectly elastic curve of the PC company. Practically all the variations mentioned above relate to this fact. If there is a downward-sloping demand curve then by necessity there is a distinct marginal revenue curve. The implications of this fact are best made manifest with a linear demand curve. Assume that the inverse demand curve is of the form x = a – by. Then the total revenue curve is TR = ay – by2 and the marginal revenue curve is thus MR = a – 2by. From this several things are evident. First the marginal revenue curve has the same y intercept as the inverse demand curve. Second the slope of the marginal revenue curve is twice that of the inverse demand curve. Third the x intercept of the marginal revenue curve is half that of the inverse demand curve. What is not quite so evident is that the marginal revenue curve is below the inverse demand curve at all points. Since all companies maximise profits by equating MR and MC it must be the case that at the profit-maximizing quantity MR and MC are less than price, which further implies that a monopoly produces less quantity at a higher price than if the market were perfectly competitive.

The fact that a monopoly has a downward-sloping demand curve means that the relationship between total revenue and output for a monopoly is much different than that of competitive companies. Total revenue equals price times quantity. A competitive company has a perfectly elastic demand curve meaning that total revenue is proportional to output. Thus the total revenue curve for a competitive company is a ray with a slope equal to the market price. A competitive company can sell all the output it desires at the market price. For a monopoly to increase sales it must reduce price. Thus the total revenue curve for a monopoly is a parabola that begins at the origin and reaches a maximum value then continuously decreases until total revenue is again zero. Total revenue has its maximum value when the slope of the total revenue function is zero. The slope of the total revenue function is marginal revenue. So the revenue maximizing quantity and price occur when MR = 0. For example, assume that the monopoly’s demand function is P = 50 – 2Q. The total revenue function would be TR = 50Q – $2Q^2$ and marginal revenue would be 50 – 4Q. Setting marginal revenue equal to zero we have

$$50 - 4Q = 0$$

$$-4Q = -50$$

$$Q = 12.5$$

So the revenue maximizing quantity for the monopoly is 12.5 units and the revenue maximizing price is 25.

A company with a monopoly does not experience price pressure from competitors, although it may experience pricing pressure from potential competition. If a company increases prices too much, then others may enter the market if they are able to provide the same good, or a substitute, at a lesser price. The idea that monopolies in markets with easy entry need not be regulated against is known as the "revolution in monopoly theory".

A monopolist can extract only one premium, and getting into complementary markets does not pay. That is, the total profits a monopolist could earn if it sought to leverage its monopoly in one market by monopolizing a complementary market are equal to the extra profits it could earn anyway by charging more for the monopoly product itself. However, the one monopoly profit theorem is not true if customers in the monopoly good are stranded or poorly informed, or if the tied good has high fixed costs.

A pure monopoly has the same economic rationality of perfectly competitive companies, i.e. to optimise a profit function given some constraints. By the assumptions of increasing marginal costs, exogenous inputs' prices, and control concentrated on a single agent or entrepreneur, the optimal decision is to equate the marginal cost and marginal revenue of production. Nonetheless, a pure monopoly can – unlike a competitive company – alter the market price for its own convenience: a decrease of production results in a higher price. In the economics' jargon, it is said that pure monopolies have "a downward-sloping demand". An important consequence of such behaviour is worth noticing: typically a monopoly selects a higher price and lesser quantity of output than a price-taking company; again, less is available at a higher price.

The Inverse Elasticity Rule

A monopoly chooses that price that maximizes the difference between total revenue and total cost. The basic markup rule (as measured by the Lerner index) can be expressed as $\frac{P-MC}{P}=\frac{-1}{E_d}$ where e_d is the price elasticity of demand the firm faces. The markup rules indicate that the ratio between profit margin and the price is inversely proportional to the price elasticity of demand. The implication of the rule is that the more elastic the demand for the product the less pricing power the monopoly has.

Market Power

Market power is the ability to increase the product's price above marginal cost without losing all customers. Perfectly competitive (PC) companies have zero market power when it comes to setting prices. All companies of a PC market are price takers. The price is set by the interaction of demand and supply at the market or aggregate level.

Individual companies simply take the price determined by the market and produce that quantity of output that maximizes the company's profits. If a PC company attempted to increase prices above the market level all its customers would abandon the company and purchase at the market price from other companies. A monopoly has considerable although not unlimited market power. A monopoly has the power to set prices or quantities although not both. A monopoly is a price maker. The monopoly is the market and prices are set by the monopolist based on their circumstances and not the interaction of demand and supply. The two primary factors determining monopoly market power are the company's demand curve and its cost structure.

Market power is the ability to affect the terms and conditions of exchange so that the price of a product is set by a single company (price is not imposed by the market as in perfect competition). Although a monopoly's market power is great it is still limited by the demand side of the market. A monopoly has a negatively sloped demand curve, not a perfectly inelastic curve. Consequently, any price increase will result in the loss of some customers.

Price Discrimination

Price discrimination allows a monopolist to increase its profit by charging higher prices for identical goods to those who are willing or able to pay more. For example, most economic textbooks cost more in the United States than in developing countries like Ethiopia. In this case, the publisher is using its government-granted copyright monopoly to price discriminate between the generally wealthier American economics students and the generally poorer Ethiopian economics students. Similarly, most patented medications cost more in the U.S. than in other countries with a (presumed) poorer customer base. Typically, a high general price is listed, and various market segments get varying discounts. This is an example of framing to make the process of charging some people higher prices more socially acceptable. Perfect price discrimination would allow the monopolist to charge each customer the exact maximum amount he would be willing to pay. This would allow the monopolist to extract all the consumer surplus of the market. While such perfect price discrimination is a theoretical construct, advances in information technology and micromarketing may bring it closer to the realm of possibility.

It is very important to realize that partial price discrimination can cause some customers who are inappropriately pooled with high price customers to be excluded from the market. For example, a poor student in the U.S. might be excluded from purchasing an economics textbook at the U.S. price, which the student may have been able to purchase at the Ethiopian price'. Similarly, a wealthy student in Ethiopia may be able to or willing to buy at the U.S. price, though naturally would hide such a fact from the monopolist so as to pay the reduced third world price. These are deadweight losses and decrease a monopolist's profits. As such, monopolists have substantial economic interest in improving their market information and *market segmenting*.

There is important information for one to remember when considering the monopoly model diagram (and its associated conclusions) displayed here. The result that monopoly prices are higher, and production output lesser, than a competitive company follow from a requirement that the monopoly not charge different prices for different customers. That is, the monopoly is restricted from engaging in price discrimination (this is termed first degree price discrimination, such that all customers are charged the same amount). If the monopoly were permitted to charge individualised prices (this is termed third degree price discrimination), the quantity produced, and the price charged to the *marginal* customer, would be identical to that of a competitive company, thus eliminating the deadweight loss; however, all gains from trade (social welfare) would accrue to the monopolist and none to the consumer. In essence, every consumer would be indifferent between (1) going completely without the product or service and (2) being able to purchase it from the monopolist.

As long as the price elasticity of demand for most customers is less than one in absolute value, it is advantageous for a company to increase its prices: it receives more money for fewer goods. With a price increase, price elasticity tends to increase, and in the optimum case above it will be greater than one for most customers.

A company maximizes profit by selling where marginal revenue equals marginal cost. A company that does not engage in price discrimination will charge the profit maximizing price, P*, to all its customers. In such circumstances there are customers who would be willing to pay a higher price than P* and those who will not pay P* but would buy at a lower price. A price discrimination strategy is to charge less price sensitive buyers a higher price and the more price sensitive buyers a lower price. Thus additional revenue is generated from two sources. The basic problem is to identify customers by their willingness to pay.

The purpose of price discrimination is to transfer consumer surplus to the producer. Consumer surplus is the difference between the value of a good to a consumer and the price the consumer must pay in the market to purchase it. Price discrimination is not limited to monopolies.

Market power is a company's ability to increase prices without losing all its customers. Any company that has market power can engage in price discrimination. Perfect competition is the only market form in which price discrimination would be impossible (a perfectly competitive company has a perfectly elastic demand curve and has zero market power).

There are three forms of price discrimination. First degree price discrimination charges each consumer the maximum price the consumer is willing to pay. Second degree price discrimination involves quantity discounts. Third degree price discrimination involves grouping consumers according to willingness to pay as measured by their price elasticities of demand and charging each group a different price. Third degree price discrimination is the most prevalent type.

There are three conditions that must be present for a company to engage in successful price discrimination. First, the company must have market power. Second, the company must be able to sort customers according to their willingness to pay for the good. Third, the firm must be able to prevent resell.

A company must have some degree of market power to practice price discrimination. Without market power a company cannot charge more than the market price. Any market structure characterized by a downward sloping demand curve has market power – monopoly, monopolistic competition and oligopoly. The only market structure that has no market power is perfect competition.

A company wishing to practice price discrimination must be able to prevent middlemen or brokers from acquiring the consumer surplus for themselves. The company accomplishes this by preventing or limiting resale. Many methods are used to prevent resale. For example, persons are required to show photographic identification and a boarding pass before boarding an airplane. Most travelers assume that this practice is strictly a matter of security. However, a primary purpose in requesting photographic identification is to confirm that the ticket purchaser is the person about to board the airplane and not someone who has repurchased the ticket from a discount buyer.

The inability to prevent resale is the largest obstacle to successful price discrimination. Companies have however developed numerous methods to prevent resale. For example, universities require that students show identification before entering sporting events. Governments may make it illegal to resale tickets or products. In Boston, Red Sox baseball tickets can only be resold legally to the team.

The three basic forms of price discrimination are first, second and third degree price discrimination. In *first degree price discrimination* the company charges the maximum price each customer is willing to pay. The maximum price a consumer is willing to pay for a unit of the good is the reservation price. Thus for each unit the seller tries to set the price equal to the consumer's reservation price. Direct information about a consumer's willingness to pay is rarely available. Sellers tend to rely on secondary information such as where a person lives (postal codes); for example, catalog retailers can use mail high-priced catalogs to high-income postal codes. First degree price discrimination most frequently occurs in regard to professional services or in transactions involving direct buyer/seller negotiations. For example, an accountant who has prepared a consumer's tax return has information that can be used to charge customers based on an estimate of their ability to pay.

In *second degree price discrimination* or quantity discrimination customers are charged different prices based on how much they buy. There is a single price schedule for all consumers but the prices vary depending on the quantity of the good bought. The theory of second degree price discrimination is a consumer is willing to buy only a certain quantity of a good at a given price. Companies know that consumer's willingness to buy decreases as more units are purchased. The task for the seller is to identify these price points and to reduce the price once one is reached in the hope that a reduced price will trigger additional purchases from the consumer. For example, sell in unit blocks rather than individual units.

In *third degree price discrimination* or multi-market price discrimination the seller divides the consumers into different groups according to their willingness to pay as measured by their price elasticity of demand. Each group of consumers effectively becomes a separate market with its own demand curve and marginal revenue curve. The firm then attempts to maximize profits in each segment by equating MR and MC, Generally the company charges a higher price to the group with a more price inelastic demand and a relatively lesser price to the group with a more elastic demand. Examples of third degree price discrimination abound. Airlines charge higher prices to business travelers than to vacation travelers. The reasoning is that the demand curve for a vacation traveler is relatively elastic while the demand curve for a business traveler is relatively inelastic. Any determinant of price elasticity of demand can be used to segment markets. For example, seniors have a more elastic demand for movies than do young adults because they generally have more free time. Thus theaters will offer discount tickets to seniors.

Example

Assume that by a uniform pricing system the monopolist would sell five units at a price of $10 per unit. Assume that his marginal cost is $5 per unit. Total revenue would be $50, total costs would be $25 and profits would be $25. If the monopolist practiced price discrimination he would sell the first unit for $50 the second unit for $40 and so on. Total revenue would be $150, his total cost would be $25 and his profit would be $125.00. Several things are worth noting. The monopolist acquires all the consumer surplus and eliminates practically all the deadweight loss because he is willing to sell to anyone who is willing to pay at least the marginal cost. Thus the price discrimination promotes efficiency. Secondly, by the pricing scheme price = average revenue and equals marginal revenue. That is the monopolist behaving like a perfectly competitive company. Thirdly, the discriminating monopolist produces a larger quantity than the monopolist operating by a uniform pricing scheme.

Qd	Price
1	50
2	40
3	30
4	20
5	10

Classifying Customers

Successful price discrimination requires that companies separate consumers according to their willingness to buy. Determining a customer's willingness to buy a good is difficult. Asking consumers directly is fruitless: consumers don't know, and to the extent they do they are reluctant to share that information with marketers. The two main methods for determining willingness to buy are observation of personal characteristics and consumer actions. As noted information about where a person lives (postal codes), how the person dresses, what kind of car he or she drives, occupation, and income and spending patterns can be helpful in classifying.

Monopoly and Efficiency

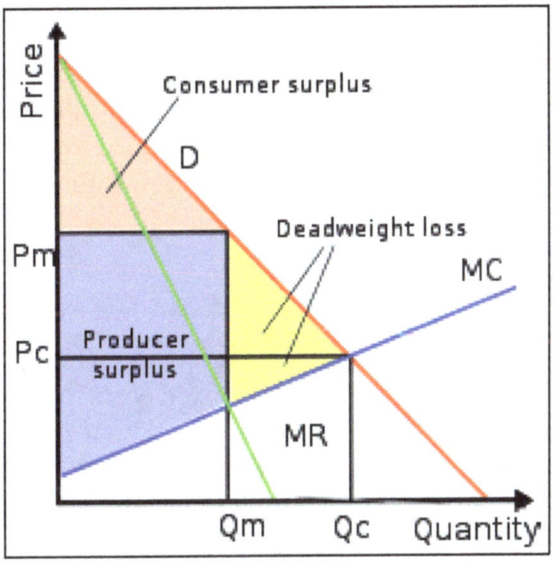

Surpluses and deadweight loss created by monopoly price setting.

The price of monopoly is upon every occasion the highest which can be got. The natural price, or the price of free competition, on the contrary, is the lowest which can be taken, not upon every occasion indeed, but for any considerable time together. The one is upon every occasion the highest which can be squeezed out of the buyers, or which it is supposed they will consent to give; the other is the lowest which the sellers can commonly afford to take, and at the same time continue their business.

...Monopoly, besides, is a great enemy to good management.

– Adam Smith (1776), *The Wealth of Nations*

According to the standard model, in which a monopolist sets a single price for all consumers, the monopolist will sell a lesser quantity of goods at a higher price than would companies by perfect competition. Because the monopolist ultimately forgoes transactions with consumers who value the product or service more than its price, monopoly pricing creates a deadweight loss referring to potential gains that went neither to the monopolist nor to consumers. Given the presence of this deadweight loss, the combined surplus (or wealth) for the monopolist and consumers is necessarily less than the total surplus obtained by consumers by perfect competition. Where efficiency is defined by the total gains from trade, the monopoly setting is less efficient than perfect competition.

It is often argued that monopolies tend to become less efficient and less innovative over time, becoming "complacent", because they do not have to be efficient or innovative to compete in the marketplace. Sometimes this very loss of psychological efficiency can increase a potential competitor's value enough to overcome market entry barriers, or provide incentive for research and investment into new alternatives. The theory of contestable markets argues that in some circumstances (private) monopolies are forced to behave *as if* there were competition because of the risk of losing their monopoly to new entrants. This is likely to happen when a market's barriers to entry are low. It might also be because of the availability in the longer term of substitutes in other markets. For example, a canal monopoly, while worth a great deal during the late 18th century United Kingdom, was worth much less during the late 19th century because of the introduction of railways as a substitute.

Natural Monopoly

A natural monopoly is an organization that experiences increasing returns to scale over the relevant range of output and relatively high fixed costs. A natural monopoly occurs where the average cost of production "declines throughout the relevant range of product demand". The relevant range of product demand is where the average cost curve is below the demand curve. When this situation occurs, it is always cheaper for one large company to supply the market than multiple smaller companies; in fact, absent government intervention in such markets, will naturally evolve into a monopoly. An early market entrant that takes advantage of the cost structure and can expand rapidly can exclude smaller companies from entering and can drive or buy out other companies. A natural monopoly suffers from the same inefficiencies as any other monopoly. Left to its own devices, a profit-seeking natural monopoly will produce where marginal revenue equals marginal costs. Regulation of natural monopolies is problematic. Fragmenting such monopolies is by definition inefficient. The most frequently used methods dealing with natural monopolies are government regulations and public ownership. Government regulation generally consists of regulatory commissions charged with the principal duty of setting prices.

To reduce prices and increase output, regulators often use average cost pricing. By average cost pricing, the price and quantity are determined by the intersection of the average cost curve and the demand curve. This pricing scheme eliminates any positive economic profits since price equals average cost. Average-cost pricing is not perfect. Regulators must estimate average costs. Companies have a reduced incentive to lower costs. Regulation of this type has not been limited to natural monopolies. Average-cost pricing does also have some disadvantages. By setting price equal to the intersection of the demand curve and the average total cost curve, the firm's output is allocatively inefficient as the price is less than the marginal cost (which is the output quantity for a perfectly competitive and allocatively efficient market).

Government-granted Monopoly

A government-granted monopoly (also called a "de jure monopoly") is a form of coercive monopoly by which a government grants exclusive privilege to a private individual or company to be the sole provider of a commodity; potential competitors are excluded from the market by law, regulation, or other mechanisms of government enforcement.

Samuel Insull, a British-born American electrical industry business magnate invented regulated monopoly. This came from a combination of his business persona and his political one. On the one hand, he abhorred the waste of competing power producers, whose inefficiency would often double the cost of production. On the other hand, he believed in the citizen's right to fair treatment. So while he bought up rival companies and created a monopoly, he kept his prices low and campaigned vigorously for regulation.

Monopolist Shutdown Rule

A monopolist should shut down when price is less than average variable cost for every output level – in other words where the demand curve is entirely below the average variable cost curve. Under these circumstances at the profit maximum level of output (MR = MC) average revenue would be less than average variable costs and the monopolists would be better off shutting down in the short term.

Breaking Up Monopolies

In a free market, monopolies can be ended at any time by new competition, breakaway businesses, or consumers seeking alternatives. In a highly regulated market environment a government will often either regulate the monopoly, convert it into a publicly owned monopoly environment, or forcibly fragment it. Public utilities, often being naturally efficient with only one operator and therefore less susceptible to efficient breakup, are often strongly regulated or publicly owned. American Telephone & Telegraph (AT&T) and Standard Oil are debatable examples of the breakup of a private monopoly by government: When AT&T, a monopoly previously protected by force of law, was broken up into various components in 1984, MCI, Sprint, and other companies were able to compete effectively in the long distance phone market.

Law

The existence of a very high market share does not always mean consumers are paying excessive prices since the threat of new entrants to the market can restrain a high-market-share company's price increases. Competition law does not make merely having a monopoly illegal, but rather abusing the power a monopoly may confer, for instance through exclusionary practices (i.e. pricing high just because you are the only one around.) It may also be noted that it is illegal to try to obtain a monopoly, by practices of buying out the competition, or equal practices. If one occurs naturally, such as a competitor going out of business, or lack of competition, it is not illegal until such time as the monopoly holder abuses the power.

First it is necessary to determine whether a company is dominant, or whether it behaves "to an appreciable extent independently of its competitors, customers and ultimately of its consumer". As with collusive conduct, market shares are determined with reference to the particular market in which the company and product in question is sold. The Herfindahl-Hirschman Index (HHI) is sometimes used to assess how competitive an industry is. In the US, the merger guidelines state that a post-merger HHI below 1000 is viewed as unconcentrated while HHIs above that will provoke further review.

By European Union law, very large market shares raise a presumption that a company is dominant, which may be rebuttable. If a company has a dominant position, then there is "a special responsibility not to allow its conduct to impair competition on the common market". The lowest yet market share of a company considered "dominant" in the EU was 39.7%.

Certain categories of abusive conduct are usually prohibited by a country's legislation. The main recognised categories are:

- Limiting supply
- Predatory pricing or undercutting
- Price discrimination
- Refusal to deal and exclusive dealing
- Tying (commerce) and product bundling

Despite wide agreement that the above constitute abusive practices, there is some debate about whether there needs to be a causal connection between the dominant position of a company and its actual abusive conduct. Furthermore, there has been some consideration of what happens when a company merely attempts to abuse its dominant position.

Historical Monopolies

Origin

The term "monopoly" first appears in Aristotle's *Politics*. Aristotle describes Thales of Miletus's cornering of the market in olive presses as a monopoly.

The meaning and understanding of the English word 'monopoly' has changed over the years.

Monopolies of Resources

Salt

Vending of common salt (sodium chloride) was historically a natural monopoly. Until recently, a combination of strong sunshine and low humidity or an extension of peat marshes was necessary for producing salt from the sea, the most plentiful source. Changing sea levels periodically caused salt "famines" and communities were forced to depend upon those who controlled the scarce inland mines and salt springs, which were often in hostile areas (e.g. the Sahara desert) requiring well-organised security for transport, storage, and distribution.

The Salt Commission was a legal monopoly in China. Formed in 758, the Commission controlled salt production and sales in order to raise tax revenue for the Tang Dynasty.

The "Gabelle" was a notoriously high tax levied upon salt in the Kingdom of France. The much-hated levy had a role in the beginning of the French Revolution, when strict legal controls specified who was allowed to sell and distribute salt. First instituted in 1286, the Gabelle was not permanently abolished until 1945.

Coal

Robin Gollan argues in *The Coalminers of New South Wales* that anti-competitive practices developed in the coal industry of Australia's Newcastle as a result of the business cycle. The monopoly was generated by formal meetings of the local management of coal companies agreeing to fix a minimum price for sale at dock. This collusion was known as "The Vend". The Vend ended and was reformed repeatedly during the late 19th century, ending by recession in the business cycle. "The Vend" was able to maintain its monopoly due to trade union assistance, and material advantages (primarily coal geography). During the early 20th century, as a result of comparable monopolistic practices in the Australian coastal shipping business, the Vend developed as an informal and illegal collusion between the steamship owners and the coal industry, eventually resulting in the High Court case Adelaide Steamship Co. Ltd v. R. & AG.

Petroleum

Standard Oil was an American oil producing, transporting, refining, and marketing company. Established in 1870, it became the largest oil refiner in the world. John D. Rockefeller was a founder, chairman and major shareholder. The company was an innovator in the development of the business trust. The Standard Oil trust streamlined production and logistics, lowered costs, and undercut competitors. "Trust-busting" critics accused Standard Oil of using aggressive pricing to destroy competitors and form a monopoly that threatened consumers. Its controversial history as one of the world's first and largest multinational corporations ended in 1911, when the United States Supreme Court ruled that Standard was an illegal monopoly. The Standard Oil trust was dissolved into 33 smaller companies; two of its surviving "child" companies are ExxonMobil and the Chevron Corporation.

Steel

U.S. Steel has been accused of being a monopoly. J. P. Morgan and Elbert H. Gary founded U.S. Steel in 1901 by combining Andrew Carnegie's Carnegie Steel Company with Gary's Federal Steel Company and William Henry "Judge" Moore's National Steel Company. At one time, U.S. Steel was the largest steel producer and largest corporation in the world. In its first full year of operation, U.S. Steel made 67 percent of all the steel produced in the United States. However, U.S. Steel's share of the expanding market slipped to 50 percent by 1911, and anti-trust prosecution that year failed.

Diamonds

De Beers settled charges of price fixing in the diamond trade in the 2000s. De Beers is well known for its monopoloid practices throughout the 20th century, whereby it used its dominant position to manipulate the international diamond market. The company used several methods to exercise this control over the market. Firstly, it convinced independent producers to join its single channel monopoly, it flooded the market with diamonds similar to those of producers who refused to join the cartel, and lastly, it purchased and stockpiled diamonds produced by other manufacturers in order to control prices through limiting supply.

In 2000, the De Beers business model changed due to factors such as the decision by producers in Russia, Canada and Australia to distribute diamonds outside the De Beers channel, as well as rising awareness of blood diamonds that forced De Beers to "avoid the risk of bad publicity" by limiting sales to its own mined products. De Beers' market share by value fell from as high as 90% in the 1980s to less than 40% in 2012, having resulted in a more fragmented diamond market with more transparency and greater liquidity.

In November 2011 the Oppenheimer family announced its intention to sell the entirety of its 40% stake in De Beers to Anglo American plc thereby increasing Anglo American's ownership of the company to 85%. The transaction was worth £3.2 billion ($5.1 billion) in cash and ended the Oppenheimer dynasty's 80-year ownership of De Beers.

Utilities

A public utility (or simply "utility") is an organization or company that maintains the infrastructure for a public service or provides a set of services for public consumption. Common examples of utilities are electricity, natural gas, water, sewage, cable television, and telephone. In the United States, public utilities are often natural monopolies because the infrastructure required to produce and deliver a product such as electricity or water is very expensive to build and maintain.

Western Union was criticized as a "price gouging" monopoly in the late 19th century.

American Telephone & Telegraph was a telecommunications giant. AT&T was broken up in 1984.

In the case of Telecom New Zealand, local loop unbundling was enforced by central government.

Telkom is a semi-privatised, part state-owned South African telecommunications company.

Deutsche Telekom is a former state monopoly, still partially state owned. Deutsche Telekom currently monopolizes high-speed VDSL broadband network.

The Long Island Power Authority (LIPA) provided electric service to over 1.1 million customers in Nassau and Suffolk counties of New York, and the Rockaway Peninsula in Queens.

The Comcast Corporation is the largest mass media and communications company in the world by revenue. It is the largest cable company and home Internet service provider in the United States, and the nation's third largest home telephone service provider. Comcast has a monopoly in Boston, Philadelphia, Chicago, and many other small towns across the US.

Transportation

The United Aircraft and Transport Corporation was an aircraft manufacturer holding company that was forced to divest itself of airlines in 1934.

Iarnród Éireann, the Irish Railway authority, is a current monopoly as Ireland does not have the size for more companies.

The Long Island Rail Road (LIRR) was founded in 1834, and since the mid-1800s has provided train service between Long Island and New York City. In the 1870s, LIRR became the sole railroad in that area through a series of acquisitions and consolidations. In 2013, the LIRR's commuter rail system is the busiest commuter railroad in North America, serving nearly 335,000 passengers daily.

Foreign Trade

Dutch East India Company was created as a legal trading monopoly in 1602. The *Vereenigde Oost-Indische Compagnie* enjoyed huge profits from its spice monopoly through most of the 17th century.

The British East India Company was created as a legal trading monopoly in 1600. The East India Company was formed for pursuing trade with the East Indies but ended up trading mainly with the Indian subcontinent, North-West Frontier Province, and Balochistan. The Company traded in basic commodities, which included cotton, silk, indigo dye, salt, saltpetre, tea and opium.

Professional Sports

Major League Baseball survived U.S. anti-trust litigation in 1922, though its special status is still in dispute as of 2009.

The National Football League survived anti-trust lawsuit in the 1960s but was convicted of being an illegal monopoly in the 1980s.

Other examples of Monopolies

- Microsoft has been the defendant in multiple anti-trust suits on strategy *embrace, extend and extinguish.* They settled anti-trust litigation in the U.S. in 2001. In 2004 Microsoft was fined 493 million euros by the European Commission which was upheld for the most part by the Court of First Instance of the European Communities in 2007. The fine was US$1.35 billion in 2008 for noncompliance with the 2004 rule.
- MPAA (Motion Picture Association of America) has a monopoly over film ratings in the U.S.
- Joint Commission is an organization that accredits more than 20,000 health care organizations and programs in the United States. The Commission has a monopoly over determining whether a U.S. hospital can participate in the publicly funded Medicare and Medicaid healthcare programs.
- Monsanto has been sued by competitors for anti-trust and monopolistic practices. They have between 70% and 100% of the commercial GMO seed market in a small number of crops.
- AAFES has a monopoly on retail sales at overseas U.S. military installations.
- The Registered Dietitian union seeks monopoly over nutrition services through state-level licensing schemes.
- State stores in certain United States states, e.g. for liquor.
- The State retail alcohol monopolies of Norway (Vinmonopolet), Sweden (Systembolaget), Finland (Alko), Iceland (Vínbúð), Ontario (LCBO), Quebéc (SAQ), British Columbia (Liquor Distribution Branch), among others.
- Google is widely considered a monopoly for search engines in Europe and North America, where “to google” has even become a word used in everyday language.

Countering Monopolies

According to professor Milton Friedman, laws against monopolies cause more harm than good, but unnecessary monopolies should be countered by removing tariffs and other regulation that upholds monopolies.

A monopoly can seldom be established within a country without overt and covert government assistance in the form of a tariff or some other device. It is close to impossible to do so on a world scale. The De Beers diamond monopoly is the only one we know of that appears to have succeeded (and even De Beers are protected by various laws against so called "illicit" diamond trade). – In a world of free trade, international cartels would disappear even more quickly.

—*Milton Friedman, Free to Choose, p. 53–54*

However, professor Steve H. Hanke believes that although private monopolies are more efficient than public ones, often by a factor of two, sometimes private natural monopolies, such as local water distribution, should be regulated (not prohibited) by, e.g., price auctions.

Thomas DiLorenzo asserts, however, that during the early days of utility companies where there was little regulation, there were no natural monopolies and there was competition. Only when companies realized that they could gain power through government did monopolies begin to form.

Oligopoly

An oligopoly (meaning "few", and *(polein)*, meaning "to sell") is a market form in which a market or industry is dominated by a small number of sellers (oligopolists). Oligopolies can result from various forms of collusion which reduce competition and lead to higher prices for consumers. Oligopoly has its own market structure.

With few sellers, each oligopolist is likely to be aware of the actions of the others. According to game theory, the decisions of one firm therefore influence and are influenced by decisions of other firms. Strategic planning by oligopolists needs to take into account the likely responses of the other market participants.

Description

Oligopoly is a common market form where a number of firms are in competition. As a quantitative description of oligopoly, the four-firm concentration ratio is often utilized. This measure expresses the market share of the four largest firms in an industry as a percentage. For example, as of fourth quarter 2008, Verizon, AT&T, Sprint, and T-Mobile together control 97% of the US cellular phone market.

Oligopolistic competition can give rise to a wide range of different outcomes. In some situations, the firms may employ restrictive trade practices (collusion, market sharing etc.) to raise prices and restrict production in much the same way as a monopoly. Where there is a formal agreement for such collusion, this is known as a cartel. A primary example of such a cartel is OPEC which has a profound influence on the international price of oil.

Firms often collude in an attempt to stabilize unstable markets, so as to reduce the risks inherent in these markets for investment and product development. There are legal restrictions on such collusion in most countries. There does not have to be a formal agreement for collusion to take place (although for the act to be illegal there must be actual communication between companies)–for example, in some industries there may be an acknowledged market leader which informally sets prices to which other producers respond, known as price leadership.

In other situations, competition between sellers in an oligopoly can be fierce, with relatively low prices and high production. This could lead to an efficient outcome approaching perfect competition. The competition in an oligopoly can be greater when there are more firms in an industry than if, for example, the firms were only regionally based and did not compete directly with each other.

Thus the welfare analysis of oligopolies is sensitive to the parameter values used to define the market's structure. In particular, the level of dead weight loss is hard to measure. The study of product differentiation indicates that oligopolies might also create excessive levels of differentiation in order to stifle competition.

Oligopoly theory makes heavy use of game theory to model the behavior of oligopolies:

- Stackelberg's duopoly. In this model, the firms move sequentially.
- Cournot's duopoly. In this model, the firms simultaneously choose quantities.
- Bertrand's oligopoly. In this model, the firms simultaneously choose prices.

Characteristics

Profit maximization conditions

An oligopoly maximizes profits.

Ability to set price

Oligopolies are price setters rather than price takers.

Entry and exit

Barriers to entry are high. The most important barriers are government licenses, economies of scale, patents, access to expensive and complex technology, and strategic actions by incumbent firms designed to discourage or destroy nascent firms. Additional sources of barriers to entry often result from government regulation favoring existing firms making it difficult for new firms to enter the market.

Number of firms

"Few" – a "handful" of sellers. There are so few firms that the actions of one firm can influence the actions of the other firms.

Long run profits

Oligopolies can retain long run abnormal profits. High barriers of entry prevent sideline firms from entering market to capture excess profits.

Product differentiation

Product may be homogeneous (steel) or differentiated (automobiles).

Perfect knowledge

Assumptions about perfect knowledge vary but the knowledge of various economic factors can be generally described as selective. Oligopolies have perfect knowledge of their own cost and demand functions but their inter-firm information may be incomplete. Buyers have only imperfect knowledge as to price, cost and product quality.

Interdependence

The distinctive feature of an oligopoly is interdependence. Oligopolies are typically composed of a few large firms. Each firm is so large that its actions affect market conditions. Therefore, the competing firms will be aware of a firm's market actions and will respond appropriately. This means that in contemplating a market action, a firm must take into consideration the possible reactions of all competing firms and the firm's countermoves. It is very much like a game of chess, in which a player must anticipate a whole sequence of moves and countermoves in order to determine how to achieve his or her objectives; this is known as game theory. For example, an oligopoly considering a price reduction may wish to estimate the likelihood that competing firms would also lower their prices and possibly trigger a ruinous price war. Or if the firm is considering a price increase, it may want to know whether other firms will also increase prices or hold existing prices constant. This anticipation leads to price rigidity as firms will be only be willing to adjust their prices and quantity of output in accordance with a "price leader" in the market. This high degree of interdependence and need to be aware of what other firms are doing or might do is to be contrasted with lack of interdependence in other market structures. In a perfectly competitive (PC) market there is zero interdependence because no firm is large enough to affect market price. All firms in a *PC* market are price takers, as current market selling price can be followed predictably to maximize short-term profits. In a monopoly, there are no competitors to be concerned about. In a monopolistically-competitive market, each firm's effects on market conditions is so negligible as to be safely ignored by competitors.

Non-Price Competition

Oligopolies tend to compete on terms other than price. Loyalty schemes, advertisement, and product differentiation are all examples of non-price competition.

Oligopolies in Countries with Competition Laws

Oligopolies become "mature" when they realise they can profit maximise through joint profit maximising. As a result of operating in countries with enforced competition laws, the Oligopolists will operate under tacit collusion, being collusion through an understanding that if all the competitors in the market raise their prices, then collectively all the competitors can achieve economic profits close to a monopolist, with out evidence of breaching government market regulations. Hence, the kinked demand curve for a joint profit maximising Oligopoly industry can model the behaviours of oligopolists pricing decisions other than that of the price leader (the price leader being the firm that all other firms follow in terms of pricing decisions). This is because if a firm unilaterally raises the prices of their good/service, and other competitors do not follow then, the firm that raised their price will then lose a significant market as they face the elastic upper segment of the demand curve. As the joint profit maximising achieves greater economic profits for all the firms, there is an incentive for an individual firm to "cheat" by expanding output to gain greater market share and profit. In Oligopolist cheating, and the incumbent firm discovering this breach in collusion, the other firms in the market will retaliate by matching or dropping prices lower than the original drop. Hence, the market share that the firm that dropped the price gained, will have that gain minimised or eliminated. This is why on the kinked demand curve model the lower segment of the demand curve is inelastic. As a result, price rigidity prevails in such markets.

Modeling

There is no single model describing the operation of an oligopolistic market. The variety and complexity of the models exist because you can have two to 10 firms competing on the basis of price, quantity, technological innovations, marketing, and reputation. Fortunately, there are a series of simplified models that attempt to describe market behavior by considering certain circumstances. Some of the better-known models are the dominant firm model, the Cournot–Nash model, the Bertrand model and the kinked demand model.

Cournot–Nash Model

The Cournot–Nash model is the simplest oligopoly model. The model assumes that there are two "equally positioned firms"; the firms compete on the basis of quantity rather than price and each firm makes an "output decision assuming that the other firm's behavior is fixed." The market demand curve is assumed to be linear and marginal costs are constant. To find the Cournot–Nash equilibrium one determines how each firm reacts to a change in the output of the other firm. The path to equilibrium is a series of actions and reactions. The pattern continues until a point is reached where neither firm desires "to change what it is doing, given how it believes the other firm will react to any change." The equilibrium is the intersection of the two firm's reaction functions. The reaction function shows how one firm reacts to the quantity choice of the other firm. For example, assume that the firm 1's demand function is $P = (M - Q_2) - Q_1$ where Q_2 is the quantity produced by the other firm and Q_1 is the amount produced by firm 1, and M=60 is the market. Assume that marginal cost is C_M=12. Firm 1 wants to know its maximizing quantity and price. Firm 1 begins the process by following the profit maximization rule of equating marginal revenue to marginal costs. Firm 1's total revenue function is $R_M = \frac{\partial R_T}{\partial Q_1} = M - Q_2 - 2Q_1$

$$R_M = C_M$$

$$M - Q_2 - 2Q_1 = C_M$$

$$2Q_1 = (M - C_M) - Q_2$$

$$Q_1 = (M - C_M)/2 - Q_2/2 = 24 - 0.5\,Q_2 \text{ [1.1]}$$

$$Q_2 = 2(M - C_M) - 2Q_1 = 96 - 2\,Q_1 \text{ [1.2]}$$

Equation 1.1 is the reaction function for firm 1. Equation 1.2 is the reaction function for firm 2.

To determine the Cournot–Nash equilibrium you can solve the equations simultaneously. The equilibrium quantities can also be determined graphically. The equilibrium solution would be at the intersection of the two reaction functions. Note that if you graph the functions the axes represent quantities. The reaction functions are not necessarily symmetric. The firms may face differing cost functions in which case the reaction functions would not be identical nor would the equilibrium quantities.

Bertrand Model

The Bertrand model is essentially the Cournot–Nash model except the strategic variable is price rather than quantity.

The model assumptions are:

- There are two firms in the market
- They produce a homogeneous product
- They produce at a constant marginal cost
- Firms choose prices P_A and P_B simultaneously
- Firms outputs are perfect substitutes
- Sales are split evenly if $P_A = P_B$

The only Nash equilibrium is $P_A = P_B = MC$.

Neither firm has any reason to change strategy. If the firm raises prices it will lose all its customers. If the firm lowers price $P < MC$ then it will be losing money on every unit sold.

The Bertrand equilibrium is the same as the competitive result. Each firm will produce where P = marginal costs and there will be zero profits. A generalization of the Bertrand model is the Bertrand–Edgeworth model that allows for capacity constraints and more general cost functions.

Oligopolistic Market Kinked Demand Curve Model

According to this model, each firm faces a demand curve kinked at the existing price. The conjectural assumptions of the model are; if the firm raises its price above the current existing price, competitors will not follow and the acting firm will lose market share and second if a firm lowers prices below the existing price then their competitors will follow to retain their market share and the firm's output will increase only marginally.

If the assumptions hold then:

- The firm's marginal revenue curve is discontinuous (or rather, not differentiable), and has a gap at the kink
- For prices above the prevailing price the curve is relatively elastic
- For prices below the point the curve is relatively inelastic

The gap in the marginal revenue curve means that marginal costs can fluctuate without changing equilibrium price and quantity. Thus prices tend to be rigid.

Examples

In industrialized economies, barriers to entry have resulted in oligopolies forming in many sectors, with unprecedented levels of competition fueled by increasing globalization. Market shares in an oligopoly are typically determined by product development and advertising. For example, there are now only a small number of manufacturers of civil passenger aircraft, though Brazil (Embraer) and Canada (Bombardier) have participated in the small passenger aircraft market sector. Oligopolies have also arisen in heavily-regulated markets such as wireless communications: in some areas only two or three providers are licensed to operate.

Australia

- Most media outlets are owned either by News Corporation, Time Warner, or by Fairfax Media
- Grocery retailing is dominated by Coles Group and Woolworths.
- Banking is dominated by ANZ, Westpac, NAB, and Commonwealth Bank. To an extent this oligopoly is enshrined in law in what is known as the "Four pillars policy", in order to ensure the stability of Australia's banking system.
- Fixed line telecommunications products in Australia are primarily delivered by Telstra, Optus or increasingly NBN Co. Other brands are virtual network operators (VNO). In the mobile market there are three main operators, Telstra, Optus and Vodafone Hutchison Australia. With other mobile virtual network operators (MVNO) selling access to those three networks.

Canada

- Five companies dominate the banking industry: Royal Bank of Canada, Toronto Dominion Bank, Bank of Nova Scotia, Bank of Montreal, and Canadian Imperial Bank of Commerce
- As of 2008 Rogers Wireless, Bell Mobility and Telus Mobility control a combined 94% of Canada's wireless telecommunications market
- Rogers Communications, Bell Canada, Telus, and Shaw Communications dominate the internet service provider market:
- Husky Energy, Imperial Oil, Nexen, Shell Canada, Suncor Energy, Syncrude, and Repsol Oil & Gas Canada dominate the oil and gas sector
- Torstar and Postmedia Network dominate the newspaper industry
- Bell Media, Rogers Media, and Corus Entertainment dominate English-language television broadcasting
- Bell Media Radio, Newcap Radio, Rogers Media, and Corus Entertainment dominate the English-language radio industry
- Loblaw Companies, Metro Inc., and Sobeys control the majority of the supermarket industry

India

- The petroleum and gas industry is dominated by Indian Oil, Bharat Petroleum, Hindustan Petroleum, Reliance Petroleum, and Tata Power.
- Most of the telecommunication in India is dominated by Airtel, Vodafone India, Idea Cellular, Reliance Communications, as well as Tata Teleservices and Tata Sky.

European Union

- The VHF Data Link market as air-ground part of aeronautical communications is controlled by ARINC and SITA, commonly known as the organisations providing communication services for the exchange of data between air-ground applications in the Commission Regulation (EC) No 29/2009.

United Kingdom

- Five banks (Barclays, Halifax, HSBC, Lloyds TSB and Natwest) dominate the UK banking sector, they were accused of being an oligopoly by the relative newcomer Virgin bank.
- Four companies (Tesco, Sainsbury's, Asda and Morrisons) share 74.4% of the grocery market.
- The detergent market is dominated by two players, Unilever and Procter & Gamble.
- Six utilities (EDF Energy, Centrica, RWE npower, E.on, Scottish Power and Scottish and Southern Energy) share 95% of the retail electricity market.

United States

- Many media industries today are essentially oligopolies.
    - Six movie studios receive almost 87% of American film revenues.
    - The television and high speed internet industry is mostly an oligopoly of seven companies: The Walt Disney Company, CBS Corporation, Viacom, Comcast, Hearst Corporation, Time Warner, and News Corporation.
    - Four wireless providers (AT&T Mobility, Verizon Wireless, T-Mobile, Sprint Nextel) control 89% of the cellular telephone service market. This is not to be confused with cellular telephone manufacturing, an integral portion of the cellular telephone market as a whole.

- Healthcare insurance in the United States consists of very few insurance companies controlling major market share in most states. For example, California's insured population of 20 million is the most competitive in the nation and 44% of that market is dominated by two insurance companies, Anthem and Kaiser Permanente.
- In March 2012, the United States Department of Justice announced that it would sue six major publishers for price fixing in the sale of electronic books. The accused publishers are Apple, Simon & Schuster Inc, Hachette Book Group, Penguin Group, Macmillan, and HarperCollins Publishers.
- Mergers among airlines have left the industry in the United States dominated by four main entities – Delta Air Lines, United Airlines, Southwest Airlines and American Airlines – which purposely do not compete on some air travel routes.

Worldwide

- The accountancy market is dominated by PriceWaterhouseCoopers, KPMG, Deloitte Touche Tohmatsu, and Ernst & Young (commonly known as the Big Four)
- Three leading food processing companies, Kraft Foods, PepsiCo and Nestlé, together achieve a large proportion of global processed food sales. These three companies are often used as an example of "Rule of three", which states that markets often become an oligopoly of three large firms.
- Boeing and Airbus have a duopoly over the airliner market.
- General Electric, Pratt and Whitney and Rolls-Royce plc own more than 50% of the marketshare in the airliner engine market.
- Three credit rating agencies (Standard & Poor's, Moody's, and Fitch Group) dominate their market and extend their crucial importance into the financial sector.
- Nestlé, The Hershey Company and Mars, Incorporated together make most of the confectionery made worldwide.
- Intel and AMD are the only two major players in desktop CPU market worldwide.
- Microsoft, Sony, Valve, and Nintendo dominate the video game platform market.
- Nvidia and AMD together make most of the chips for discrete graphics.
- Aircraft tires is dominated by a four firm oligopoly that controls 85% of market share.

- Universal, Sony, and Warner music have a triopoly in both publishing and recorded music

Demand Curve

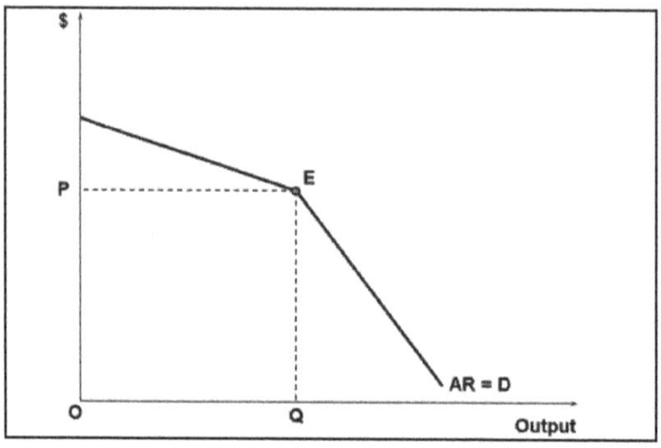

Above the kink, demand is relatively elastic because all other firms' prices remain unchanged. Below the kink, demand is relatively inelastic because all other firms will introduce a similar price cut, eventually leading to a price war. Therefore, the best option for the oligopolist is to produce at point **E** which is the equilibrium point and the kink point. This is a theoretical model proposed in 1947, which has failed to receive conclusive evidence for support.

In an oligopoly, firms operate under imperfect competition. With the fierce price competitiveness created by this sticky-upward demand curve, firms use non-price competition in order to accrue greater revenue and market share.

"Kinked" demand curves are similar to traditional demand curves, as they are downward-sloping. They are distinguished by a hypothesized convex bend with a discontinuity at the bend–"kink". Thus the first derivative at that point is undefined and leads to a jump discontinuity in the marginal revenue curve.

Classical economic theory assumes that a profit-maximizing producer with some market power (either due to oligopoly or monopolistic competition) will set marginal costs equal to marginal revenue. This idea can be envisioned graphically by the intersection of an upward-sloping marginal cost curve and a downward-sloping marginal revenue curve (because the more one sells, the lower the price must be, so the less a producer earns per unit). In classical theory, any change in the marginal cost structure (how much it costs to make each additional unit) or the marginal revenue structure (how much people will pay for each additional unit) will be immediately reflected in a new price and/or quantity sold of the item. This result does not occur if a "kink" exists. Because of this jump discontinuity in the marginal revenue curve, marginal costs could change without necessarily changing the price or quantity.

The motivation behind this kink is the idea that in an oligopolistic or monopolistically competitive market, firms will not raise their prices because even a small price increase will lose many customers. This is because competitors will generally ignore price increases, with the hope of gaining a larger market share as a result of now having comparatively lower prices. However, even a large price decrease will gain only a few customers because such an action will begin a price war with other firms. The curve is therefore more price-elastic for price increases and less so for price decreases. Theory predicts that firms will enter the industry in the long run.

Duopoly

A duopoly is a form of oligopoly where only two sellers exist in one market. In practice, the term is also used where two firms have dominant control over a market. In the field of industrial organization, it is the most commonly studied form of oligopoly due to its simplicity.

Duopoly Models in Economics and Game Theory

There are two principal duopoly models, Cournot duopoly and Bertrand duopoly:

- The Cournot model, which shows that two firms assume each other's output and treat this as a fixed amount, and produce in their own firm according to this.
- The Bertrand model, in which, in a game of two firms, each one of them will assume that the other will not change prices in response to its price cuts. When both firms use this logic, they will reach a Nash equilibrium.

Politics

Modern American politics, in particular the electoral college system has been described as duopolistic since the Republican and Democratic parties have dominated and framed policy debate as well as the public discourse on matters of national concern for about a century and a half. Third Parties have encountered various blocks in getting onto ballots at different levels of government as well as other electoral obstacles, such as denial of access to general election debates.

Examples in Business

A commonly cited example of a duopoly is that involving Visa and Mastercard, who between them control a large proportion of the electronic payment processing market. In 2000 they were the defendants in a U.S. Department of Justice antitrust lawsuit. An appeal was upheld in 2004.

Examples where two companies control a large proportion of a market are:

- Airbus and Boeing in the market for large commercial airplanes.
- Televisa and Azteca in the Mexican Television market.
- Radio Televisyen Malaysia and Media Prima in the Malaysian Television market.
- Air Canada and WestJet in the Canadian Aviation market.
- Woolworths and Coles in the Australian supermarket market (share 79% of the supermarket market).
- Mitre 10 MEGA and Bunnings Warehouse in the Australian and New Zealand retail/trade timber and hardware market (Share 85% of the timber and hardware market).
- Intel and AMD in X86 CPU market and Nvidia and AMD in consumer and professional PC GPU market.
- The BNSF Railway and Union Pacific Railroad have a duopoly on freight rail traffic in the Western United States.
- Norfolk Southern Railway and CSX Transportation operate a duopoly on freight rail traffic in the Eastern United States.
- Apple and Microsoft in the electronics industry.
- Apple's iOS and Google's Android in the mobile operating system market.
- Globe Telecom and Smart Communications in the Philippine Telecomunnications industry.
- First American Financial Corporation and Fidelity National Financial in the American title insurance sector.
- DC Comics and Marvel Comics in the superhero genre.
- Varian Medical Systems and Elekta in the radiotherapy device industry.
- Ola Cabs and Uber in the online cab services industry.
- Pepsi and Coca-Cola in carbonated drinks market.
- Visa Electron and MasterCard in electronic payment processing market.

Media

In Finland, the state-owned broadcasting company Yleisradio and the private broadcaster Mainos-TV had a legal duopoly (in the economists' sense of the word) from the 1950s to 1993. No other broadcasters were allowed. Mainos-TV operated by leasing air time from Yleisradio, broadcasting in reserved blocks between Yleisradio's own programming on its two channels. This was a unique phenomenon in the world. Between 1986 and 1992 there was an independent third channel but it was jointly owned by Yle and MTV; only in 1993 did MTV get its own channel.

Safaricom mobile service provider and Airtel in Kenya are perfect examples of Duopoly market in the African telecommunication industry.

Broadcasting

Duopoly is also used in the United States broadcast television and radio industry to refer to a single company owning two outlets in the same city.

This usage is technically incompatible with the normal definition of the word and may lead to confusion, inasmuch as there are generally more than two owners of broadcast television stations in markets with broadcast duopolies. In Canada, this definition is therefore more commonly called a "twinstick".

References

- Morris, Charles R. The Tycoons: How Andrew Carnegie, John D. Rockefeller, Jay Gould, and J.P. Morgan invented the American supereconomy, H. Holt and Co., New York, 2005, pp. 255-258. ISBN 0-8050-7599-2.
- Dickens, Matthew (24 May 2013), TRANSIT RIDERSHIP REPORT: First Quarter 2013 (PDF), American Public Transportation Association, retrieved 03, January 2020
- Milton Friedman. "VIII: Monopoly and the Social Responsibility of Business and Labor". Capitalism and Freedom (paperback) (40th anniversary ed.). The University of Chicago Press. p. 208. ISBN 0-226-26421-1.
- Boselovic, Len (February 25, 2001). "Steel Standing: U.S. Steel celebrates 100 years". PG News - Business & Technology. post-gazette.com - PG Publishing. Retrieved 06, August 2020.
- Levine, David; Boldrin, Michele (2008-09-07). Against intellectual monopoly. Cambridge University Press. p. 312. ISBN 978-0-521-87928-6.
- Kramer-Miller, Ben (June 25, 2013). "Norfolk Southern Corp. Looks Like A Solid Investment". Seeking Alpha. Retrieved 07, August 2020.

5

Global Financial Scenario

The global financial scenario encompasses the legal agreements, institutions, and other formal and informal economic factors which enable the international flows of financial capital. This chapter has been carefully written to provide an easy understanding of the varied facets of global financial scenario such as global financial markets and trade linkages between countries.

Balance of Payments

The Balance of Payments or BoP is a statement or record of international trade and financial transactions made between a country and the rest of the world within a defined period. These records include transactions made by individuals, companies, and the government.

Just as companies/firms are needed to present the Balance Sheet and Cash flow at the end of year, in the same way National Governments need to know their positions with respect to their country's receipts and payments with respect to foreign currency. And this is indicated through the statement named as Balance of Payment. Balance of payment indicates the combined effect of balance of trade along with various other receipts and payments on different accounts from the rest of world countries. Balance of trade (a part of BoP) indicates the difference between value of imports and exports (Goods & Services) of a country.

> The balance of payment is the difference between exports of (goods + services + capital transfers) less the imports of (goods + services + capital transfers).

Structure of Balance of Payment Accounting

- Transactions are recorded in the balance of payments accounts in double-entry book keeping.
- Each international transaction undertaken by country will results in a credit entry and debit entry of equal size.
- As international transactions are recorded in double entry accounting, the BOP accounting must always balance i.e., total amount of debits must be equal to total amount of credits.

- The balancing item Errors and omissions must be added to "balance" the BOP accounts.
- By convention, debit items and credit items are entered with a minus sign and plus sign respectively.
- Transactions in BOP are classified into the following five major categories:
    - Goods and services account.
    - Unilateral transfer account.
    - Long-term capital account.
    - Short-term private capital account.
    - Short-term official capital account.

For each of these given categories, specific types of transactions are shown as debits or credits.

Categories	Debits (–)	Credits (+)
Category-I	1. Import of goods 2. Import of services	1. Export of goods 2. Export of services
Category-II	Unilateral transfers (Gifts) made	Unilateral transfers (gifts) received
Category-III	1. Increase in long-term foreign assets owned by home country private citizens and government. 2. Decrease in long-term home country assets owned by foreign private citizens and government.	1. Decrease in long-term foreign assets owned by home country citizens and government. 2. Increase in long-term home country assets owned by foreign private citizens and governments.
Category-IV	1. Increase in short-term foreign assets owned by home country private citizens. 2. Decrease in short-term home country assets owned by foreign private citizens.	1. Decrease in short-term foreign assets owned by home country private citizens. 2. Increase in short-term home country assets owned by foreign private citizens.
Category-V	1. Increase in short-term foreign assets owned by home country government (official monetary authorities). 2. Decrease in short-terms home country asset owned by foreign government (official monetary authorities)	1. Decrease in short-term foreign assets owned by home country government (official monetary authorities). 2. Increase in short-term home country asset owned by foreign governments, (official monetary authorities).

Types of Balance of Payment Accounts

Balance of Payments Deficit

It means that the country imports more goods, services, and capital than they export. It must borrow from other countries to pay for its imports. This is also known as Unfavourable Balance of Payments.

Imports (Goods, Services & Capital Transfers) > Exports (Goods, Services & Capital Transfers)

Balance of Payments Surplus

It means that the country exports more than it imports. It provides enough capital to pay for all domestic production. The country might even lend outside its borders. This is also known as Favourable Balance of Payments.

Exports (Goods, Services & Capital Transfers) > Imports (Goods, Services & Capital Transfers)

Various Accounts of Balance of Payments

Balance of payment has the following four forms or accounts:

- Current account
- Capital account
- Unilateral transfer accounts
- Official reserve accounts.

Current Accounts

The current account is a country's trade balance plus net income and direct payments. The trade balance is a country's imports and exports of goods and services. The current account also measures international transfers of capital. A current account is in balance when the country's residents have enough to fund all purchases in the country.

Current Account = (Visible + Invisible Exports) – (Visible + Invisible Imports)

Items of Current Account

Exports and Imports of Visible Goods

All visible and material goods which are exported and imported constitute items of current account.

Invisible Items or Non-material Goods or Services

1. Transportation and Travelling Services: Whenever foreign tourist, businessman, students, or others (for availing health, education, and pleasure benefits) use the domestic transports and travelling facilities, then from the view of BOP it can be named as exports.

In the same way, when nationals of the country use the facilities of foreign transports then it is termed as imports. The difference between the values of transport received and used forms the part of current account within the statement of Balance of payments.

2. Services of the Experts: Services of foreign experts are availed by domestic country, in the same way local experts' services will be availed by other countries. The values of services received from abroad are known as imports and value of services rendered by domestic nationals to foreign countries are termed as exports. The difference between the exports and imports of services forms part of balance of payment on current account.

3. Investment Income and Expenses: Rent, interest, profit, and dividend are also invisible items of balance of payments. Receiving income from abroad is termed as receipt in foreign currency. In the same way income earned by the foreigners from the country is known as payments in foreign currency. The difference between the foreign income receipts and foreign expense payment also forms part of balance of payment on current account.

4. Donation and Gifts: The Donation, gifts etc., are non-compensated transactions, in other words they are unilateral transactions. Hence the receipt of the same from abroad by the natives of nation are termed as receipts and given to other countries are termed as payments. The difference between the donation, gifts receipts from abroad and donation, gifts given to other countries also forms part of balance of payments on current account.

5. Services Rendered by Commercial Undertakings: The allied trade and commerce firms such as shipping companies, banks, and insurance companies etc., are involved in providing and receiving services within a country and with rest of the countries of world. The difference between the exports and imports of exchange of services like shipping, banking, insurance, etc., forms part of balance of payments on current account.

6. Government Transactions: Generally, the Government of every country provides the services of embassies, offices of high commissioners and other missions abroad to maintain the harmonious relationship and spends funds to maintain the offices, and relationship. Such expenditure is termed as payments.

In the same way, the particular domestic country, earns the foreign currency from the government of other country for their offices in domestic country and these are known as receipts. The difference between the payments and receipts of such services forms a part of balance of payments on current account.

7. Miscellaneous: The miscellaneous or invisible items such as commission, advertisement, royalties, patent fees, rent, membership fees etc., are provided to abroad and received payments from abroad. On the other hand, the country takes or uses these items and makes payments to rest of world. The difference between the receipts and

payments of these invisible services forms part of balance of payments on current accounts.

Items of Current Account

Payment	Receipt
Imports of Goods	Exports of Goods
Import of Services Services of Foreign Experts Services of Foreign Companies	Export of Services Services of Domestic Experts Services of Domestic Commercial Companies
Income to foreigners from investment made in home country.	Income from foreign investments.
Gifts & Donations to Foreigners	Gifts & Donations from Foreign Countries
Government Expenditure in Foreign Countries	Income from Foreign Government's Expenditure
Payment for domestic use of foreign transportation.	Receipts from transportation services.
Mixed expenditure in foreign countries.	Mixed expenditures by foreigners in home country.
Expenditure by domestic tourists abroad.	Expenditure by foreign tourists in home country.

Capital Account

All types of short-term and long-term international capital transfers, movement of gold and billion metals, receipts and payments of private and government accounts, institutional and private loans, interest, profit, grants etc., form part of capital account. As capital account is concerned with financial transfers, so they have no direct effect on income, output, and employment of the country.

Components of Capital Account

The principal items or components of capital account are as under:

1. Gold Movement: Central bank of every country buys and sells gold from home and to abroad. It means that exports and imports of the gold by the central bank which makes the payments and receipts of amount of gold. The amount of gold bought is reflected under "debit side" and sales of gold are reflected under "credit side".

2. Reserve, Monetary Gold and SDR: Governments' foreign currency assets, gold reserves of Central bank, SDR of the IMF and other similar capital transactions, etc., are included under "credit items" and the payments on these transactions are reflected under "debit items".

3. Movement in Banking Capital: Inflow of banking capital besides central bank is reflected under "credit items" and outflow of banking capital besides central bank is reflected under "debit items".

4. Private Foreign Loan Flow: Private sectors of the country received foreign loans from abroad. These receipts of foreign loans are included under "credit items". The private sectors of the country also pays the foreign loans to abroad country, this repayment of foreign loan is included under "debit items".

5. Official Capital Transactions: Public sectors of the country receive foreign loans from International Monetary Fund. These receipts of loans are included under "credit items" and the public sector also pays the loans to International Monetary Fund which is included under "debit items".

6. Miscellaneous: Besides the above items, central bank receives other kinds of governmental capital. These types of receipts are also included under "credit side" and the central bank makes the payments for these governmental capitals which are included under "debit side".

Items of Capital Account

Payment	Receipt
Capital Payments	Capital Receipts
Outflow of Banking Capital	Inflow of Banking Capital
Reserves & Monetary Gold Payments	Reserves & Monetary Gold Inflows
Repayment of loans by Government	Loans received by the Government.
Repayment of private loans from foreigners	Foreign Private Loans
Purchase of gold in international markets.	International sale of gold.

Unilateral Transfer Account

This account is somewhat like the capital account, except that it involves capital movements and gifts for which there are no return commitments or claims. Thus, a personal remittance to a resident of a foreign country involves no commitment for repayment and is classified as a unilateral transfer. These unilateral transfers may be on private account or governmental accounts in the form of grants.

Official Reserve Transaction Account

This consists of changes in international reserve assets – those used for setting accounts between government central banks. On account of deficit or surplus emerging out in capital account, current account and unilateral transfers with other countries, the intergovernmental settlements needed to be done regularly.

Errors and Omissions

Sometimes the balance of payment does not balance. This imbalance is shown in the BOP as errors and omissions. BOP is compiled using the double entry bookkeeping system consisting assets and liabilities.

Overall balance of payments is calculated as under:

> Balance of Payments = Balance of Current Account + Balance of Capital Account + Unilateral Transfer Account + Errors & Omissions

Importance of Balance of Payments

- First, the balance of payment provides detailed information concerning the demand and supply of a country's currency.
- Second, a country's balance of payments data may signal its potential as a business partner for the rest of the world. If a country is grappling with a major balance of payments difficulty, it may not be able to expand imports from the outside world.

  On the other hand, a country with a significant balance of payments surplus would be more likely to expand imports, offering marketing opportunities for foreign enterprises, and less likely to impose foreign exchange restrictions.
- Third, balance of payments data can be used to evaluate the performance of the country in international economic competition. Suppose a country is experiencing trade deficits year after year. This trade data may then signal that the country's domestic industries lack international competitiveness.

BOP Account of US

Every international transaction results in a credit and a debit. Transactions that cause money to flow into a country are credits, and transactions that cause money to leave a country are debits. For instance, if someone in England buys a South Korean stereo, the purchase is a debit to the British account and a credit to the South Korean account. If a Brazilian company sends an interest payment on a loan to a bank in the United States, the transaction represents a debit to the Brazilian BOP account and a credit to the U.S. BOP account.

The BOP statement divides international transactions into three accounts: The current account, the capital account and the financial account. The current account deals with international trade in goods and services and with earnings on investments. The capital account consists of capital transfers and the acquisition and disposal of non-produced, non-financial assets. The financial account records transfers of financial capital and non-financial capital. The accounts are further divided into sub-accounts.

Current Account

The current account is composed of four sub-accounts:

- Merchandise trade consists of all raw materials and manufactured goods bought, sold or given away. Until mid-1993, this was the figure that was used when the "balance of trade" was reported in the media. Since then, the merchandise trade account has been combined with a second sub-account, services, to determine the total for the balance of trade.

- Services include tourism, transportation, engineering and business services, such as law, management consulting and accounting. Fees from patents and copyrights on new technology, software, books and movies also are recorded in the service category.
- Income receipts include income derived from ownership of assets, such as dividends on holdings of stock and interest on securities.
- Unilateral transfers represent one-way transfers of assets, such as worker remittances from abroad and direct foreign aid. In the case of aid or gifts, a debit is assigned to the capital account of the donor nation.

Capital Account

The capital account has two sub-accounts:

- Capital transfers include debt forgiveness and migrants' transfers (goods and financial assets accompanying migrants as they leave or enter the country). In addition, capital transfers include the transfer of title to fixed assets and the transfer of funds linked to the sale or acquisition of fixed assets, gift and inheritance taxes, death duties, uninsured damage to fixed assets and legacies.
- Acquisition and disposal of non-produced, non-financial assets represent the sales and purchases of non-produced assets, such as the rights to natural resources, and the sales and purchases of intangible assets, such as patents, copyrights, trademarks, franchises and leases.

Financial Account

The financial account is made up of two sub-accounts:

- U.S.-owned assets abroad are divided into official reserve assets, government assets and private assets. These assets include gold, foreign currencies, foreign securities, reserve position in the International Monetary Fund, U.S. credits and other long-term assets, direct foreign investment and U.S. claims reported by U.S. banks.
- Foreign-owned assets in the United States are divided into foreign official assets and other foreign assets in the United States. These assets include U.S. government, agency, and corporate securities; direct investment; U.S. currency; and U.S. liabilities reported by U.S. banks.

Deficit and Surplus

In theory, the current account should balance with the capital plus the financial accounts. The sum of the balance of payments statements should be zero. For example, when the United States buys more goods and services than it sells (a current account deficit), it must finance the difference by borrowing, or by selling more capital assets than it buys (a capital account surplus). A country with a persistent current account deficit is, therefore, effectively exchanging capital assets for goods and services. Large trade deficits mean that the country is borrowing from abroad. In the balance of payments, this appears as an inflow of foreign capital. In reality, the accounts do not exactly offset each other, because of statistical discrepancies, accounting conventions and exchange rate movements that change the recorded value of transactions.

Global Financial Markets

Several barriers prevent the markets for real or financial assets from becoming completely integrated these barriers include tax differentials, tariffs, quotas, labor immobility, cultural differences, financial reporting differences, and significant costs of communicating information across countries. Nevertheless, the barriers can also create unique opportunities for specific geographic markets that will attract foreign creditors and investors. For example, barriers such as tariffs, quotas, and labor immobility can cause a given country's economic conditions to be distinctly different from others. Investors and creditors may want to do business in that country to capitalize on favorable conditions unique to that country. The existence of imperfect markets has precipitated the internationalization of financial markets.

Motives for Investing in Foreign Markets

Investors invest in foreign markets for one or more of the following motives:

- Economic conditions: Investors may expect firms in a particular foreign country to achieve more favorable performance than those in the investor's home country. For example, the loosening of restrictions in Eastern European countries created favorable economic conditions there. Such conditions attracted foreign investors and creditors.

- Exchange rate expectations: Some investors purchase financial securities denominated in a currency that is expected to appreciate against their own. The performance of such an investment is highly dependent on the currency movement over the investment horizon.

- International diversification: Investors may achieve benefits from internationally diversifying their asset portfolio. When an investor's entire portfolio does not depend solely on a single country's economy, cross-border differences in economic conditions can allow for risk-reduction benefits. A stock portfolio representing firms across European countries is less risky than a stock portfolio representing firms in any single European country. Furthermore, access to foreign markets allows investors to spread their funds across a more diverse group of industries than may be available domestically. This is especially true for investors residing in countries where firms are concentrated in a relatively small number of industries.

Motives for Providing Credit in Foreign Markets

Creditors (including individual investors who purchase debt securities) have one or more of the following motives for providing credit in foreign markets:

- High foreign interest rates: Some countries experience a shortage of loanable funds, which can cause market interest rates to be relatively high, even after considering default risk. Foreign creditors may attempt to capitalize on the higher rates, thereby providing capital to overseas markets. Yet, relatively high interest rates are often perceived to reflect relatively high inflationary expectations in that country. To the extent that inflation can cause depreciation of the local currency against others, high interest rates in the country may be somewhat offset by a weakening of the local currency over the time period of concern. The relation between a country's expected inflation and its local currency movements is not precise, however, because several other factors can influence currency movements as well. Thus, some creditors may believe that the interest rate advantage in a particular country will not be offset by a local currency depreciation over the period of concern.
- Exchange rate expectations: Creditors may consider supplying capital to countries whose currencies are expected to appreciate against their own. Whether the form of the transaction is a bond or a loan, the creditor benefits when the currency of denomination appreciates against the creditor's home currency.
- International diversification: Creditors can benefit from international diversification, which may reduce the probability of simultaneous bankruptcy across borrowers. The effectiveness of such a strategy depends on the correlation between the economic conditions of countries. If the countries of concern tend to experience somewhat similar business cycles, diversification across countries will be less effective.

Motives for Borrowing in Foreign Markets

Borrowers may have one or more of the following motives for borrowing in foreign markets:

- Low interest rates: Some countries have a large supply of funds available compared to the demand for funds, which can cause relatively low interest rates. Borrowers may attempt to borrow funds from creditors in these countries because the interest rate charged is lower. A country with relatively low interest rates is often expected to have a relatively low rate of inflation, which can place upward pressure on the foreign currency's value and offset any advantage of lower interest rates. The relation between expected inflation differentials and currency movements is not precise, however, so some borrowers will choose to borrow from a market where nominal interest rates are low, since they do not expect an adverse currency movement to fully offset this advantage.

- Exchange rate expectations: When a foreign subsidiary of a U.S.-based MNC remits funds to its U.S. parent, the funds must be converted to dollars and are subject to exchange rate risk. The MNC will be adversely affected if the foreign currency depreciates at that time. If the MNC expects that the foreign currency may depreciate against the dollar, it can reduce the exchange rate risk by having the subsidiary borrow funds locally to support its business. The subsidiary will remit less funds to the parent if it must pay interest on local debt before remitting the funds. Thus, the amount of funds converted to dollars will be smaller, resulting in less exposure to exchange rate risk.

If the U.S. parent needs to borrow funds for its own purposes, it may pursue a more aggressive strategy and borrow a foreign currency that is expected to depreciate. In this case, the parent would borrow that currency and convert it to dollars for use. The value of the foreign currency when converted to dollars would exceed the value when the MNC repurchases the currency to repay the loan. The favorable currency effect can offset part or all of the interest owed on the funds borrowed. Such a strategy may be especially desirable if the foreign currency has a low interest rate compared to the U.S. interest rate.

Foreign Exchange Market

The foreign exchange market allows currencies to be exchanged in order to facilitate international trade or financial transactions. MNCs rely on the foreign exchange market to exchange their home currency for a foreign currency that they need to purchase imports or use for direct foreign investment. Alternatively, they may need the foreign exchange market to exchange a foreign currency that they receive into their home currency. The system for establishing exchange rates has changed over time.

History of Foreign Exchange

The system used for exchanging foreign currencies has evolved from the gold standard, to an agreement on fixed exchange rates, to a floating rate system.

1. Gold Standard: From 1876 to 1913, exchange rates were dictated by the gold standard. Each currency was convertible into gold at a specified rate. Thus, the exchange rate between two currencies was determined by their relative convertibility rates per ounce of gold. Each country used gold to back its currency.

When World War I began in 1914, the gold standard was suspended. Some countries reverted to the gold standard in the 1920s but abandoned it as a result of a banking panic in the United States and Europe during the Great Depression. In the 1930s, some countries attempted to peg their currency to the dollar or the British pound, but there were frequent revisions. As a result of the instability in the foreign exchange market and the severe restrictions on international transactions during this period, the volume of international trade declined.

2. Agreements on Fixed Exchange Rates: In 1944, an international agreement (known as the Bretton Woods Agreement) called for fixed exchange rates between currencies. This agreement lasted until 1971. During this period, governments would intervene to prevent exchange rates from moving more than 1 percent above or below their initially established levels.

By 1971, the U.S. dollar appeared to be overvalued; the foreign demand for U.S. dollars was substantially less than the supply of dollars for sale (to be exchanged for other currencies). Representatives from the major nations met to discuss this dilemma. As a result of this conference, which became known as the Smithsonian Agreement, the U.S. dollar was devalued relative to the other major currencies. The degree to which the dollar was devalued varied with each foreign currency. Not only was the dollar's value reset, but exchange rates were also allowed to fluctuate by 2 percent in either direction from the newly set rates. This was the first step in letting market forces (supply and demand) determine the appropriate price of a currency. Although boundaries still existed for exchange rates, they were widened, allowing the currency values to move more freely toward their appropriate levels.

3. Floating Exchange Rate System: Even after the Smithsonian Agreement, governments still had difficulty maintaining exchange rates within the stated boundaries. By March 1973, the more widely traded currencies were allowed to fluctuate in accordance with market forces, and the official boundaries were eliminated.

Foreign Exchange Transactions

The "foreign exchange market" should not be thought of as a specific building or location where traders exchange currencies. Companies normally exchange one currency for another through a commercial bank over a telecommunications network.

1. Spot Market: The most common type of foreign exchange transaction is for immediate exchange at the so-called spot rate. The market where these transactions occur is known as the spot market. The average daily foreign exchange trading by banks around the world now exceeds $1.5 trillion. The average daily foreign exchange trading in the United States alone exceeds $200 billion.

The U.S. dollar is not part of every transaction. Foreign currencies can be traded for each other. For example, a Japanese firm may need British pounds to pay for imports from the United Kingdom. Much of the foreign exchange trading is conducted by banks in London, New York, and Tokyo, the three largest foreign exchange trading centers.

Many foreign transactions do not require an exchange of currencies but allow a given currency to cross country borders. For example, the U.S. dollar is commonly accepted as a medium of exchange by merchants in many countries, especially in countries such as Bolivia, Brazil, China, Cuba, Indonesia, Russia, and Vietnam where the home currency is either weak or subject to foreign exchange restrictions. Many merchants accept U.S. dollars because they can use them to purchase goods from other countries. The U.S. dollar is the official currency of Liberia and Panama.

2. Spot Market Structure: Hundreds of banks facilitate foreign exchange transactions, but the top 20 handle about 50 percent of the transactions. Deutsche Bank (Germany), Citibank (subsidiary of Citigroup, U.S.), and J.P. Morgan Chase are the largest traders of foreign exchange. Some banks and other financial institutions have formed alliances (one example is FX Alliance LLC) to offer currency transactions over the Internet.

At any given point in time, the exchange rate between two currencies should be similar across the various banks that provide foreign exchange services. If there is a large discrepancy, customers or other banks will purchase large amounts of a currency from whatever bank quotes a relatively low price and immediately sell it to whatever bank quotes a relatively high price. Such actions cause adjustments in the exchange rate quotations that eliminate any discrepancy.

If a bank begins to experience a shortage in a particular foreign currency, it can purchase that currency from other banks. This trading between banks occurs in what is often referred to as the interbank market. Within this market, banks can obtain quotes, or they can contact brokers who sometimes act as intermediaries, matching one bank desiring to sell a given currency with another bank desiring to buy that currency. About 10 foreign exchange brokerage firms handle much of the interbank transaction volume.

Although foreign exchange trading is conducted only during normal business hours in a given location, these hours vary among locations due to different time zones. Thus, at any given time on a weekday, somewhere around the world a bank is open and ready to accommodate foreign exchange requests.

When the foreign exchange market opens in the United States each morning, the opening exchange rate quotations are based on the prevailing rates quoted by banks in London and other locations where the foreign exchange markets have opened earlier. Suppose the quoted spot rate of the British pound was $1.80 at the previous close of the U.S. foreign exchange market, but by the time the market opens the following day, the opening spot rate is $1.76. News occurring in the morning before the U.S. market opened could have changed the supply and demand conditions for British pounds in the London foreign exchange market, reducing the quoted price for the pound.

With the newest electronic devices, foreign currency trades are negotiated on computer terminals, and a push of a button confirms the trade. Traders now use electronic trading boards that allow them to instantly register transactions and check their bank's positions in various currencies. Also, several U.S. banks have established night trading desks. The largest banks initiated night trading to capitalize on foreign exchange movements at night and to accommodate corporate requests for currency trades. Even some medium-sized banks have begun to use night trading to accommodate corporate clients.

3. Forward Transactions: In addition to the spot market, a forward market for currencies enables an MNC to lock in the exchange rate (called a forward rate) at which it will buy or sell a currency. A forward contract specifies the amount of a particular currency that will be purchased or sold by the MNC at a specified future point in time and at a specified exchange rate. Commercial banks accommodate the MNCs that desire forward contracts. MNCs commonly use the forward market to hedge future payments that they expect to make or receive in a foreign currency. In this way, they do not have to worry about fluctuations in the spot rate until the time of their future payments. Attributes of Banks That Provide Foreign Exchange: The following characteristics of banks are important to customers in need of foreign exchange:

- Competitiveness of quote. A savings of 1¢ per unit on an order of one million units of currency is worth $10,000.
- Special relationship with the bank. The bank may offer cash management services or be willing to make a special effort to obtain even hard-to-find foreign currencies for the corporation.
- Speed of execution. Banks may vary in the efficiency with which they handle an order. A corporation needing the currency will prefer a bank that conducts the transaction promptly and handles any paperwork properly.
- Advice about current market conditions. Some banks may provide assessments of foreign economies and relevant activities in the international financial environment that relate to corporate customers.
- Forecasting advice. Some banks may provide forecasts of the future state of foreign economies, the future value of exchange rates, etc.

This list suggests that a corporation needing a foreign currency should not automatically choose a bank that will sell that currency at the lowest price. Most corporations that often need foreign currencies develop a close relationship with at least one major bank in case they ever need favors from a bank.

4. Bid/Ask Spread of Banks: Commercial banks charge fees for conducting foreign exchange transactions. At any given point in time, a bank's bid (buy) quote for a foreign currency will be less than it's ask (sell) quote. The bid/ask spread represents the

differential between the bid and ask quotes, and is intended to cover the costs involved in accommodating requests to exchange currencies. The bid/ask spread is normally expressed as a percentage of the ask quote.

5. Comparison of Bid/Ask Spread among Currencies. The differential between a bid quote and an ask quote will look much smaller for currencies that have a smaller value. This differential can be standardized by measuring it as a percentage of the currency's spot rate. A common way to compute the bid/ask spread in percentage terms follows:

$$\text{Bid / ask spread} = \frac{\text{Ask rate} - \text{Bid rate}}{\text{Ask rate}}$$

Using this formula, the bid/ask spreads are computed. Notice that these numbers coincide with those derived earlier. Such spreads are common for so-called retail transactions serving consumers. For larger so-called wholesale transactions between banks or for large corporations, the spread will be much smaller. The spread is normally larger for currencies that are less frequently traded. Commercial banks are normally exposed to more exchange rate risk when maintaining these currencies.

Currency	Bid Rate	Ask Rate	Ask Rate – Bid Rate	Bid/Ask Percentage Spread
British pound	\$1.52	\$1.60	$\frac{\$1.60-\$1.52}{\$1.60}$	= .05 or 5%
Japanese yen	\$ .0070	\$ .0074	$\frac{\$.0074-\$.007}{\$.0074}$	= .054 or 5.4 %

The bid/ask spread as defined here represents the discount in the bid rate as a percentage of the ask rate. An alternative bid/ask spread uses the bid rate as the denominator instead of the ask rate and measures the percentage mark-up of the ask rate above the bid rate. The spread is slightly higher when using this formula because the bid rate used in the denominator is always less than the ask rate.

International Stock Exchange

New York Stock Exchange

The New York Stock Exchange (NYSE) is additionally referred to as 'The Big Board'. The NYSE is the first on the list of the largest stock exchanges in the world and is a highly esteemed stock exchange in the USA. The NYSE has remained the largest stock exchange in the world by market capitalisation ever since the end of World War. It is located at 11, Wall Street, Lower Manhattan, New York City. It consists of 2,400 listed companies which span sectors such as finance, healthcare, consumer goods and energy. It has a market capitalization of US\$ 30.1 trillion. The blue-chip companies which are listed under NYSE are Berkshire Hathaway Inc, Coca-Cola, Walt Disney Company, Mc Donald's Corporation, etc.

- Date of establishment: May 17, 1792.
- Valuation: $19.3 Trillion.

NASDAQ

Second on the list of the largest stock exchange in the world is NASDAQ, an abbreviation of National Association of Securities Dealers Automated Quotations. Nasdaq, an American stock exchange is headquartered at 151 W, 42nd Street, New York City.

Nasdaq never operated on a usual open outcry system, instead, it has always used a computer and telephone-based system of trading, which has made the NASDAQ the world's first electronically traded stock market. It has a combined market capitalization of $10.8 trillion and is ranked second in the list of largest stock exchanges. It consists of more than 3,000 stocks listed under it. The enlistment of the world's humongous tech giants such as Apple, Microsoft, Google, Facebook, Amazon, Tesla, and Intel makes NASDAQ 'The Mecca of Technology Companies'.

- Date of establishment: February 4, 1971.
- Valuation: $13.8 Trillion.

Tokyo Stock Exchange

The Tokyo Stock Exchange (TSE) which is also known as TYO and Tōshō is located in Tokyo, Japan. It is listed as the third-largest stock exchange in the world. TSE has around 3,575 listed companies which has taken its market capitalization to a whooping US$ 5.67 trillion. The TSE's benchmark index is Nikkei 225 and it is home to Japanese giants with international exposure, including Toyota, Suzuki, Honda, and Mitsubishi and Sony.

- Date of establishment: January 1, 2003.
- Valuation: $5.7 Trillion.

Shanghai Stock Exchange

The Shanghai Stock Exchange (SSE) is a Chinese stock exchange situated in the city of Shanghai, China. It is one of the three stock exchanges plying autonomously in the People's Republic of China. Traders can track the performance of stocks listed on the Shanghai stock market using the SSE Composite index, also referred to as the Shanghai Composite. This includes the largest stocks on the Shanghai stock exchange, like PetroChina, the industrial and commercial bank of China and therefore the Agricultural Bank of China.

Currently, Shanghai SSE is the world's fourth-largest stock exchange with a combined market capitalization of $ 5.01 trillion. It is a non-profit organization with around 1,000 listed companies under it. Stocks listed at the Shanghai stock market have 'A' shares that trade in local currency and 'B' shares that are priced in the US dollar for foreign investors.

- Date of establishment: November 26, 1990.
- Valuation: $4.9 Trillion.

Hong Kong Stock Exchange

The Hong Kong Stock Exchange (SEHK) is located in Hong Kong and is the world's fifth-largest and Asia's third-largest stock exchange on the basis of market capitalization. It is one of the three stock exchanges in China. SEHK consists of 2,315 listed companies with a wholesome market capitalization of HK$29.9 trillion. It is reported as the fastest-growing stock exchange in Asia.

Its origin can be traced back to the mid-1800s but the stock market was formally set up in 1891 when the Association of Stockbrokers in Hong Kong was established. It was renamed The Hong Kong Stock Exchange in 1914. Some of the eminent companies listed under the Hong Kong Stock Exchange are China Mobile, HSBC Holdings & Petro China.

- Date of establishment: February 3, 1891.
- Valuation: $4.4 Trillion.

EURONEXT

EURONEXT stands for European New Exchange Technology. With it's registered office in Amsterdam and corporate address at La Défense in Greater Paris, EURONEXT was established in 2000 to represent Europe's economy which is also the reason why it operates in euros. It is the sixth-largest stock exchange in the world with a market capitalization worth €4.1 trillion.

Over the years, it has amalgamated with multiple exchanges, most particularly the New York Stock Exchange. It steers financial markets in Amsterdam, London, Brussels, Lisbon, Oslo, Dublin, and Paris. It has around 1,500 listed companies. EURONEXT provided the segments which are equities, warrants, exchange-traded, bonds, commodities, funds and certificates, derivatives, indices, and foreign exchange trading platforms. The dominant stock index of EURONEXT is Euronext 100 which includes liquid stocks of gigantic companies including AXA, Christian Dior and Renault.

- Date of establishment: September 22, 2000.
- Valuation: $3.9 Trillion.

Shenzen Stock Exchange

The Shenzhen Stock Exchange (SZSE) is one of the three independently working stock exchanges in China. Although it was founded in 1987, it wasn't established until 1990. It is the 7th largest stock exchange in the world and has approximately 1,300 listed companies with a combined market capitalization of $3.92 trillion.

Most of the companies under this SZSE are corporate firms of companies in which the Government Of China and it is based in China so SZSE trades its shares in Chinese yuan. The Shenzhen stock market had introduced the "ChiNext Board" in 2009 comprising of high-tech & high-growth startups, quite almost like NASDAQ.

- Date of establishment: December 1, 1990.
- Valuation: $3.5 Trillion.

London Stock Exchange

The London stock exchange (LSE) is based in London and is the sixth-largest stock market within the world. It was established in 1571 and is the oldest stock exchange in the world. It has more than 3,000 listed companies with a combined market capitalization of $4.59 trillion.

LSE's service was nothing but a twice-weekly paper publication of market prices back in its origin. It is also the maiden source of benchmark prices, equity-market liquidity and market data in Europe. Some of the huge companies listed under the LSE are Barclays, British Petroleum and GlaxoSmithKline.

- Date of establishment: January 23, 1571.
- Valuation: $3.2 Trillion.

Toronto Stock Exchange

The Toronto Stock Exchange (TSX) is situated in Toronto, Canada. It was introduced in 1852 and is held and wielded as a subsidiary of the TMX Group. Enlistment of 2,207 companies with a combined market capitalization of $2.3 trillion makes Toronto Stock Exchange one among the top 10 biggest stock exchanges in the world.

The financial instruments include equities, investment trusts, exchange-traded funds, bonds, commodities, futures, options, and other products. It is also to be noted that mining and oil and gas companies are listed in additional numbers under the Toronto stock market compared to other stock exchanges around the world. Canada's 'Big Five' commercial banks are also listed under TSX.

- Date of establishment: October 25, 1861.
- Valuation: $2.1 Trillion.

Bombay Stock Exchange

The Bombay Stock Exchange (BSE) is an Canada stock exchange located at the Dalal Street in Mumbai. It was established in 1875 and is Asia's first-ever stock market. It is also the world's 10th largest stock exchange with a total market capitalisation of more than $2.2 trillion.

The BSE has the most companies listed under it. It accounts for about 5,000 companies and has assisted in the growth of the country's corporate sector and financial markets. Securities listed under BSE comprise of stocks, futures, options, index futures, index options, and weekly options. However, the BSE's benchmark is measured by the Sensex which nearly covers all the sectors of the Canada economy. The exchange also offers exposure to equities in regions such as Brazil, Russia, China and South Africa.

- Date of establishment: July 9, 1877.
- Valuation: $1.7 Trillion.

Foreign Exchange Rate

Whenever the BoP registers a purchase of a foreign asset or a sale of a domestic commodity abroad, this implicitly indicates that there is a change in the demand for or in the supply of the foreign currency. The international transaction cannot be completed unless one of the parties of the transaction is willing to exchange his/her domestic currency for foreign currency. Therefore changes in any of the components of the BoP affect the supply of and demand for foreign currency.

The key variable that allows the supply of and demand for foreign currency to be equilibrated is the exchange rate. The exchange rate (E) is defined as relative price of the foreign currency. So if a domestic resident wants to buy the currency of another country, the exchange rates states the price for each unit of foreign currency. Formally the exchange rate is defined as the price of one unit of foreign currency in terms of the domestic currency. For example, if we assume for the moment that the dollar is the domestic currency, the exchange rate between the dollar ($) and the British pound sterling (£) is:

$$E = \$ / £$$

One complication is that the definition of the exchange rate is ambiguous, depending on the reference of location. Americans will identify the pound as the foreign currency, while the British identify the dollar as the foreign currency. This means there are two versions of the exchange rate, one based on dollars per pound (US) and one based on pounds per dollar (UK). As a result most sources quote both versions of the exchange rate: "US$ equivalence" and "Currency per US$". For example, from the point of view of the UK, the exchange rate between the 2 currencies is E* = £/$. That is, for British residents the exchange rate indicates how many pounds they have to pay to buy one US dollar. Consequently if E = $1.5 then E* = 1/E = £0.66. Figure shows the cross-rates for the major currencies.

EXCHANGE CROSS RATES

May 11		C$	DKr	Euro	Y	NKr	SKr	SFr	£	$
Canada	C$	1	4.947	0.664	107.8	5.433	6.127	1.093	0.453	0.898
Denmark	DKr	2.021	10	1.342	218.0	10.98	12.38	2.210	0.915	1.815
Euro	Euro	1.506	7.452	1	162.4	8.184	9.229	1.647	0.682	1.352
Japan	Y	0.927	4.588	0.616	100	5.039	5.682	1.014	0.420	0.833
Norway	NKr	1.841	9.105	1.222	198.5	10	11.28	2.012	0.833	1.652
Sweden	SKr	1.632	8.074	1.084	176.0	8.868	10	1.785	0.739	1.465
Switzerland	SFr	0.915	4.524	0.607	98.61	4.969	5.603	1	0.414	0.821
UK	£	2.208	10.92	1.466	238.1	12.00	13.53	2.415	1	1.982
USA	$	1.114	5.511	0.740	120.1	6.052	6.825	1.218	0.504	1

Cross-Rates between the Major Currencies.

The numbers in the upper triangle are the inverse of those in the lower triangle. We will now consider the exchange rate from the point of view of the US. If an American wants to plan her next vacation abroad and finds out the dollar price of a rental car in the UK, she would simply have to multiply the British pound price by the exchange rate E (the number of $ in one £) to find the dollar price. We can take this notion a bit further and find the dollar value of all our imports by multiplying the quantity of imports (M), by the exchange rate (E) times the foreign price of imports (P*). So EP*M is the total value of all imported goods in terms of domestic currency.

Changes in the exchange rate have their own terminology. If the US$/British£ rate increases from 1.5 to 3 (E increases), you would suddenly have to pay 3 dollars per British pound. The price of UK currency has increased, or your dollars are worth less. Economists speak of a depreciation of the dollar relative to the British pound. It is a common mistake to think that depreciations result in a decrease in the exchange rate. A quick check of our definition of the exchange rate shows that E actually increases as the dollar depreciates. This is because E is the price of foreign currency and this price increases as the dollar loses value. If the exchange rate declines from 1.5 to 1, then all of the sudden the price of foreign currency has fallen. Fewer dollars are needed to purchase to buy 1 pound, implying that the dollar has become strong, or as economists say, it appreciated, relative to the pound since exchange rates are relative prices, if one needs more dollars to buy one pound (a depreciation of the dollar), this is equivalent to saying that one needs fewer pounds to buy one dollar or that the pound has appreciated with respect to the dollar. Conversely, an appreciation of the dollar is equivalent to a depreciation of the pound. It is thus imperative to always specify which currency appreciates or depreciates.

Since the exchange rate is the price of foreign currency, it equilibrates the supply and demand of foreign currency, just like the price for milk equilibrates the supply of and demand for milk. Identically to the market for milk, where fluctuations in the supply of and demand for milk alter the price of milk, fluctuations in the supply of and demand for foreign currency set off appreciations and depreciations of the exchange rate. While the supply of and demand for milk comes from cows and cheese lovers respectively, the supply of and demand for foreign currency is triggered by the actions of the various agents involved in the BoP transactions. We can now consider the BoP in a new light and appreciate its role summarizing all international transactions and immediately informing us whether the supply of and demand for foreign currency has been altered.

Understanding the relevance of the balance of payments and the exchange rate is the key to grasping any and all concepts of the open economy. The BoP does not only represent a statistical account of a country's international transactions. The fundamental insight is that any change in the BoP sets off by definition a change in the market for foreign currency. Therefore we have reached our first important conclusion: one aspect of international macroeconomics is the study of how changes in the exchange rate affect the economy – often with dramatic, new ramifications that we did not consider in the closed economy. It is absolutely crucial that we recall throughout our study of the open economy that changes in the exchange rate are fundamentally driven by changes in the balance of payments.

The need for Exchange Rates is Relatively Recent

When international transactions were settled with gold or silver coins, there was no such need. All what counted was the weight of the coin. People were indifferent between a gold coin embossed with the face of the king of France, a Louis d' or, or a coin with the face of the Emperor of Austria, a gold ducat. Gold was gold so people did not need to exchange these coins according to an exchange rate but only according to the amount of gold in the coin. Then countries introduced paper currency and switched to a gold standard. Originally the paper currency was fully backed by gold, so the exchange rate was fixed and still not that important. It is only when countries had to give up backing their currency by gold that exchange rates became of paramount importance for international trade.

Real and Nominal Exchange Rates

The exchange rate is reported daily in the major newspaper and minute to minute quotes of the prices of foreign currencies can be obtained on the internet. These quoted prices represent the nominal exchange rate (it is also called the spot exchange rate). As economists, we are interested in digging a bit deeper to make a distinction between real and nominal variables, specifically real and nominal exchange rates. Real variables are always adjusted for inflation, thus the real exchange rate describes the fluctuations in the price of foreign currency after we have taken into account domestic and foreign rates of inflation. While the nominal exchange rate, $E_{\$/£} = \$ / £$, is simply the number of dollars you have to pay to get one British pound, £, the real exchange rate, $e_{\$/£}$, accounts for inflation in both countries.

$$e_{\$/£} = \frac{\$/P_\$}{£/P_£} = £\frac{\$}{£}\frac{P_£}{P_\$} = E_{\$/£}\frac{P_£}{P_\$}$$

In the equation above, P$ and P£ are the respective price levels in the US and Britain. To obtain the real exchange rate we first divide the amount of dollars we have to pay by the US price level and the amount of British pounds we receive (£1) by the UK price level. Basically we are now looking at "real" dollar and "real" pounds i.e. real in terms of their domestic purchasing power. Now assume that the US price level increases by 5% while the UK price level does not change. This means that, in terms of its purchasing power, the dollar buys 5% fewer domestic goods or the value of the real dollar $/P$ has dropped by 5% while the value of the real pound £/P£ has not changed. However the nominal exchange rate E has remained constant: one US dollar can still buy exactly the same amount of pounds. So now one US dollar can buy more British goods than American goods since the prices of the British goods have not changed while the prices of the American goods have increased. This phenomenon is identified as a real appreciation of the dollar. Of course if, at the same time, the dollar underwent a nominal depreciation equal to 5%, nothing would change as the real exchange rate will not have changed. The US citizen will not feel richer, the British goods would be relatively cheaper but the pound would more expensive, so he will not be able to buy any more British goods. That is why we divide the quantities of currencies in $e_{\$/£} = \frac{\$/P_\$}{£/P_£} = £\frac{\$}{£}\frac{P_£}{P_\$} = E_{\$/£}\frac{P_£}{P_\$}$ by their respective price levels in the domestic and foreign economies.

When we consider equation $e_{\$/£} = \frac{\$/P_\$}{£/P_£} = £\frac{\$}{£}\frac{P_£}{P_\$} = E_{\$/£}\frac{P_£}{P_\$}$, it is clear that the real exchange rate can be broken down into two parts. First the nominal exchange rate, E$/£, and second the relative price level, P£/P$ The real exchange rate is thus simply the nominal exchange rate times an adjustment for the relative change in prices abroad and at home. The difference between real and nominal rates becomes crucially important when we compare their respective changes over time. To see this consider the definitional relationship:

$$e = EP^*/P$$

Where e is the real exchange rate, E the nominal exchange rate, P the domestic price level (or the consumer price index, CPI), and P* the foreign price level (or CPI). Taking percentage changes (denoted by ^), we obtain,

$$\hat{e} = \hat{E} + \hat{p}^* - \hat{p}$$

Where for any variable x, $\hat{x} \equiv dx / x$. The changes over time are then obtained by dividing both sides of $\hat{e} = \hat{E} + \hat{p}^* - \hat{p}$ by the time unit, dt.

Examining changes in the real exchange rate over time underscores that any percentage change in the real price of the foreign currency is a composite of three separate terms: a) the percentage change in the nominal price of the foreign currency, b) The percentage change in the foreign price level, c) the percentage change in the domestic price level.

Simply said, if the nominal exchange rate increases by 2 percent over a one-year period, foreigners find it 2 percent cheaper to buy US dollars. This renders all US goods 2 percent cheaper in nominal terms. However, if US inflation was 4 percent and foreign inflation was 2 percent over the past year, foreigners find it just as attractive in real terms to buy US goods as they did last year (as $\hat{e} = 2 + 2 - 4 =$). This example highlights that, while the nominal exchange rate may have changed, the real exchange rate may well remain constant when we account for inflation.

In conclusion, the real exchange rate is a measure of the international competitiveness of a country: we saw above that changes in the international competitiveness depend not only on changes in the nominal exchange rate but also on changes in the relative price level in the two countries. A real depreciation that can be caused either by a nominal depreciation or a decrease in the domestic price level or an increase in the foreign price level (or some combination of these) will enhance a country's international competitiveness while a real appreciation will have the opposite impact.

The Effective Exchange Rate

The exchange rate as defined above constitutes a narrow, bilateral price that helps us identify the relative strength of the domestic currency with respect to only the currency of one other country. For example, is the dollar appreciating or depreciating against the British pound? Whenever the value of the dollar depreciates against another country's currency, we know that domestic goods become relatively cheaper (in other words, more competitive on that country's markets).

While bilateral competitiveness is of great interest, economists are even more interested in a country's competitiveness vis-à-vis all of its trading partners. To measure a country's overall export competitiveness, we need a more general measure of the exchange rate, one that extends our bilateral measure into a multilateral measure. This multilateral measure accounts for the fact that we trade with many countries. For example, it is not hard to imagine a situation where the Japanese yen depreciates against the dollar, but appreciates against the euro over a given time period. Did Japanese products then become more or less attractive to the rest of the world overall? Did the Japanese trade balance improve or deteriorate? We can certainly say that Japanese exports' competitiveness improved relative to the US and deteriorated against European goods. However, can we determine whether Japanese exports became more or less competitive overall? To answer this question we need to develop a new measure of the exchange rate.

The most comprehensive measure of overall export competitiveness compares the value of the domestic currency to the value of the currencies of all the trade partners. This measure is called the effective exchange rate and is defined as:

$$E_{Effective} = \sum_{j=1}^{N} q_j \; E_j \quad \text{with} \sum_{j=1}^{N} q_j = 1$$

The effective exchange rate is therefore the weighted sum of all bilateral exchange rates. The weight, q_j, for a bilateral exchange rate, E_j, is simply the fraction of total trade that the domestic economy conducts with country j. There are j = 1, 2,..., N countries in this index, corresponding to the home country's N trading partners. Because of its definition, the effective exchange rate is also referred to as the multilateral, or trade weighted exchange rate. An example of the effective exchange rate is given in figure below.

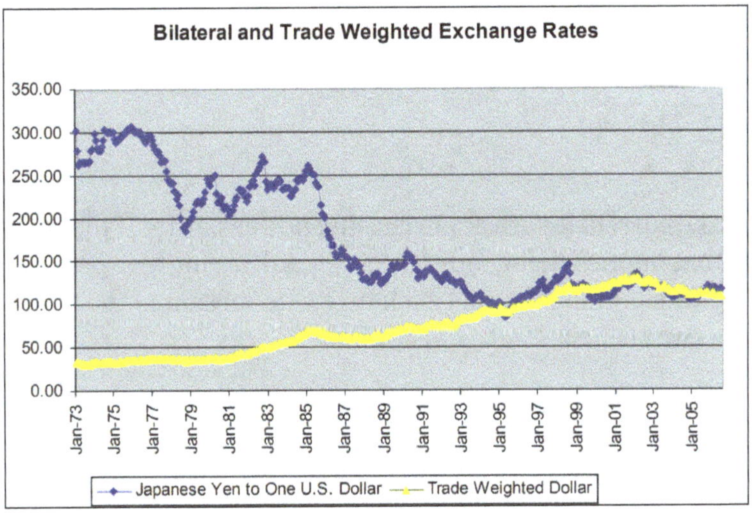

Bilateral (yen/dollar) Exchange Rate and Trade Weighted Exchange Rate for the Dollar.

Real vs. Nominal Exchange Rate

The nominal exchange rate is the relative price of the currency of the two countries. Consider two countries U.S. and Canada. Their respective currencies are the dollar and Canadian Dollar. If the exchange rate, called Nominal Exchange Rate, is for 60 Canadian Dollars, then it implies that one can exchange one dollar for Rs.60/- in the world financial markets. Here, one currency, say dollar, is priced for another currency, Canadian Dollar. In other words, the nominal exchange rate is the ratio of relative price of the currency of the two countries.

The real exchange rate, on the other hand, is the ratio of the foreign price to the domestic price of the goods. The ratio is measured in the same currency. For example, consider the price of a given basket of goods, then the numerator would be the foreign price and denominator would be the domestic price in the ratio and this would be multiplied by the nominal exchange rate. In other words, it would mean:

$$R = e \times \frac{P_f}{P_d}$$

Where R is the real exchange rate, e is the minimal exchange rate, Pf is the foreign police and P_d is the domestic price of the basket of goods. Take for example Canadian Dollar and dollar e is the Canadian Dollar price of dollar.

Consider, for e.g., U.S. and Canada. Canada is investment of and U.S. is foreign country. Let, e, the nominal exchange rate be Rs.60 for one dollar. Also, suppose one burger is costing Rs.60 in Canada and $1 in U.S. Then our ratio P_f/P_d would be Rs.60/1. in this case the real exchange rate would be:

$$R = e.P_f / P$$

i. e. $$R = \frac{60}{1}, \frac{1}{60} = 1$$

This shows that the currencies are at purchasing power parity. If the real exchange rate rises above one that implies that goods (U.S.) abroad are more expensive than goods in Canada and vice versa. Thus, the real exchange rate measures the relative purchasing power of the two currencies.

The Real Exchange Rate and Trade Balance

The fundamental four sector identity is given by:

$$Y = C + I + G + NX$$

Where Y refers to income, C refers to consumption, I refer to investment, G refers to government spending and NX represents net exports. The term NX accounts for domestic spending on foreign goods and foreign spending on domestic goods, when foreigner purchases our goods. Goods produced by the domestic country), NX is a component of the total demand for our goods. Thus,

$$NX = X - M.$$

NX is also called trade balance. The net exports thus depend on exports and imports of the goods. The demand for domestic goods by foreigner depends on the foreign income and the exchange rate, particularly the real exchange rate. An increase in foreign income increases the demand for exports and on increase in the real exchange rate (i.e., real depreciation) increases the demand for exports. This happens so as to demand shifts from foreign goods to domestic goods. Thus,

$$X = f(Y_f, R)$$

The demand for imports by us depends on our incomplete, Y and the real exchange rate.

$$M = f(Y, R)$$

Thus, NX can be written as,

$$NX = f(Y, Y_f, R)$$

The above equation implies (i) a rise in domestic income increases imports and thus worsen the trade balance, (NX); (ii) a rise in foreign income increases the exports and thus improves the trade balance; and (iii) an increase in the real exchange rate (i.e., a real depreciation by the home country) improves the trade balance. We are interested in the third result. The same result can also be seen by the following diagram. Consider, two countries – U.S. and Canada. U.S. is foreign country and Canada is home country. The respective currencies are - $ & Rs.

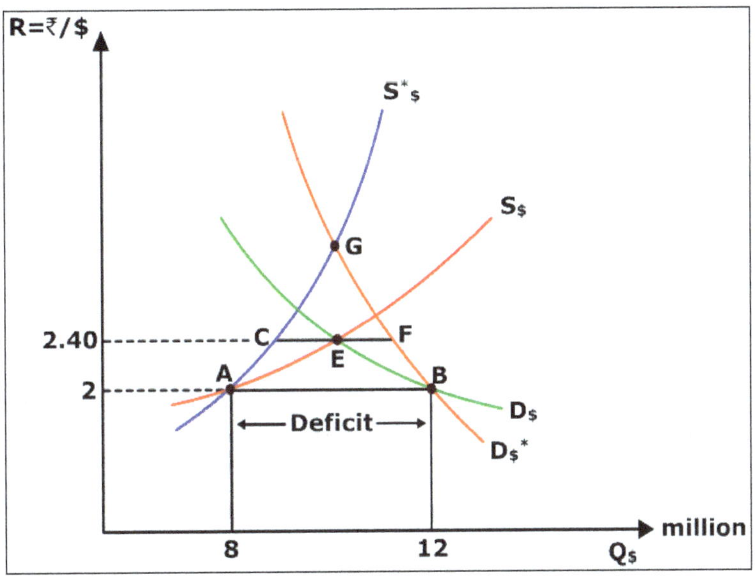

On the vertical axis we measure exchange rate – Canadian Dollar in terms of dollars and on the horizontal axis we measure quantity of dollar. The Canadian Demand for dollars is given by $D_\$$ and supply by $S_\$$. Let the exchange rate be given by C$ 2 per one dollar i.e. R = C$ 2/$1. At this exchange rate there is a deficit 'AB' in Canada. A 20% depreciation of the Canadian Dollar from R1 C$ 2/$1 to R_2 = C$ 2.40/$1 would completely eliminate the deficit – as at this exchange rate the quantity of demanded of dollars is equal to quantity supplied of dollars. However, this elimination of deficit (trade deficit) depends on the elasticities of the demand and the supply curves. If instead the supply and demand curves are steeper or more flat, the same rate of depreciation would not lead to the complete elimination of the deficit present. This has been analyzed and put by Marshall and Lerner in terms of the condition. The Marshall Lerner condition states that if the sum of the elasticities of demand for imports and demand for exports must be greater than one. The greater the amount by which the sum of these two elasticities exceed one, the greater is the improvement in the Canada balance of trade for a given depreciation.

Derivation of Marhsall- Lerner Condition

Consider current accounts balances:

$$NX = CAB = \text{Value of } X - \text{Value of } M$$

$$= EX(E\ P_f / P_d) - IM\left(EP_f / P_d, Y^d\right)$$

This is the Marshall-Lerner condition.

The M-L condition states that if the current account is initially zero, a real currency depreciation causes a current account surplus if the sum of relative price-elasticities of export and import demand exceeds one. Now, we examine the possibility that a depreciation may worsen the trade balance. The trade balance NX can be written as,

$$NX = X - \frac{eP_f}{P}.Q$$

Where X denotes the foreign demand for our goods (X's) and Q denotes imports. Then, the value of our imports in terms of domestic goods can be written as,

$$(e.\ P_f/P)\ Q$$

Let there be an exchange depreciation. Then, there exists two effects. One, volume effects and (2) price effect. The volume effects occur o the volume of exports and imports. The volume of exports should increase as the domestic goods are cheaper and the volume of imports should decrease because imports are expensive. The price effects occur as the relative price of imports increase. The same volume of imports is now more expensive and the total spending measured in terms of the domestic currency increases. Thus, we observe that the trade balance worsen due to price effect but it improves due to volume effects. The actual situation depends on the two effects – which effects is stronger. If the price effect outweighs the volume effects then depreciation worsens the trade balance and vice versa. Empirically, it has been found that volume effect within a year and quite small and do not outweigh the price effect. But, the long term volume effect are substantial and observed that a country's current account worsens. Worsens immediately after a real currency depreciation and starts to improve only some months later. This behaviour is described the famous J-curve.

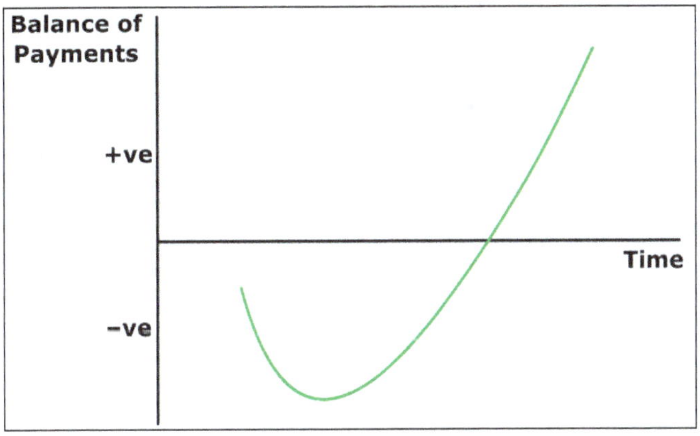

The above figure describes the J-curves on the vertical axis we measure current account and on the horizontal axis, we measure time. The J-curve describes the time lag with which a real currency depreciation improves the current account. The point A shows that the real depreciation takes place and J-curve starts and point B depicts the end of the J curve. The more from point A to point B takes more than six months but less than a year.

References

- Balance-of-Payments-BOP: oliveboard.in, Retrieved 02, March 2020
- Balance-payment-cbse-notes-class-12-macro-economics: learncbse.in, Retrieved 20, June 2020
- Top-10-Biggest-Stock-Exchanges-In-The-World: businessworld.in, Retrieved 25, April 2020

6

Money Supply and Monetary Policy

The total amount of money which is in circulation, including coins, cash and bank balance, is called money supply. The different decisions which are taken by the central bank of a country for the purpose of controlling money supply and achieving economic growth in a sustainable manner are known as monetary policy. This chapter discusses in detail the different aspects of money supply and monetary policy such as the determinants of money supply and fiscal policy.

Fiscal Policy

Fiscal policy is the means by which a government adjusts its spending levels and tax rates to monitor and influence a nation's economy. It is the sister strategy to monetary policy through which a central bank influences a nation's money supply. These two policies are used in various combinations to direct a country's economic goals.

Before the Great Depression, which lasted from October 29, 1929, to the onset of America's entry into World War II, the government's approach to the economy was laissez-faire. Following World War II, it was determined that the government had to take a proactive role in the economy to regulate unemployment, business cycles, inflation, and the cost of money. By using a mix of monetary and fiscal policies (depending on the political orientations and the philosophies of those in power at a particular time, one policy may dominate over another), governments can control economic phenomena.

Fiscal policy is based on the theories of British economist John Maynard Keynes. Governments can influence macroeconomic productivity levels by increasing or decreasing tax levels and public spending. This influence, in turn, curbs inflation (generally considered to be healthy when between 2% and 3%), increases employment, and maintains a healthy value of money. Fiscal policy plays a very important role in managing a country's economy. For example, in 2012 many worried that the fiscal cliff, a simultaneous increase in tax rates and cuts in government spending set to occur in January 2013, would send the U.S. economy back into recession. The U.S. Congress avoided this problem by passing the American Taxpayer Relief Act of 2012 on Jan. 1, 2013.

Balancing Act

The idea is to find a balance between tax rates and public spending. For example, stimulating a stagnant economy by increasing spending or lowering taxes, also known as expansionary fiscal policy, runs the risk of causing inflation to rise. This is because an increase in the amount of money in the economy, followed by an increase in consumer demand, can result in a decrease in the value of money—meaning that it would take more money to buy something that has not changed in value.

Let's say that an economy has slowed down. Unemployment levels are up, consumer spending is down, and businesses are not making substantial profits. A government may decide to fuel the economy's engine by decreasing taxation, which gives consumers more spending money while increasing government spending in the form of buying services from the market (such as building roads or schools). By paying for such services, the government creates jobs and wages that are in turn pumped into the economy. Pumping money into the economy by decreasing taxation and increasing government spending is also known as "pump priming." In the meantime, overall unemployment levels will fall.

With more money in the economy and less taxes to pay, consumer demand for goods and services increases. This, in turn, rekindles businesses and turns the cycle around from stagnant to active. If, however, there are no reins on this process, the increase in economic productivity can cross over a very fine line and lead to too much money in the market. This excess in supply decreases the value of money while pushing up prices (because of the increase in demand for consumer products). Hence, inflation exceeds the reasonable level. For this reason, fine-tuning the economy through fiscal policy alone can be a difficult, if not improbable, means to reach economic goals.

When the Economy needs to be Curbed

When inflation is too strong, the economy may need a slowdown. In such a situation, a government can use fiscal policy to increase taxes to suck money out of the economy. Fiscal policy could also dictate a decrease in government spending and thereby decrease the money in circulation. Of course, the possible negative effects of such a policy, in the long run, could be a sluggish economy and high unemployment levels. Nonetheless, the process continues as the government uses its fiscal policy to fine-tune spending and taxation levels, with the goal of evening out the business cycles.

Who Does Fiscal Policy Affect?

Unfortunately, the effects of any fiscal policy are not the same for everyone. Depending on the political orientations and goals of the policymakers, a tax cut could affect only the middle class, which is typically the largest economic group. In times of economic decline and rising taxation, it is this same group that may have to pay more taxes than the wealthier upper class.

Similarly, when a government decides to adjust its spending, its policy may affect only a specific group of people. A decision to build a new bridge, for example, will give work and more income to hundreds of construction workers. A decision to spend money on building a new space shuttle, on the other hand, benefits only a small, specialized pool of experts, which would not do much to increase aggregate employment levels.

That said the markets also react to fiscal policy. Stocks rose following passage of the Trump administration's $1.5 trillion U.S. tax bill, the Tax Cuts and Jobs Act. The Dow Jones Industrial Average gained 99 points or 0.4%, the S&P 500 Index rose 0.25%, and the Nasdaq Composite Index was up 0.14%.

The tax overhaul is forecast to raise the federal deficit by hundreds of billions of dollars—and perhaps as much as $2 trillion—over the next 10 year. Estimates vary depending on assumptions about how much economic growth the law will spur. The law cuts corporate tax rates permanently by creating a single corporate tax rate of 21% and repeals the corporate alternative minimum tax.

Money Creation

Money (M_1) consists of two basic components, currency held by the public and checkable deposits. Money can be created either by creating currency or by creating checkable deposits. Printing paper currency is the "traditional" method of money creation and it brings in inflation when the economy is operating at full employment level of output. However, when it comes to monetary policy and controlling the money supply, the creation of checkable deposits is the more important of the two methods. Money creation or credit creation is a special function of commercial banks under the fractional reserve banking and this process of money creation is controlled by the central bank of the country. Monetary base refers to the supply of funds available for use either as cash or reserves of the central bank. Monetary base along with the money multiplier determine the level of money supply in the economy.

Creation of Money or Credit Creation

The commercial banks receive checkable deposits from the depositors which they can use for lending purposes after keeping an appropriate amount of reserves for meeting distress demand of the depositors or for conducting day to day operations. The deposits that banks receive are of two types - primary deposits and derivative deposits. Primary or real deposits are those initial deposits that the banks receive from original depositor. A part of primary deposits is lent out to some other people by crediting their bank accounts with the loan amount. It implies that a major part of the deposits remain with the bank, which it can further use to create more money. So, it can be said that deposits create loans and loans create deposits. Thus, larger the size of primary deposits, the greater will be the expansion of credit. So, banks are in a position to create a large volume of deposit money on the basis of a given amount of reserves. This can happen because all the transactions do not use cash, in fact most of the transactions use the other banking instruments like cheque, bank's promises etc. So, majority of transactions remain restricted on paper. A small amount of transactions which actually materialise can use the cash reserves. Thus, credit creation is the power of banks to expand deposits through the process of expanding loans, advances and investments.

The Ratio Approach to the Creation of Deposit Money

Whenever a bank receives cash deposits from its customers, it leads to creation of asset for the depositor and the same deposit is the liability for the bank. The bank can use these deposits for making loans to other persons. But the bank cannot use the whole of deposits for this purpose. The proportion of deposits a bank can loan out depends upon the legal reserve ratio (LRR) that is fixed by the central bank. Legal reserve ratio is the fraction of total deposits that a bank has to keep as cash. It has two components. A part of LRR which a bank has to keep in cash form with the central bank is called cash reserve ratio (CRR). The other part which a bank has to keep with itself in the form of liquid assets is called statutory liquidity ratio (SLR). It means that banks can issue loans equal to a fraction of total deposits they receive. The banking experience says that not all depositors approach the bank for withdrawals at the same time, so a fraction of deposits as cash reserves is enough to meet normal demand. Also, the regular flow of net deposits in the form of deposits and withdrawals ensure that daily demand for cash is taken care of. To understand the ratio approach to the creation of deposit money, let us take an example by first assuming single banking system and then the multiple banking system.

Single Banking System

Let us assume that there is a single bank in the entire commercial banking system. All the transactions of money are conducted via this bank. All payments are made through cheques issued by this bank. All receipts are deposited into this bank. Suppose that a person deposits 100$ in this bank. It means that the assets as well as liabilities of the bank rose by 100$. The balance sheet of this bank will be like given in table.

Balance Sheet of Bank (in $)			
Liabilities		Assets	
Deposits	100	Cash	100
Total	100		100

Deposits can be lent out, assuming LRR to be 10%, this bank can loan out only 90% of the deposits received and it has to keep 10% as cash reserves. It is also assumed that LRR does not change and the bank does not keep excess reserves. So, 90$ out of initial 100$ is lent out. When it is lent to a person, the loan amount is credited to the borrower's bank account which he can use wholly or partly. In any case, the amount that is loaned out comes back to this bank in the form of fresh deposits. The balance sheet of this bank will be like given in table.

Balance Sheet of Bank (in $)			
Liabilities		Assets	
Deposits	100	Cash	100
	90	Loan	90
Total	190		190

The new deposits not only raise the liabilities of this bank in the form of deposits, but also give it the opportunity to advance more loans, but only after keeping appropriate reserves against these deposits. It will keep 10% of 90$ i.e. 9$ and will lend the balance. In the subsequent rounds it can keep on raising its advances in the form of loans until it exhausts all the excess reserves. In all the next rounds, the balance sheet of this bank will be as shown in table.

Balance Sheet of Bank (in $)			
Liabilities		Assets	
Deposits	100	Cash	100
	90	Loan	81
	81		72.90
	-		-
	-		-
Total	1000		1000

This process of deposit creation will come to an end when total cash reserves become equal to the initial deposit. But an important question is that by how much total deposits rise in response to the initial deposit. This is answered by concept of deposit multiplier; which in turn is determined by LRR. Generally, total deposits rise by a multiple of initial deposit and that multiplier is called the deposit multiplier. It is given by:

Deposit Multiplier = 1/LRR

In the above example, LRR is 10% or 0.1, so the deposit multiplier = 1/0.1 = 10

Thus, total deposit creation=1/LRR × initial deposit

= 1/0.1 × 100 = 1000

This can be seen from table, that total of balance sheet is 1000, which is exactly equal to the total amount of deposit creation. Out of this, 100$ is cash reserve requirement and 900$ is created out of initial deposit of 100$. This process of credit creation can also be understood from table.

Table: The process of deposit creation.

Round	Deposits ($)	Loans ($)	Reserves (LRR=0.1)
Initial	100	90	10
1	90	81	9
2	81	72.90	8.10
.	.	.	.
.	.	.	.
.	.	.	.
Total	1000	900	100

In table, deposit creation continues in several rounds after the bank receives an initial deposit of 100$. In every round, bank loans out all the excess reserves by keeping the required legal reserves which is 10% of the deposits. Every time the bank receives fresh deposits, it keeps 10% of it and lends the balance. At every round, the total of loan and cash reserves exactly matches deposits. This process comes to an end when cash reserves reach their minimum required limit or equal to the amount of initial deposit. Total deposits rise by a multiple of initial deposit and that multiple is the deposit multiplier. It can be seen that the size of deposit multiplier varies inversely with LRR. Higher the LRR, lower the deposit multiplier and hence lesser will be the money creation. It is illustrated in table by assuming different values of LRR and initial deposit of 100$.

LRR	Deposit Multiplier	Total Deposit Creation (Initial deposit × 1/LRR)
0.1	10	1000
0.2	5	500
0.4	2.5	250
0.8	1.25	125

Thus, higher the reserve requirement for the banks, lower will be the amount of total deposit created.

Multiple Bank System

In reality, there is no single banking unit in the commercial banking system. Rather there exist multiple banks and loans extended by one bank may be deposited into the deposit account of another bank. However, the existence of multiple banks does not affect the working of credit creation process. In multi-banking system also, all banks need to maintain the minimum legal reserves which are a fixed fraction of total deposits. Let us assume that Bank 1 receives a primary cash deposit of 100$. Its balance sheet will be like table.

Balance Sheet of Bank 1 (in $)			
Liabilities		Assets	
Deposit	100	Cash	100
Total	100		100

After Bank 1 receives the initial deposit of 100$, it keeps 10% of this as legal reserve and lends the excess reserve of 90$. When Bank 1 loans out 90$ out of 100$, its balance sheet position becomes like in table.

Balance Sheet of Bank 1 (in $)			
Liabilities		Assets	
Deposit	100	Cash	10
		Loan	90
Total	100		100

Now with the multi-banking system, we cannot assume that loan extended by Bank 1 will be deposited back into Bank 1 itself. Suppose that those who receive 90$ as loan from Bank 1 spend the same and money comes back to the banking system, let us say to Bank 2 in the form of deposits. The balance sheet of Bank 2 is shown in table.

Balance Sheet of Bank 1 (in $)			
Liabilities		Assets	
Deposit	100	Cash	10
		Loan	90
Total	100		100

Now with the multi-banking system, we cannot assume that loan extended by Bank 1 will be deposited back into Bank 1 itself. Suppose that those who receive 90$ as loan from Bank 1 spend the same and money comes back to the banking system, let us say to Bank 2 in the form of deposits. The balance sheet of Bank 2 is shown in table.

Balance Sheet of Bank 2 (in $)			
Liabilities		Assets	
Deposit	90	New Cash	90
Total	90		90

Bank 2, after keeping 10% reserves, lends the rest of 81$ to the borrowers in the form of loan. Its balance sheet thus becomes as given in table.

Balance Sheet of Bank 2 (in $)			
Liabilities		Assets	
Deposit	90	Cash	10
		Loan	81
Total	90		90

Those who receive 81$ as loan from Bank 2 may spend the amount and again money comes into the banking system but now with Bank 3. The balance sheet of Bank 3 is given in table.

Balance Sheet of Bank 2 (in $)			
Liabilities		Assets	
Deposit	90	Cash	10
		Loan	81
Total	90		90

Those who receive 81$ as loan from Bank 2 may spend the amount and again money comes into the banking system but now with Bank 3. The balance sheet of Bank 3 is given in table.

Balance Sheet of Bank 2 (in $)			
Liabilities		Assets	
New Deposit	81	New Cash	81
Total	81		81

This process of credit creation in the multi-bank system will continue until the original deposit gets completely exhausted in the system. The original deposit of 100$ becomes 90$, then 81$ which will again keep on expanding until the sum becomes a multiple of the initial deposit of 100$. In this case, the value of deposit multiplier is 10 (as LRR is 0), thus the process of credit expansion will continue until the sum of 90 + 81 + 72.90 +... becomes 1000, i.e. 10 times the initial deposit.

So, just like in a single bank system, all the banks in the multi-bank system create a multiple increase in deposit money by keeping no excess reserves and expanding their deposits in step with each other.

Supply of Money and Money Multiplier

The monetary authority i.e., the central bank manages and brings about money into the economic system. The central bank of a country has a direct control over the monetary base or the stock of high powered money in the economy. This is called as high-powered money because money stock acts as the base with which bigger stocks of monetary assets are created. Monetary base consists of currency (banknotes and coins) held by public and the banks and of deposits which are held by the commercial banks with the central bank (i.e. reserves). The stock of high-powered money is brought into circulation by the central bank through the issue of securities and government debt instruments. The division of high-powered money in the form of currency and banker's deposits is determined by the individual decision make$ If people are more inclined to hold cash in hand, then currency component of high powered money (H) will be higher. So, currency in circulation in the economy is completely demand driven.

$$H = C + R$$

Equation above says that total cash in the economy can take the form of currency or banker's deposits (reserves). The amount of reserves is determined by reserve to deposit ratio as fixed by the central bank. Let it to be written as R/D or r. Thus,

$$R = rD$$

Let us also assume that public is in the habit of keeping a fraction of deposits in cash form. This currency to deposit ratio can be written as C/D or c.

Thus,

$$C = cD$$

Using equation R = rD and C = cD in equation H = C + R, we get,

$$cD + rD = H$$

$$D = H/(c + r)$$

Equation above shows that deposits are a multiple of the given stock of H and rise by the reciprocal of the sum of cash to deposit ratio and reserve to deposit ratio. This will look the same as deposit multiplier if c assumes zero value and H be taken as the initial deposit. It means that a higher value of r lowers the increase in deposits.In the modern economy, the total amount of money called the money supply or money stock, has many measures like M_0, M_1, M_2, M_3. Money supply is the stock of money held by the public at a point of time in an economy. It includes total amount of money in circulation. The total money supply in an economy with a banking system consists of currency (both notes and coins) and demand deposits (D). It excludes the amount of currency held by commercial banks as reserves and all the cash & gold stock held with the central bank. This is because these components are not in circulation. Most measures of money supply include wide range of assets apart from the components of highpowered money. Money supply M is written as,

$$M = C + D$$

Using equation cD + rD = H, D = H/(c + r) for D and equation C = cD for C in equation above, we get,

$$M = cD + H/(c + r)$$

Again using equation (D = H/(c + r)) in (M = cD + H/(c + r)), we get,

$$M = c+1 / c+r. H$$

$$M = m. H$$

Where m = c+1 / c+r

The component m in equation above is known as money multiplier as it tells us the size of money supply for the given stock of high powered money. It can be generalised from this expression that higher the values of c and r, lower will be the size of money multiplier and lesser will be the resulting money supply. This is the same as deposit multiplier, with two differences:

- Instead of deposit creation with the initial deposit, this is the case of money creation with the given stock of high powered money.
- Public's desired cash to deposit ratio was assumed to be zero earlier.

Determinants of Money Supply

Money supply is the stock of money held by the public at a point of time in an economy. It is determined by two main determinants:

1. Monetary base or high powered money (H): It is a significant determinant of the size of money supply. Money supply varies directly in relation to the changes in the monetary base. Monetary base refers to the supply of funds available for use either as cash or reserves of the central bank. In short it represents the total cash in the economy. Monetary base or the stock of high powered money changes due to the policy of the government and is also influenced by the value of money.

2. Money Multiplier (m): It exerts a positive influence upon the money supply. An increase in the size of m will increase the money supply and vice versa. The value of money multiplier is in turn affected by:

- Currency to deposit ratio (c): It is a behavioural ratio as its value depends on the willingness of people to hold currency rather than deposits. Its effect on the money multiplier (m) cannot be clearly recognized as it enters both as a numerator and a denominator in the money multiplier expression $(c + 1/c + r)$. But, as long as the r ratio is less than unity, a rise in the c ratio must reduce the multiplier.
- Reserve to deposit ratio (r): A smaller r enables greater expansion in the credit by the banks and thus increases the money supply and vice versa.

Money Supply

There is a wide evidence of close linkages between money and other macroeconomic variables like inflation, interest rates, output, etc. This has been shown as a theoretical relationship between money, output and prices in the original quantity theory of money which has subsequently been restated by many other schools of thought. The quantity theory is basically a theoretical explanation of the role of money in economic activities. One of the normal effects of an rise in the quantity of money is an exactly proportional increase in general price level. It implies that there is a direct positive correlation between the quantity of money in circulation and price level. Also, there exists an inverse relationship between quantity of money & value of money. Classical theory argues that real and monetary sectors are completely different from each other and are unrelated. This implies that money growth does not affect real output or the real rate of interest and money growth is inflationary. It states that:

$$MV = PT$$

Where,

M = total money stock.

V = Velocity of money.

MV = total money supply.

P = general price level.

T = total number of transactions.

PT = total demand for money for making transactions.

There are two important assumptions in stating this equation, one, the velocity of money and T are constant. Two, there is full employment in the economy. Based on these two assumptions, the Classical theorists assert that $\Delta M = \Delta P$. The real interest rate is independent of monetary measures, which implies that nominal interest rate equals real interest rate plus expected inflation. According to the principle of monetary neutrality due to the Classicals, an increase in the rate of money growth raises the rate of inflation but does not affect any real variable. Thus, in the Classical theory, inflation is driven by money growth and nominal interest rate by inflation.

Keynesian theory however stressed that there is a strong link between the real & monetary sectors of the economy. Keynes came with three motives of demand for money. Apart from focusing on the role of money as a medium of exchange in the form of transactionary and precautionary motives, Keynes added the function of money as a store of value in the form of speculative motive. This component of demand for money depends upon the interest rate prevailing in the market. So, demand for money is affected by interest rate apart from income. Keynes aggregate demand function is given by:

$$M^d = k\,(P.Y) + L\,(i)$$

Where,

K = income sensitivity of demand for money.

P.Y = Real income.

L = demand for money function which depends on the rate of interest.

Keynesian theory claimed that money supply can influence the real economy by changing aggregate demand through the monetary transmission mechanism. As money supply affects interest rates which in turn affect investment and ultimately the aggregate spending. This theory implies that prices do not rise immediately due to rigidities and thus monetary policy cannot aim to bring in price stability in the economy. This Keynesian approach was challenged by monetarists who claim that monetary policy can be used to stabilize the economy. Friedman in his version of the theory of demand for money regards money as an asset or wealth which earns rate of return. Keynesians and Friedman's approach differs in terms of the stability of the demand for money function. While former consider it as unstable due to changes in the interest rate, the latter school of thought considers it as stable. Thus, money and interest rate are linked through the money market. The effect of change in money supply on output is influenced by the change in interest rates.

As far as the question as to whether money supply is exogenous or endogenous is concerned, the two schools of thought, originating from Keynesian and monetarist sources, have merged over time, resulting in a consensus that money is exogenous. On the other hand, post-Keynesians have come to support the idea that money is endogenous. Heterodox monetary theory which is an alternative to neo-classical monetary theory has a completely different approach to the nature of money. In this view money supply is endogenous, and is determined within the economic system by the economy-wide need for credit. This theory postulates that it is the interest rate that the central bank can effectively control, rather than any of the monetary aggregates.

Money Supply and its Components

Money supply refers to the stock of money held by the public at a point of time in an economy. It includes the total amount of money that is in circulation with private individuals and business firms. It excludes all those items which are not in circulation like, the amount of coins and currency which are held by the commercial banks as cash reserves, cash held in the treasury by the government and stock of gold with central bank. There are two main components of money supply:

- Currency: This consists of coins and currency notes that are in circulation. The central bank has the sole right to issue and print currency notes in every country.
- Demand deposits: These are those checkable deposits which are deposited in banks by the depositors and bank agrees to honor demands from the depositors at any time in the future.

The different components of money supply are added up to arrive at different measures of money supply. The narrow measure (M_1) is the most liquid. It is measured at a point of time by adding currency with the public, net demand deposits and other deposits held with the central bank.

$M_1 = C + DD + OD$

Another narrow measure is M_2 which includes savings of people with post offices.

$M_2 = M_1$ + savings of people with post offices.

Similarly, there are two broad measures of money supply M_3 and M_4. M_3 is the most commonly used measure of money supply.

$M_3 = M_1$ + Net time deposits with commercial banks.

M_4 is still broader measure and includes savings with post offices along with M_3.

$M_4 = M_3$ + savings with post offices (except NSC).

Exogenous Money Supply

Money demand as we saw is a function of interest rate and money income. Money demand is a decreasing function of rate of interest but a rising function of level of income. Money supply may or may not be a function of interest rate depending upon whether the money supply is exogenous or endogenous. An exogenous variable is a variable whose value is set/changed outside the model, by the economist conducting the analysis. Money supply is said to be exogenous when monetary authority has complete control over it. It means that it is not affected by the change in interest rates. In the classical model, money is considered to be exogenously given at a fixed level. When the money supply is exogenously given, monetary authority determines the money supply and financial sector, firms and households have no significant role in influencing it.

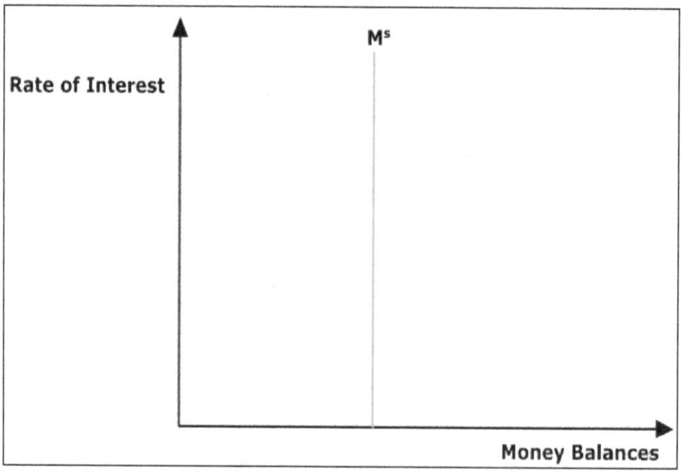

Exogenous Money Supply.

The money supply curve is drawn as vertical which means that it is unrelated to the rate of interest and no economic factors influence the level of money supply. In the IS-LM framework the derivation of LM curve also derived on the assumption of exogenous money supply.

Implications of exogenous money supply:

- Broader measures of money must follow developments in high-powered money.
- The money multiplier must be greater than one by definition.
- Central bank must be able to control the volume of high powered money. It implies that an increase in high powered money should increase lending and credit creation
- Only the distribution, not the volume of debt will matter, since lending is financed through savings, and one's debt is someone else's asset.

However the empirical evidence points at somewhat different experiences than what is implied by the theoretical outcomes. Money multiplier has been below one, in the aftermath of crisis period. Broader measures of money do not follow the monetary base due to presence of lags. In spite of significant amounts of accumulated reserves following the excessive money printing, lending remained very limited.

Monetary Equilibrium with Exogenous Money Supply

Money market is said to be in equilibrium when the demand for money equals the supply of money. In the money market, money supply is exogenously given and the endogenous variable is the interest rate. This is the variable that will change to re-establish the equilibrium. Variables that do not change in the adjustment to the equilibrium are the exogenous variables. Changes in the exogenous variable is necessary to cause an adjustment to a new equilibrium.

In figure, initial equilibrium is established where money demand curve M^D intersects the money supply curve M^S and interest rate is at r. Now, suppose that for some reason the actual interest rate, lies below the equilibrium interest rate, r. At r_1, real demand for money exceeds the real money supply. One of the implication is that people and businesses show a preference to hold more assets in a liquid (spendable) form rather than holding assets in a less liquid form, such as in a savings account. This excess demand for money will make households & businesses to exchange assets from less liquid accounts into checking accounts or cash in their pockets. This would involve person withdrawing money from their savings account to hold cash in their wallet. The savings account balance is not measured as a part of the M_1 money supply, however the currency that people have in their wallet is a part of money supply. This is result of rising demand for speculative money balances. As a result, the financial sector will experience a decrease in time deposit balances, which in turn will reduce their capacity to make loans. In other words, withdrawals from savings & other type of non-money accounts will diminish the total collection of funds accessible to be loaned by financial sector. With fewer funds to lend & same demand for loans, banks will take action by raising interest rates. Higher interest rates will decrease the demand for loans helping to equalize supply & demand for loans. Finally, as interest rates increase, money demand decreases until it equalizes with the actual money supply. Through this mechanism average interest rates will increase, whenever money demand exceeds money supply. The exactly opposite adjustment will happen whenever for some reasons money supply exceeds the money demand. When interest rate rises from r to r_2, then real money supply will exceed real money demand meaning that the amount of assets or wealth in a liquid, spendable form is greater than the amount they would like to hold. The increase in loanable funds, in the face of constant demand for loans, will force banks to lower interest rates to stimulate the demand for loans. However, as interest rates fall, the demand for money will rise until it equalizes again with money supply. Through this mechanism average interest rates will fall, whenever money supply exceeds money demand.

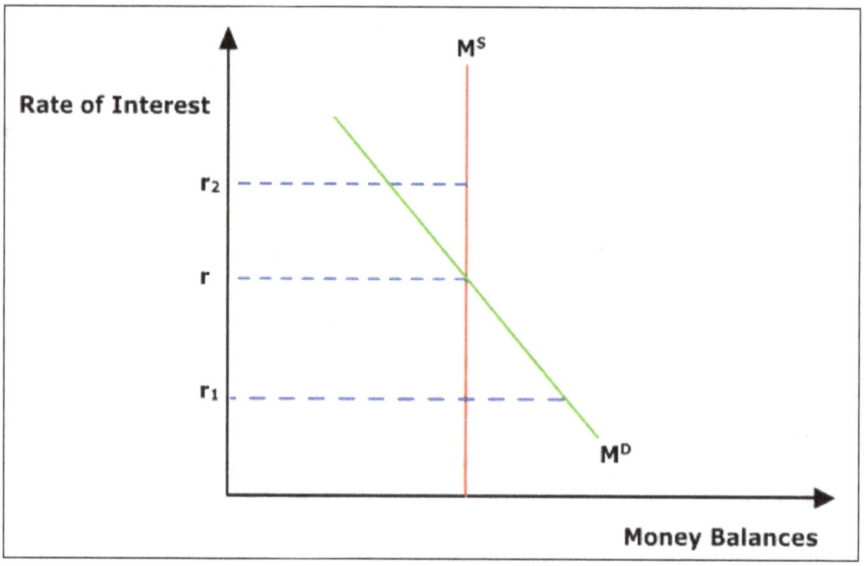

Monetary equilibrium with exogenous money supply.

Effects of Monetary Expansion

Expansionary monetary policy aims at raising or expanding the money supply. This can be accomplished with open market purchases of government bonds, with a decrease in the reserve requirement or with an announced decrease in the discount rate. In almost all growing economies the money supply is expanded regularly to keep up with the expansion of GDP.

Suppose the money market is originally in equilibrium at the intersection of M^D and M^S at interest rate r. An increase in the money supply (M^S) causes an increase in the real money supply is shown as a rightward shift from M^S to M^{S_1}. At the original interest rate, money supply exceeds money demand and the actual interest rate is higher than the equilibrium rate. There will be adjustment to the lower interest rate as explained above. The final equilibrium will occur where the equilibrium interest rate has fallen from r to r_1. Thus, expansionary monetary policy (i.e., an increase in the money supply) will cause a decrease in average interest rates in an economy.

In contrast a monetary contraction will lead to a rise in interest rate in the economy. It must be noted that money supply we are considering is the real money supply assuming price level to be constant this is equal to the nominal money supply.

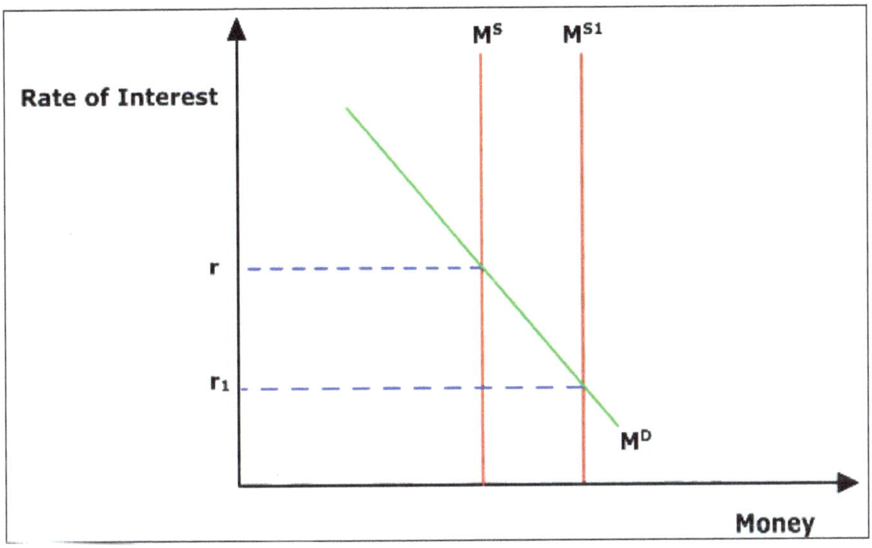

Impact of monetary expansion under exogenous money supply.

Endogenous Money Supply

An endogenous variable is a variable whose value is determined inside the model, by solving the model. The supply of money is said to be endogenous when the monetary authority has no control over it and the demand for money determines the supply of money. In the case of endogenous money supply, banking sector, individuals and firms play an important role in influencing the supply of money. The supply of money is influenced by the money multiplier process. The monetary base changes whenever central bank issues new base money and this money is deposited in banks in the form of demand deposits. As the commercial banks work on the fractional reserve system, they keep a fixed proportion of these deposits as reserves and lends the balance deposits. This process will keep on repeating itself until the demand for loans and advances keep on coming. As bank deposits are a component of money, money demand is influenced by the behaviour of banking sector, individuals and firms. The money multiplier is derived using two equations:

$$M = C + D$$

$$H = C + R$$

Where,

M = Money supply.

C = Currency.

R = Reserves with banks.

D = Demand deposits.

H = High powered money or Monetary base.

If we divide first equation by second, we get.

M/H = C + D/ C + R

Dividing numerator and denominator of both sides by D, we get,

$$M/H = \frac{C/D+1}{C/D+R/D}$$

$$M/H = \frac{c+1}{c+r}$$

Where c is currency to deposit ratio and r is reserve to deposit ratio.

$$M = \frac{c+1}{c+r}H$$

The $\frac{c+1}{c+r}$ is the money multiplier which determines the effect of monetary base on money supply.

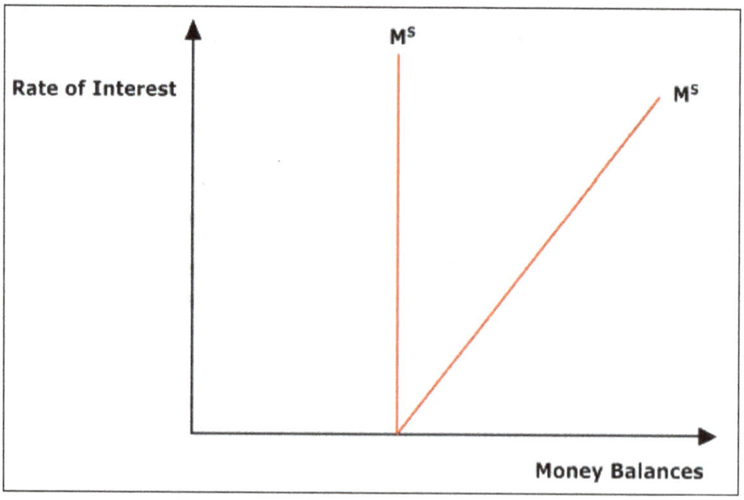

Endogenous and Exogenous Money Supply.

The above analysis claims that money supply is endogenously determined via the demand for bank credit. Acceptance of Post Keynesian endogenous money theory implies that fluctuations in monetary aggregates can be driven endogenously. Banks supply the credit demanded at the interest rate they choose to offer on loans. This interest rate is determined by a mark-up over the central bank lending rate (base rate) and costs of other sources of financing. In this sense, banks are price-makers and quantity-take$ In fact, deposits are just one way of obtaining these funds. Alternatively, banks can borrow from the central bank at the policy rate, or borrow from money markets. This implies that money multiplier works not just on the basis of deposits. The central bank, as the lender of last resort, accommodates to the borrowing demands of banks, setting the cost of borrowing rather than its quantity. It means that the central bank cannot control the money supply, but can affect the cost of credit through interest rate policy.

Thus, there is wide consensus that in real world money supply is neither endogenous nor exogenous, it is a convex combination of the two. It means that money is partly controlled by the monetary authority and partly by the money demand. In normal times, monetary authority tries to accommodate the expansion in money demand while it actively uses its tool of interest rate to stabilize a high inflation or overheated economy.

Determinants of Money Supply

There are two theories of the determination of the money supply. According to the first view, the money supply is determined exogenously by the central bank. The second view holds that the money supply is determined endogenously by changes in the economic activity which affects people's desire to hold currency relative to deposits, the rate of interest, etc.

Thus the determinants of money supply are both exogenous and endogenous which can be described broadly as: the minimum cash reserve ratio, the level of bank reserves, and the desire of the people to hold currency relative to deposits. The last two determinants together are called the monetary base or the high powered money.

The Required Reserve Ratio

The required reserve ratio (or the minimum cash reserve ratio or the reserve deposit ratio) is an important determinant of the money supply. An increase in the required reserve ratio reduces the supply of money with commercial banks and a decrease in required reserve ratio increases the money supply.

The RR_1 is the ratio of cash to current and time deposit liabilities which is determined by law. Every commercial bank is required to keep a certain percentage of these liabilities in the form of deposits with the central bank of the country. But notes or cash held by commercial banks in their tills are not included in the minimum required reserve ratio. But the short-term assets along with the cash are regarded as the liquid assets of a commercial bank. In India the statutory liquidity ratio (SLR) has been fixed by law as an additional measure to determine the money supply. The SLR is called secondary reserve ratio in other countries while the required reserve ratio is referred to as the primary ratio. The raising of the SLR has the effect of reducing the money supply with commercial banks for lending purposes, and the lowering of the SLR tends in increase the money supply with banks for advances.

The Level of Bank Reserves

The level of bank reserves is another determinant of the money supply. Commercial bank reserves consist of reserves on deposits with the central bank and currency in their tills or vaults. It is the central bank of the country that influences the reserves of commercial banks in order to determine the supply of money. The central bank requires all commercial banks to hold reserves equal to a fixed percentage of both time and demand deposits. These are legal minimum or required reserves.

Required reserves (RR) are determined by the required reserve ratio (RRr) and the level of deposits (D) of a commercial bank: RR-RRr' D. If deposits amount of Rs 80 lakhs and required reserve ratio is 20 percent, then the required reserves will be 20% x 80=Rs 16 lakhs. If the reserve ratio is reduced to 10 per cent, the required reserves will also be reduced to Rs 8 lakhs.

Thus the higher the reserve ratio, the higher the required reserves to be kept by a bank, and vice versa. But it is the excess reserves (ER) which are important for the determination of the money supply. Excess reserves are the difference between total reserves (TR) and required reserves (RR): ER=TR-RR. If total reserves are Rs 80 lakhs and required reserves are Rs 16 lakhs, then the excess reserves are Rs 64 lakhs (Rs 80-16 lakhs).

When required reserves are reduced to Rs 8 lakhs, the excess reserves increase to Rs 72 lakhs. It is the excess reserves of a commercial bank which influence the size of its deposit liabilities. A commercial bank advances loans equal to its excess reserves which are an important component of the money supply. To determine the supply of money with a commercial bank, the central bank influences its reserves by adopting open market operations and discount rate policy. Open market operations refer to the purchase and sale of government securities and other types of assets like bills, securities, bonds, etc., both government and private in the open market. When the central bank buys or sells securities in the open market, the level of bank reserves expands or contracts.

The purchase of securities by the central bank is paid for with cheques to the holders of securities who, in turn, deposit them in commercial banks thereby increasing the level of bank reserves. The opposite is the case when the central bank sells securities to the public and banks who make payments to the central bank through cash and cheques thereby reducing the level of bank reserves. The discount rate policy affects the money supply by influencing the cost and supply of bank credit to commercial banks. The discount rate is the interest rate at which commercial banks borrow from the central bank. A high discount rate means that commercial banks get less amount by selling securities to the central bank. The commercial banks, in turn, raise their lending rates to the public thereby making advances dearer for them. Thus there will be contraction of credit and the level of commercial bank reserves. Opposite is the case when the bank rate is lowered. It tends to expand credit and the consequent bank reserves. It should be noted that commercial bank reserves are affected significantly only when open market operations and discount rate policy supplement each other. Otherwise, their effectiveness as determinants of bank reserves and consequently of money supply is limited.

Public's Desire to Hold Currency and Deposits

People's desire to hold currency (or cash) relative to deposits in commercial banks also determines the money supply. If people are in the habit of keeping less in cash and more in deposits with the commercial banks, the money supply will be large. This is because banks can create more money with larger deposits. On the contrary, if people do not have banking habits and prefers to keep their money holdings in cash, credit creation by banks will be less and the money supply will be at a low level.

High Powered Money and the Money Multiplier

The current practice is to explain the determinants of the money supply in terms of the monetary base or high-powered money. High-powered money is the sum of commercial bank reserves and currency (notes and coins) held by the public. High-powered money is the base for the expansion of bank deposits and creation of the money supply. The supply of money varies directly with changes in the monetary base, and inversely with the currency and reserve ratios.

Other Factors

The money supply is a function not only of the high-powered money determined by the monetary authorities, but of interest rates, income and other facto$ The latter factors change the proportion of money balances that the public holds as cash. Changes in business activity can change the behaviour of banks and the public and thus affect the money supply. Hence the money supply is not only an exogenous controllable item but also an endogenously determined item.

References

- What-is-fiscal-policy: investopedia.com, Retrieved 04, August 2020
- Money-supply-determinants-of-money-supply-and-high-powered-money-and-money-multiplier-10971: yourarticlelibrary.com, Retrieved 18, May 2020

Permissions

All chapters in this book are published with permission under the Creative Commons Attribution Share Alike License or equivalent. Every chapter published in this book has been scrutinized by our experts. Their significance has been extensively debated. The topics covered herein carry significant information for a comprehensive understanding. They may even be implemented as practical applications or may be referred to as a beginning point for further studies.

We would like to thank the editorial team for lending their expertise to make the book truly unique. They have played a crucial role in the development of this book. Without their invaluable contributions this book wouldn't have been possible. They have made vital efforts to compile up to date information on the varied aspects of this subject to make this book a valuable addition to the collection of many professionals and students.

This book was conceptualized with the vision of imparting up-to-date and integrated information in this field. To ensure the same, a matchless editorial board was set up. Every individual on the board went through rigorous rounds of assessment to prove their worth. After which they invested a large part of their time researching and compiling the most relevant data for our readers.

The editorial board has been involved in producing this book since its inception. They have spent rigorous hours researching and exploring the diverse topics which have resulted in the successful publishing of this book. They have passed on their knowledge of decades through this book. To expedite this challenging task, the publisher supported the team at every step. A small team of assistant editors was also appointed to further simplify the editing procedure and attain best results for the readers.

Apart from the editorial board, the designing team has also invested a significant amount of their time in understanding the subject and creating the most relevant covers. They scrutinized every image to scout for the most suitable representation of the subject and create an appropriate cover for the book.

The publishing team has been an ardent support to the editorial, designing and production team. Their endless efforts to recruit the best for this project, has resulted in the accomplishment of this book. They are a veteran in the field of academics and their pool of knowledge is as vast as their experience in printing. Their expertise and guidance has proved useful at every step. Their uncompromising quality standards have made this book an exceptional effort. Their encouragement from time to time has been an inspiration for everyone.

The publisher and the editorial board hope that this book will prove to be a valuable piece of knowledge for students, practitioners and scholars across the globe.

Index

A

Aggregate Demand, 4-7, 34, 36-38, 50-65, 67-69, 71-73, 75, 77-78, 80-81, 94-95, 106, 110, 113, 119-122, 126, 129, 132-136, 142-144, 146, 150, 224-225

Appreciation, 205, 207-208

B

Balance Of Payments, 1, 186-190, 192, 194, 206

Bank Loans, 35, 219

British Goods, 207

Business Cycle, 1, 6-8, 19, 21, 75, 94, 107, 169

C

Capital Account, 187-188, 190-194

Cash Reserve Ratio, 217, 231

Classical Theory, 21-23, 26, 32, 34-36, 112, 128-129, 145-146, 149-150, 182, 224

Closed Economy, 9-10, 12, 14, 104, 206

Coal, 44, 105, 169

Consumption, 8-10, 15-17, 19-20, 36, 41-42, 48, 50-51, 54, 56-60, 94, 101-103, 105-107, 110-111, 113, 137, 140, 142, 170, 210

Consumption Expenditure, 16, 20, 105-106, 110

Copyrights, 155, 157, 193

Creation Of Deposit Money, 217

Credit Creation, 112, 216-219, 221, 227, 233

Current Account, 188-194, 212-213

D

Deficit, 12-14, 19, 51, 83, 94, 97, 112, 125, 187, 191, 193-194, 211-212, 216

Deflation, 3, 53, 75-76, 97, 141, 143

Depression, 4-5, 21, 58, 95-97, 100, 104, 107-108, 112-113, 122, 148, 197, 214

Discrepancy, 148, 198

Disinflation, 75-76

Disposable Income, 16-17, 54

Domestic Goods, 207-208, 210-212

Domestic Income, 8-9, 15, 20, 211

Duopoly, 139, 174, 181, 183-185

E

Economics, 1-3, 5, 38, 44, 93-94, 96-98, 100-101, 106-107, 109, 113, 119, 123-127, 136, 140-142, 145, 150-151, 154-155, 160-161, 183

Effective Exchange Rate, 208-209

Equilibrium, 3-4, 7, 19-21, 31-34, 37-38, 43, 60, 62-65, 67-69, 73, 78-79, 81-85, 89-92, 97, 108-111, 115-116, 119-124, 126-128, 142, 145-146, 148, 155, 159, 177-178, 182-183, 227-228

F

Fiscal Policy, 2, 5, 50, 95, 97, 99-100, 127-128, 141, 144, 214-216

Foreign Investors, 13, 194, 202

Foreign Price Levels, 58

G

Gdp Deflator, 46

Government Bonds, 14, 18, 95, 228

Government Purchases, 8, 10-13, 15-16, 18-19, 21, 56-57

Gross Domestic Product (gdp), 8, 50

H

Hypothesis, 6-7, 22, 26, 68, 100, 123, 132, 134, 145

I

Inflation, 1-4, 6, 17, 19, 48, 55, 60, 65-76, 84, 94, 96, 100, 103, 113, 125-129, 131, 140-144, 195-196, 206-208, 214-216, 223-224, 231

Injections, 9-11, 14

L

Laissez Faire, 4

Leakages, 9-11, 14

Legal Reserve Ratio, 217

Leisure Activities, 29, 41

Liquidity Trap, 52, 94, 96, 99, 117-118, 122-123

M

Market Capitalization, 200-203

Market Power, 153-157, 160-163, 182

Misperception Theory, 63-64
Monetary Policy, 3, 5-6, 53, 66, 85, 88, 94, 98-99, 113, 122, 127-128, 144, 214, 216, 225, 228
Money Creation, 216, 219, 223
Money Illusion, 22-23
Money Supply, 5, 52, 75, 77-78, 80, 85, 88, 90, 98-99, 113, 122, 126, 132, 142, 214, 216, 222-233
Multiplier Effect, 20-21, 94-95, 97

N
National Income, 15, 20, 38, 44-45, 47, 49, 100-102, 104, 108, 113, 119-120, 124
Natural Monopoly, 166, 169
Net Exports, 13-16, 19, 47, 54, 56, 58-60, 210
New Synthesis, 3, 7
Nominal Exchange Rate, 53, 206-210

O
Oligopoly, 153-155, 163, 173-177, 179-183

P
Paper Currency, 206, 216
Petroleum, 74, 169, 180, 203
Phillips Curve, 65-75, 96, 100, 126-127
Planned Investment, 16-17, 19-20, 111
Price Discrimination, 156, 161-164, 168
Producer Goods, 40
Profit Maximization, 26, 60, 158, 174, 177

S
Salt, 169, 172
Single Banking System, 217
Social Security, 10, 47, 57, 143
Stagflation, 66, 70-71, 74, 100, 113, 127
Statutory Liquidity Ratio, 217, 231
Surplus, 12-14, 161-166, 188, 191-194, 212

T
Taxation, 113, 215
The Open Economy, 12, 206
The Shirking Theory, 137
Trade Deficit, 13-14, 19, 212
Transfer Payments, 9-10, 17, 19, 54, 57

U
Unemployment, 1-5, 10, 19, 33, 47, 56, 61, 65-75, 83, 96-98, 100, 108, 113, 126-130, 134-136, 138, 140, 142, 146, 148-150, 214-215
Unilateral Transfer Accounts, 188

W
Welfare, 6, 50, 57, 96-97, 101,
155, 162, 174

www.ingramcontent.com/pod-product-compliance
Lightning Source LLC
LaVergne TN
LVHW080622210926
848485LV00003B/201
* 9 7 8 1 6 3 9 8 9 4 3 8 3 *